The Nordic Translation Series

Sponsored by the Nordic Cultural Commission of the Governments of Denmark, Finland, Iceland, Norway, and Sweden.

Advisory Committee
Einar Haugen, Harald S. Næss,
and Richard B. Vowles, Chairman

Fire and Ice

FIRE AND ICE

Three Icelandic plays by **INDEXED**
Jóhann Sigurjónsson, Davið Stefánsson,
and Agnar Thórðarson

with Introductions by
Einar Haugen

The University of Wisconsin Press

Madison, Milwaukee, and London 1967

Contents

General Introduction

General Introduction

The classical literature of medieval Iceland is rich in dramatic episodes, both in poetry and prose. A number of the poems in the *Poetic Edda* are cast in dialogue form: one thinks of the intellectual sparring of Odin with the giant Vafthruðnir or the ribald taunts of Loki directed at the gods in the banquet scene of *Lokasenna*, both ending with the discomfiture of the giants. The love poem *Skírnismál*, which tells of the wooing of Gerd by the god Frey, has even been called the reflection of a ritual fertility drama. The sagas of Icelanders and Norwegians are built around a series of dramatic confrontations between antagonists, whether at banquets, in the courts, or on the battlefield. Their dialogue consists of short, pithy exchanges, highlighting in unforgettable relief the personality clashes of a Hallgerd and a Gunnar, a Sigrid and an Olaf Tryggvason, or a Gunnhild and an Egill Skallagrimsson. But all attempts to recast either the poetry of the *Edda* or the prose of the sagas into modern drama have failed, as our present author, Jóhann Sigurjónsson, learned to his distress when he tried to dramatize *Njáll's Saga* in his play *Løgneren* (*The Liar*, 1917). Even Henrik Ibsen's attempts to transfer themes from the old literature to the modern drama were among his less happy efforts: *The Vikings of Helgeland* (1858) and *The Pretenders* (1864).

A viable dramatic literature is dependent on a flourishing theater, which in turn requires an audience of a certain size. Iceland as a country of scattered farmsteads, however literate its population of fishermen and herders, offered no incentives

to the writers of drama until well into the nineteenth century.
Plays had been written and performed at the cathedral school
at Skálholt (later moved to Reykjavík and Bessastaðir) as far
back as in the sixteenth century, but the productions were
one-night stands performed on the students' *Herranótt,* a kind
of winter carnival, and did not reach beyond the circle of the
school itself and its graduates. Since Iceland at this time was a
part of the Dano-Norwegian kingdom and Copenhagen was its
capital and university town, it is not surprising that the Icelandic theater developed as an offshoot of the Danish theater, and
that it represented a self-assertion by the Icelanders against the
dominance of that theater.[1]

Icelandic drama found its own special atmosphere in the play
Útilegumennirnir (*The Outlawed Men,* 1861–62) by Iceland's
national poet Matthías Jochumsson (1835–1920), whose first
book it was. This naively charming little play was clearly
influenced by the ever-popular Danish *Elverhøj* and was like it
a typical product of the Romantic era of nationalism, with
prose dialogue and interspersed songs. The author exploited
the tradition of the outlaw, here set against the fantastic background of Iceland's mountain wastes of ice and fire. We have
the word of Iceland's chief modern authority on the drama,
Professor Steingrímur J. Thorsteinsson, in an article written in
1956, that by then this play had been performed at least 500
times in Iceland, "in warehouses, in barns, in private homes,
and in every kind of meeting place, from restaurants to the
National Theater."[2]

For many Icelanders this play became their first overwhelming experience of the theater: one of them was Indriði Einarsson (1851–1939), dramatist, translator, director; another was
our present author Jóhann Sigurjónsson (1880–1919), who was
to become the first classic writer of Icelandic plays. Indriði
(Icelanders are always referred to by their first names) was the

[1] See Einarsson, *History of Icelandic Literature, passim.*
[2] Thorsteinsson, "Islandsk skuespildigtning og skuespilkunst."

leading spirit in the founding of the first Icelandic stage, the Reykjavík Dramatic Society (Leikfélag Reykjavíkur) in 1897, and the National Theater (Thjódleikhús Íslands) in 1950. Indriði's share in the preparations for the latter, which he did not live to see opened, was commemorated on its opening night, when his romantic folklore play *Nýjársnóttin* (*New Year's Night*, 1871) was performed. This was followed on the second night by Jóhann Sigurjónsson's *Fjalla-Eyvindur* (*Eyvindur of the Hills*, 1912), which deals (as we shall see) with a theme that continues very directly the tradition of *The Outlawed Men*.

That Reykjavík, a city (in 1950) of some 50,000 inhabitants, should have two repertory theaters is a source of pride to Icelanders, and rightly so, for anything like it is utterly unheard of in the United States. That the theaters are partially subsidized is in the European tradition, however, while the fact that both have difficulty maintaining themselves against the seductive power of the film industry is an international dilemma. But at least Icelandic dramatists have since 1897 had a forum for their efforts, and since 1950 they have had two. At the same time these stages have made the best of world drama directly available to the Icelandic public and to budding dramatists, either through guest performances (usually Danish) or through translations ranging from the Greeks and the Elizabethans to the latest productions of Paris and New York. Semiprofessional and professional actors have been trained, with results that are often of international quality, as visitors to Reykjavík in the theater season can testify.

The consequence has been that since the turn of the century Icelandic drama has faithfully reflected the passing fashions of the European and American theater. The romanticism of *The Outlawed Men* gave way to the problem (and problematic) realism of early Ibsen and Strindberg, only to follow these writers into the neo-romanticism and psychologizing of the fin-de-siècle. This is the point at which the first drama of our collection stands. Jóhann Sigurjónsson was one of a band of Icelandic writers who found his way from Iceland to the bright lights of Copenhagen in the hope of making a greater career there. For all its literary precociousness, Reykjavík before the wars had little to offer an ambitious young author, and a generation which had breathed the freer air of the late nineteenth century could not be confined within its provincial culture. In these years a number of Icelanders were attracted by the bracing winds of Europe that blew through the cultural life of Copenhagen. They wrote in Danish, even though they remained Icelanders in spirit and exploited Icelandic traditions and experiences for their thematic material. In this respect Jóhann's example was followed, among others, by the novelist Gunnar Gunnarsson (1889—) and the novelist-dramatist Guðmundur Kamban (1888–1945). In the years 1911–20 one could actually speak of an Icelandic school in Danish literature.[3]

But the establishment (on a modest scale) of an Icelandic university in 1911 and the independence pact with Denmark of 1918 (which gave Iceland home rule under the Danish king) presaged a new era in Icelandic dramatic literature as well. The authors who arose after 1918 generally eschewed Danish: in 1919, when Davið Stefánsson and Halldór Laxness produced their first books, they wrote in Icelandic as a matter of course, and they have always continued to do so. Hence their plays and those of their successors have also been written in Icelandic and for a primarily Icelandic audience. In so far as they have succeeded in reaching a wider audience, it has been through translations. It is hoped that through this volume Icelandic drama may come to be known even beyond the limits of the Scandinavian countries, where a number of Icelandic plays have been part of the repertory for a long time.

The plays here chosen by Icelandic critics of literature as

[3] Toldberg, "De islandske dramatikere i Danmark." See also his book on Jóhann Sigurjónsson.

representative of Iceland include one by each of three outstanding authors: Jóhann Sigurjónsson, Davið Stefánsson, and
Agnar Thórðarson. These represent three successive generations, as the introductions to their plays will demonstrate, each
with its special profile. There are others who have had to be
regretfully excluded, beginning with the previously mentioned
Matthías Jochumsson and Indriði Einarsson. There is
Guðmundur Kamban, whose play *Hadda-Padda* (1914) appeared in English translation in 1917, with a foreword by
Georg Brandes. Kamban was more cosmopolitan than Icelandic, living abroad much of his life, including two years in New
York (1915-17), which he made the setting of three plays,
Marmor (*Marble*, 1918), *Vi mordere* (*We Murderers*, 1920),
and *Ørkenens stjerner* (*Stars of the Desert*, 1925). He worked
as a theatrical director in Copenhagen; his plays were problem
pieces in the Ibsen and Strindberg tradition, deeply concerned
with the psychological relationships of marriage and the work-
ings of justice in society. In general, his novels, two of which
were translated into English in the 1930's, were more successful
than his plays. The same appears to be true of the Nobel-
prizewinner Halldór Laxness (1902——), whose plays include
Straumrof (*Short Circuit*, 1934), *Snæfriður Íslandssól* (1950),
which dramatizes his novel *Íslandsklukkan* (*The Bell of Iceland*, 1943), *Silfurtunglid* (*The Silver Moon*, 1954), *Stromp-
leikurinn* (*The Stovepipe Game*, 1961), and *Prjónastofan
Sólin* (*The Sun Knitting Factory*, 1962). In the words of his
sympathetic biographer, Peter Hallberg, the effects tend to be
obtrusive, "lacking the rich overtones, endlessly faceted and
playful, which characterize his narrative."[4] Other, younger
dramatists are at work; when the time comes for a new collection of Icelandic plays, they will demand our attention.

EINAR HAUGEN

Cambridge, Mass.
January, 1967

[4] Hallberg, *Skaldens hus*, p. 492.

Bibliography

ABOUT ICELANDIC DRAMA AND DRAMATISTS

Beck, Richard. *History of Icelandic Poets, 1800–1940.* Ithaca, New York: Cornell University Press, 1950 (= *Islandica,* 34). 247 pp.

Einarsson, Stefán. *A History of Icelandic Literature.* New York: Johns Hopkins Press for the American-Scandinavian Foundation, 1957.

————. *History of Icelandic Prose Writers 1800–1940.* Ithaca, New York: Cornell University Press, 1948 (= *Islandica* 32–33).

Gad, Carl. "Jóhann Sigurjónsson." *Litteraturen: Nordens kritiske Revue,* vol. 2 (1919), 359–371.

Hallberg, Peter. *Skaldens hus. Laxness' diktning från Salka Valka till Gerpla.* Stockholm: Rabén og Sjögren, 1956.

Hermansson, Halldór. *Icelandic Authors of To-day.* Ithaca, N.Y., 1913 (= *Islandica* 6).

Johannessen, Matthías. Introduction to Davíð Stefánsson, *Gullna hliðið.* Reykjavík: Helgafell, 1966, pp. 7–37.

Jónsson, Erlendur. *Íslenzk bókmenntasaga 1750–1950.* Reykjavík: Ríkisútgáfa námsbóka, 1960. 72 pp.

Leach, Henry Goddard. Introduction to Jóhann Sigurjónsson, *Modern Icelandic Plays.* New York: The American-Scandinavian Foundation, 1916, pp. xi–xii.

Levy, Louis. "Islandsk Teater." *Tilskueren,* vol. 35 (1918), sec. 1, pp. 282–86.

Magoun, Francis P., Jr. "Jóhann Sigurjónsson's *Fjalla-Eyvindur:* Source, Chronology, and Geography." *Publications of the Modern Language Association,* vol. 61 (1946), 269–92.

Møller, Arne. "Islandsk Digtning," in Ejnar Skovrup, ed., *Hovedtræk af Nordisk Digtning i Nytiden,* vol. 2 (Copenhagen: Aschehoug, 1920–21).

Pineau, Leon. "Un poète dramatique islandais: Jóhann Sigurjónsson." *La Revue,* vol. 109 (1914), 52–67, 188–201.

Sigurjónsson, Ingeborg. *Mindernes Besøg.* Copenhagen: 1932.

Thorsteinsson, Steingrímur J. *"Anna Pjetursdóttir og Galdra-Loftur,"* Lesbók *Morgunblaðsins,* March 18, 1951, pp. 157–61.

———. "Islandsk skuespildigtning og skuespilkunst." Lecture given at VI Nordic Theatrical Congress, in National Theater in Reykjavík, June 4, 1956. Stencilled, Reykjavík, 1956. 20 pp.

———. "Islandsk dramatik og skuespilkunst, dens oprindelse og udvikling." *The Proceedings of the First Conference on Scandinavian Studies, Held at Cambridge 2–7 July, 1956,* pp. 47–61. (Mimeo.) [Substantially identical with article listed above.]

Thuborg, Anders. "Ved Jóhann Sigurjónssons Død." *Tilskueren,* vol. 36, sec. 2 (1919), pp. 330–37.

Toldberg, Helge, "De islandske dramatikere i Danmark." *The Proceedings of the First Conference on Scandinavian Studies, Held at Cambridge 2–7 July, 1956,* pp. 41–46. (Mimeo.)

———. *Jóhann Sigurjónsson.* Copenhagen: Rasmus Fischers Forlag, 1965. [Rev. by Steingrímur J. Thorsteinsson, *Scandinavica,* vol. 5 (1966), 135–37.]

Worster, W. W. "Four Icelandic Writers." *Edinburgh Review,* vol. 238 (1923), 306–19.

For additional bibliography, especially on Jóhann Sigurjónsson, see Toldberg's book, pp. 179–82.

ABOUT ICELAND

Dufferin, Lord. *Letters from High Latitudes.* London: Everyman's Library, 1856. 252 pp.

Gjerset, Knut. *A History of Iceland.* New York: The MacMillan Company, 1925. 482 pp.

Nuechterlein, Donald E. *Iceland, Reluctant Ally.* Ithaca, New York: Cornell University Press, 1961. 213 pp.

Rothery, Agnes. *Iceland, New World Outpost.* New York:
    The Viking Press, 1948. 214 pp.
Sutton, George Miksch. *Iceland Summer, Adventures of a Bird
    Painter.* Norman, Oklahoma: Oklahoma University Press,
    1961. 254 pp.

Translator's note: All accents have been omitted on Icelandic
names occurring in the text of the translations, and *th* has
regularly been substituted for *þ*.

THE WISH

A Play in Three Acts

Galdra-Loftur, by Jóhann Sigurjónsson

Translated from Danish and Icelandic by Einar Haugen

First published in 1915

Introduction

It is a striking fact that all five of the plays which Jóhann Sigurjónsson managed to complete and publish in his short but intense creative period ended with the tragic death of the chief character. That the first of these, *Dr. Rung* (1905), should have dealt with tuberculosis and that he himself should have died of the same dread disease fourteen years later is perhaps no more than a coincidence. But there runs through his work a sense of the profound tragedy of life, which is the more intense because he was one who loved life and enjoyed it to the full. In an essay entitled, "I Love Life," he ecstatically confessed: "I love life, as a man loves a woman: I follow it helplessly, it enchants me with irresistible force. . . . I love it as a lovesick man desires a cold, disdainful dancer, and if I should lose this love, I would do so with distress, like the king of old who took the life of his beloved because he was afraid of losing himself."[1] Friends from his days in Copenhagen describe him as a man of sudden and unpredictable moods, who could shift from light-hearted gaiety to the blackest despair. Professor Árni Pálsson, who had known him then, wrote in 1920 that many thought of him as "a vacillating and unreliable enthusiast." But they agreed that "he was unlike all others, and that in his best moments sun and summer shone around him."[2]

This dual emphasis on the beauty and the tragedy of life is

[1] Jóhann Sigurjónsson, *Rit*, vol. 2, 266.

[2] *Eimreiðin* 1920, cited in theater program for *Galdra-Loftur* by Leikfélag Reykjavíkur 59. season, 2. program, 1955/56, p. 8.

projected into all of Jóhann's writings. "When I was a child,"
he once wrote, "I promised the Lord that if He would give me
the gracious gift of poetry, I would use it to honor Him and
His work. In those days His heaven was so wondrously near
and there could be no doubt that all He did was good. Later
the firmament grew larger and colder and the conditions of life
were harder to understand. But however this might be, the
inmost nerve in all my creation is the same as when I was a
child: to shape in the ringing metal of language something of
the flowing eternity of life, in simpler and if possible in more
beautiful images."[3] Beauty, as this is seen in the simple things of
life, is one of the keys to his work. He found it in nature,
especially the nature of Iceland, which is the setting of all but
one of his plays. He found it in women and children, who are
pictured with tenderness and insight. He found it above all in
love, here coupled with tragedy in each of his plays. His
thoughts, as one also sees from his published letters, circled
around a man's inescapable need for love, his fear that love
might not come, and his equal fear that if it did, it would lead
only to tragic upheaval and death. His temperament was in
many ways more lyric than dramatic, but he had set himself
the goal of becoming a great dramatic author. He was borne on
the wave of drama that had been stirred up by Ibsen, Bjørnson,
and Strindberg, but his work was more nearly akin to that of
his immediate predecessors, the Norwegians Gunnar Heiberg
and Knut Hamsun, in whose plays the irresistible force of love
and the tragic edge of happiness were basic themes. Heiberg's
Balkonen (*The Balcony*, 1894) and *Kjærlighedens tragedie*
(*The Tragedy of Love*, 1904) or Hamsun's *Ved rigets port*
(*At the Gates of the Kingdom*, 1895) all proclaim the suprem-
acy of love in its conflict with reason and common sense.

These were the great names in the theatrical life of Copenhagen when Jóhann came there in 1899 to study veterinary

---

[3] *Morgunblaðið*, 1919, reprinted in *Rit*, vol. 2, 265.

medicine. They were golden years in Danish and Norwegian literature, and Jóhann was enchanted. He soon rejected science for the muses and staked his future on his talent for drama. His friends were skeptical, and success was not exactly around the corner. His first two plays, *Dr. Rung* (1905) and *Bóndinn á Hrauni* (*The Farmer at Hraun,* 1908) were not well received. Most of his plays were written in both Danish and Icelandic, often with considerable deviation between the two versions. As he wrote to his fiancée and later wife, Ingeborg, in 1910, while he was preparing the Icelandic version of *Eyvind of the Hills*: "the very words awaken new ideas in me."[4] He had great handicaps to overcome in the fact that Danish was not his native language and that his background was very different from that of his new environment. He came from one of the remotest sections of Iceland, Laxamýri near the little fishing village of Húsavík in the northeast, and his preparation for university life consisted of the local schools plus three years of Latin School in Reykjavík, not unlike the education he attributed to his hero Loftur in our play. His enthusiasm for the dramatic art had already been awakened in his home, however, where his brother organized and starred in a performance of *The Outlawed Men*: "Then the Muse of Tragedy touched my heart for the first time with her mighty wing."[5]

Only an unshakeable purpose and great will power could have overcome the handicaps which obstructed his path to the Muse. The publication of *Bjærg-Ejvind og hans hustru* in Copenhagen in 1911 and its great success at the Dagmar Theater in December of that year was the fulfillment of his dreams.[6] Performances followed in other Scandinavian cities, including

---

[4] *Rit,* vol. 2, 274.

[5] *Ibid.,* vol. 2, 268 (written in 1915). For a survey of Jóhann's life and works see Einarsson, *History of Icelandic Prose Writers 1800–1940,* pp. 128–34, where other references will be found.

[6] For detailed information on performances and reception see Magoun, "Jóhann Sigurjónsson's *Fjalla-Eyvindur.*"

Reykjavík (Christmas Day, 1912), as well as translations into nine languages (before his death in 1919) and numerous performances abroad. The great Swedish director Victor Sjöström made from it one of his earliest films, with himself as the lead; stills of the film were used to illustrate a special edition of the play.[7] He was the first modern Icelandic author to win for himself not only publication but success outside his own country. He followed up his success with the play *Ønsket* (*The Wish*, 1915), of which more below. His last play *Løgneren* (*The Liar*, 1917) was the previously-mentioned attempt to dramatize some episodes of *Njáll's Saga*. It is perhaps a measure of his eagerness to please that he permitted and himself wrote alternate endings to two of his plays, *The Hraun Farm* and *Eyvind of the Hills*, in which the tragic catastrophes are averted by a sudden shift to sweet reasonableness on the part of the protagonists.

The central theme of all his plays may be formulated as the ambitious man's challenge to the laws of the universe, a basically Nietzschean and Dostoievskian theme. Each of his heroes is endowed with a will to exceed his grasp, and this becomes his tragic downfall. Dr. Harald Rung burns to produce a vaccine for the cure of tuberculosis and goes to the length of trying it on himself. To a friend who remonstrates with him he says: "Couldn't you want something so passionately that you would buy it with your life?" Sveinungi, the farmer at Hraun, defies an earthquake that threatens to destroy his farm, a possession more important to him than life itself. In the end it is not the earthquake that destroys him, however, but his own daughter. Her love for a man whom her father despises makes the farmer's life valueless and his efforts vain, and so he chooses to be destroyed with the farm. In *Eyvind of the Hills* it is the woman, Halla, who defies nature. She joins the man she loves in voluntary outlawry among the inhospitable mountain wastes

[7] Third ed., Copenhagen: Gyldendal, 1917.

of the interior. To one of the characters she says, "May not a strong will turn the tide of fate?" But in the end fate catches up with her also, when the hounding of the community and the inclemency of the elements bring out the basic cowardice of the man she loves. She loses her faith in her own love for him and rather than face emptiness she walks out into the snow to her death. In *The Wish* Loftur embodies perhaps more fully than any of the rest man's defiance of his limitations, here symbolized by the secret lore which Loftur seeks beyond and above the knowledge that his school conveys.

The reception of *Eyvind* was enthusiastic, and foreign critics like Georg Brandes in Denmark and Léon Pineau in France acclaimed Jóhann as a worthy successor to the great dramatists of the preceding generation. Brandes described him as having "poetic talent of a high order" and Pineau spoke of his "sublimely powerful poetry."[8]

The Wish appeared in Danish as *Ønsket* and in Icelandic as *Galdra-Loftur* (*Loftur the Magician*), both in 1915. The latter name is one that was applied to his hero Loftur because of his practice of the magic arts. Even before the appearance of *Eyvind*, Jóhann was thinking of this play. In a letter dated August 2, 1911, he wrote to his fiancée, "The play lives in my soul as one long, beautiful song, 'The Wish.' The individual scenes come into the light one by one, like a landscape emerging from the dark. The people who live there are becoming my friends,—what a joy to try to create something beautiful, but also a torment, often a frightful torment, when discouragement and doubt fill my soul."[9] When the play finally appeared, Jóhann was already a celebrity. *Eyvind* had been a sensation,

[8] Leach, ed., *Modern Icelandic Plays* (1916). This volume includes translations of *Bjærg-Ejvind og hans hustru* and *Gaarden Hraun*. For further information on the former play see the article by Magoun, cited above, footnote 6.

[9] *Rit*, vol. 2, 275.

but *The Wish* was something less than that. It was well received, however, and over the years it has proved to be rather
more enduring. The Danish critic Anders Thuborg wrote at
the time of Jóhann's death: "*The Wish* constitutes the culmi-
nation of the author's life work."[10]

It will be seen from the footnote to the list of Characters
that Jóhann described the relation of his play to its source as
being that of a "free fantasia." This is not far from the truth,
since the play is essentially one more embodiment of his own
basic concern with man's relationship to the universe. Loftur
reflects the author himself and carries his message to the audience. But much of the story and the central character are also
historical, or at least legendary. Jóhann is known to have been
familiar with the story of Galdra-Loftur from childhood, since
it appeared in the most widely read collection of Icelandic
folklore, Jón Arnason's *Íslenzkar Thjóðsögur og æfintýri* (*Icelandic Folktales and Fairystories*, Leipzig, 1864–74), a work
which was also the source of his preceding play, *Eyvind*.[11] Jón
Arnason's tale is derived from a written source, but builds on
popular narrative reflecting contemporary notions on the nature of academic activities. Loftur is reported to have been a
pupil at the cathedral school in Hólar in the north of Iceland,
and a ringleader in the secret practice of witchcraft indulged in
by some of the pupils. Although no dates are given in the
story, historical persons mentioned in it lived in the first half of
the eighteenth century. Various tricks which Loftur performed with his magic are mentioned, but the only one that
Jóhann found use for in his play was the following:

> Another time Loftur got a servant girl on the farm with child
> and then killed her by witchcraft. She had the job of carrying

[10] "Ved Jóhann Sigurjónssons Død." *Tilskueren*, vol. 36, sec. 2 (1919),
330–37.

[11] See Arnason, *Íslenzkar Thjódsögur*, vol. 1, 583–86, here taken from
the phototypic reprint of 1929, and Magoun, "Jóhann Sigurjónsson's
Fjalla-Eyvindur."

containers of food in and out of the kitchen. To speed up this work they used trough-shaped trays on which they put several containers at once. Loftur opened a passage for her right through the wall so that she went in through this. But because the girl was frightened and hesitated, the magic worked and caused the wall to close again. A long time later, when the wall was torn down, the skeleton of a woman was found standing in it, with a tray of containers in her arms and the bones of an unborn child in her womb.

It is clear that this poor little story was no more than a springboard for the poet's imagination, and he found much more to his use in *Anne Pedersdotter*, a play that had been successfully performed in Copenhagen in 1909. This play was by the Norwegian playwright Hans Wiers-Jenssen, and was performed with the same Johanne Dybwad in the main role who was to play his Halla in *Eyvind* three years later. Anne Pedersdotter was a woman of sixteenth-century Bergen, the widow of a bishop, who was accused of having killed her husband by witchcraft and was eventually burned at the stake for her supposed crime. As Wiers-Jenssen presented the theme, her sin was much the same as Loftur's: she wished her husband's death because she loved another. The Wiers-Jenssen play was later translated into English by John Masefield as *The Witch*, and this was also its title when the famous Danish producer Carl Dreyer turned it into a great film.[12] The connection between this play and *The Wish* has been demonstrated by Professor Steingrímur Thorsteinsson, but as he has also pointed out, the essential psychological content is deeper in *The Wish*. This play reflects to the full the personality and inner experience of its author.[13]

Even though the hero's dilemma is therefore less a part of the legend of Loftur than it is of the author's own experience, Jóhann returned to the legend for the final, dramatic scene of

[12] First published as *Anne Pedersdotter*, English version by John Masefield (Boston: Little, Brown, 1917); reprinted as *The Witch*, with an introduction by H. Osborne (New York: Brentano's, 1926).

[13] Thorsteinsson, "*Anna Pjetursdottir og Galdra-Loftur*."

the play. This concerns Bishop Gottskalk the Grim and his powerful book of magic, the *Rauðskinna* (*The Red Book*, lit. "Redskin"). Gottskalk appears to have been one of the last Catholic bishops of Iceland, having died in 1520.[14] That people believed, even as late as the eighteenth century, that the clergy and their pupils practiced witchcraft is abundantly clear not only from legends of this kind, but from actual court records of cases in which they were publicly accused of witchcraft and compelled to clear themselves if they wished to save their necks.[15] This is that same early modern world of Christian superstition which we know from Arthur Miller's *The Crucible*.

Loftur is said to have frightened one of his schoolmates into joining him in an attempt to raise all the dead bishops of Hólar from their rest under the ground. The friend was asked only to stand in the church steeple and hold the bell cord until Loftur gave him a signal to ring the bell. Loftur had learned all he could from the book called *Gráskinna*, *The Gray Book*, which legend said was used as a textbook at the cathedral schools, and now he wanted to lay his hands on the more advanced *Rauðskinna*. His explanation to his friend of the reasons for this is of interest:

> Those who have learned magic, as I have, can only use it for evil, and they will all be destroyed when they die. But if a person learns enough, the devil will no longer have power over him, but will have to serve him without getting anything in return, just as he served Sæmundur the Wise. Anyone who learns that much is free to use his knowledge as he pleases. This kind of knowledge cannot be acquired in our days since the Black School was disbanded, and Bishop Gottskalk the Grim had the *Rauðskinna* buried with him.[16]

In the play this is reflected in Loftur's words to the girl Dísa, who has replaced his schoolmate in the legend: "Only one path

14 Jón Arnason, *Íslenzkar Thjóðsögur*, vol. 1, 515 fn.
15 *Ibid.*, vol. 1, 446–47.
16 *Ibid.*, vol. 1, 584.

is open to me. I have to go on into darkness. I have to gain so much knowledge that I can win power over Evil. If I can then abstain from ever wanting anything for myself, I will be forgiven in the hour of my death." But the Loftur of our play is placed in a modern, Nietzschean context: "When I make use of Evil to promote the Good—what is then Good and what is Evil?"

In the legend Loftur enters the pulpit and conjures the bishops up into the moonlit church one by one; the oldest of them says to Loftur, "Stop this, thou evil man, while there is time." In the play these words are elaborated and turned into the "voices of conscience." In the legend Loftur finally succeeds in raising Bishop Gottskalk, with the red book in his right hand. "Well have you sung, my son, and better than I expected," he says, "but you will not get my *Rauðskinna*."

Loftur was seized by a veritable fury and frenzy, and conjured as he had never done before. He turned the words of benediction and the Lord's prayer against the Devil; the whole church shook and trembled. It looked to the schoolboy as if Gottskalk came nearer to Loftur and was reluctantly handing him one corner of the book. So far the boy had been brave, but now he shook with fear and all turned black before his eyes. It seemed to him as if the bishop turned the book as Loftur thrust forth his hand. He thought that Loftur was giving him the signal and he grabbed the bell cord. Immediately everything vanished into the floor with a tremendous crash. Loftur stood a moment as if frozen in the pulpit and laid his head in his hands. Then he stumbled slowly down and found his companion, groaned and said, "This went worse than it should have." [17]

The legend goes on to let Loftur explain that it was his own impatience and anger in grabbing for the book that had caused the boy's error. Loftur does not die immediately, as he does in the play, but his mind is beclouded and he knows that his fate is sealed. In spite of the friendship and vigilance of a local

[17] *Ibid.*, vol. 1, 585.

priest he vanishes into the sea one day, having been seized by a large, hairy hand.

The material as Jóhann found it in Jón Arnason's book was certainly tempting as material for dramatic reworking. The play has often been referred to as an Icelandic *Faust*, but there are more differences than similarities. The emphasis here is not on knowledge as knowledge, rather on the passion for knowledge which can become so overpowering that it crushes the humbler passion of love. Bishop Gottskalk tells Loftur: "In the darkness, before thou wert born, Evil cleft thy will." Loftur's curse is his divided will, or in psychological terms, his schizophrenia, which is symbolized in the two women he loves. The evil wish that kills Steinunn and gives the play its name is an expression of deep and mysterious forces within himself which he is unable to master and which are his fate. "In the beginning was the wish," he cries, apparently in conscious rejection of Faust's "Im Anfang war der Tat."

The play was first performed in Reykjavík on December 26, 1914, and at the Dagmar Theater in Copenhagen on January 22, 1915. The present translation into English is an entirely new one, based on the Icelandic version, but corrected so that it substantially agrees with the Danish.

E. H.

Jóhann Sigurjónsson: Bibliography

IN DANISH AND ICELANDIC

Dr. Rung. Drama in four acts. Copenhagen: Gyldendal, 1905.
Bóndinn á Hrauni (*The Farmer at Hraun*). Play in four acts. Reykjavík, 1908.
Bjærg-Ejvind og hans hustru (*Eyvind of the Hills and His Wife*). Play in four acts. Copenhagen: Gyldendal, 1911.
———. Second, revised edition. Copenhagen: Gyldendal, 1913.

————. Third, revised edition. With 40 illustrations from the Swedish film version. Copenhagen: Gyldendal, 1917.

Fjalla-Eyvindur (*Eyvind of the Hills*). Play in four acts. Reykjavík, 1912 (Icelandic version of the preceding).

Gaarden Hraun (*The Hraun Farm*). Play in three acts. Copenhagen: Gyldendal, 1912. (Danish version of *Bóndinn á Hrauni.*)

Ønsket (*The Wish*). Play in three acts. Copenhagen: Gyldendal, 1915.

Galdra-Loftur (*Loftur the Magician*). Play in three acts. Reykjavík, 1915 (Icelandic version of the preceding).

Løgneren (*The Liar*). Play in five acts with a prologue. Copenhagen: Gyldendal, 1917.

Smaadigte (*Poems*). Copenhagen: Gyldendal, 1920.

Lygarinn (*The Liar*). In *Ársritið Jólagjöfin*, Reykjavík, 1939 (Icelandic version of *Løgneren*).

Rit (*Writings*). 2 vols., ed. Kristinn Andrésson. Reykjavík: Mál og Menning, 1941–42.

IN ENGLISH

Modern Icelandic Plays. New York: The American-Scandinavian Foundation, 1916. (Contains translations by Henninge Krohn Schanche of *Bjærg-Ejvind og hans hustru* and *Gaarden Hraun*).

Eyvindur of the Mountains, tr. Frank P. Magoun. Reykjavík: Helgafell, 1961.

Loftur, tr. by Jean Young and Eleanor Arkwright. University of Reading, 1939.

Loft's Wish, tr. by Jakobina Johnson, in *Poet Lore,* vol. 46 (1940), pp. 99–146.

Characters

The Bishop of Holar
The Bishop's Wife
Disa, the Bishop's Daughter
The Bailiff at Holar
Loftur, the Bailiff's son, in his mid-twenties, one of the students
    at the Cathedral school
Olafur, Loftur's best friend and the Bailiff's right-hand man
Steinunn, a female relative of Olafur, employed on the farm
A blind almsman
His granddaughter, a ten-year-old girl
Five almsmen
A vagrant
A maid servant
Hired workmen
"Voices of conscience"
Bishop Gottskalk the Grim

Time: Early in the Eighteenth Century
The play is a free fantasia based on a legendary Icelandic
figure, Galdra-Loftur, who lived at the Bishop's seat in
Holar after the Reformation.

Act I

The Bishop's seat at Holar. The Bailiff's spacious livingroom. Lofted beams. The meadow, which slopes down to a river with low mountains in the background, is seen dimly through two windows. Between the windows, in the center of the stage, a large, old-fashioned writing desk. A cashbox beside the desk. A row of closed-in bedsteads in the corner right. Table, benches, and chairs of wood. Large, ornamented chest on the left-hand wall, front. Bookshelf filled with books. In the left corner a double shelf with mugs, candle holders, and tapers. A bench nearest the audience on the left. Another small door to the left. Sunday afternoon. Late summer. There are six almsmen in the room. One is speaking, the others are listening. Some are standing, some sitting.

FIRST ALMSMAN (*telling a story*): "I ask Thee not for Thy wisdom, for of that I have enough myself, but now I ask Thee for Thy mercy."

SECOND ALMSMAN: Were those his last words?

FIRST ALMSMAN: Yes, those were his last words.

SECOND ALMSMAN: The first time I saw him we were guests at the same farm. He sat in the livingroom with his bag on his back. (*Falls silent.*)

THE VAGRANT: What kind of a fellow was he? I'm new in this district.

THIRD ALMSMAN: It was too bad about him. He thought his

head was so heavy with wisdom that he would fall on his face if he didn't carry a bag on his back all the time.

THE VAGRANT (*laughs*): I wish I could have seen him.

FOURTH ALMSMAN: You wouldn't have laughed if you had seen him. No one is more deserving to be one of God's almsmen than those who are weak of mind.

FIFTH ALMSMAN (*looking out the window*): The river keeps rising. It must have rained good and hard up in the mountains.

(*A blind almsman enters, guided by a ten-year-old girl. He is holding a bundle under his arm.*)

THE BLIND MAN: God bless you all.

THE ALMSMEN: God bless you.

(*The blind almsman turns to the left.*)

THE GIRL: This way, grandfather.

THE BLIND MAN: It's just an old habit, daughter, from the years when we used to gather in the Bishop's room. (*He sits down.*) How many are we in here?

FOURTH ALMSMAN: We were six before you came.

(*The church bells peal.*)

FIRST ALMSMAN: This is the second time they have rung. His Highness the Bishop will soon be here.

A MAID (*enters, goes over to the little girl*): The Bishop's lady asked me to bring you in. She wants to talk to you. She caught sight of you and your grandfather out in the yard.

(*The girl presses closer to her grandfather.*)

THE BLIND MAN: Just you go, my child. The lady wishes you well in every way. I'll wait for you here.

(*The maid and the girl exit.*)

THE BLIND MAN: Who will be leading the service this evening?

FIFTH ALMSMAN: The cathedral dean.

THE BLIND MAN: When his Highness the Bishop is not in the pulpit, I am happiest about the singing. I have often wondered that such a great building could have so sweet a voice. (*Silence.*)

LOFTUR (*comes in, looks around hastily*): Here they are gathered, all of Pharaoh's lean-fleshed kine. (*He goes over to the blind man, puts his hand on his shoulder.*) I'm not referring to you. Do you have the thing I asked you to get for me?

THE BLIND MAN (*unwraps the bundle, takes out an old book in wooden covers*): The owner said that the book was not for sale, but he would lend it to you for a month's time, just because you are the Bailiff's son and a man of learning. (*Hands him the book.*) I promised to bring the book back to him.

LOFTUR (*flips the pages for a moment*): If my father should ask for me, tell him I don't feel well and have gone to bed. (*Takes a coin out of his wallet.*) Here is a small reward for your trouble. (*Opens the door to the left, exit.*)

FIRST ALMSMAN (*looks angrily at the door*): It's easy for him to mock at us poor folk. He never tried starvation.

THE BLIND MAN: Wealth does not always lead to happiness. Often enough discontent goes with a full belly.

FIRST ALMSMAN: I've heard it said that he noses around in a lot more learning than is needed for the ministry. You should be above acting as his errand boy.

THE BLIND MAN: What are you talking about that you don't dare speak out plainly?

FIRST ALMSMAN: We don't need to go back very far. In the days of the late bishop some of the pupils at the school were caught practicing witchcraft. Anything that has happened once can happen again.

(*Enter the Bishop in his vestments and the Bailiff dressed for church.*)

ALL THE ALMSMEN (*rising*): God give his Highness the Bishop a long life!

THE BISHOP (*kindly*): Please remain seated.

(*The Blind Man sits down, the others remain standing. The Bailiff goes to the writing desk, pulls out a drawer, takes out a key and opens the cashbox.*)

THE BISHOP (*still in a kindly tone*): It has been brought to my ears that some of you are not satisfied with my gifts. Do you feel that I give you too little?

THE ALMSMEN: No, heaven help us, no.

THE BISHOP (*in the same gentle voice*): You need have no fears about coming to me with all your troubles. Sincerity is a virtue.

FIRST ALMSMAN (*picks up his courage*): It is only that we, who come here constantly, feel that we are more closely attached to the bishop's see than these vagrants, who turn up now and then. (*More boldly.*) Isn't that the truth?

ALL THE ALMSMEN (*except the Blind Man and the Vagrant*): Yes.

THIRD ALMSMAN: Your Highness treats everyone alike.

THE BISHOP: Which of you is the least in need? I'll reduce his portion and add to the portion of one who needs it more. (*The almsmen fall silent.*)

THE BAILIFF: The Bishop is waiting for an answer. (*Hands the Bishop the money.*)

FIRST ALMSMAN: I am not the one who is least in need, but the one who deserves the least, your Highness.

THE BISHOP (*coldly*): I did not ask about that. (*Distributes the alms.*) Now take your usual portion, each of you, and pray to God that he will cleanse your hearts of envy. Go in peace. (*The almsmen bow to the Bishop, mumble words of gratitude, leave. The Blind Man remains seated.*)

THE BLIND MAN (*shaking his head*): I gave thee the sun and the stars, and thou thanked me not.

THE BAILIFF (*writing in the account book*): If they could do as they wished, they would divide the property of the Bishop's see among themselves, with no other excuse than their envy.

THE BISHOP: We are well enough off so that God's almsmen need not leave here empty-handed. (*The Bishop's wife enters, stops in the doorway.*)

THE BAILIFF: Better roads and bridges would improve the welfare of the bishopric and add to the income of the see. Then there would be means enough for a new church, which would raise its rafters higher than all other buildings in Iceland. (*Closes the book.*)

THE BISHOP: The poorest of almsmen is a temple of God, even though it should fall into dust sooner than those which are built of stone.

THE BISHOP'S WIFE: Your bailiff is always full of cares. Are you ready to go to church?

THE BISHOP: Yes, I am, my dear.

THE BISHOP'S WIFE (*to the Blind Man*): Your little darling will be here any moment now, as soon as we have fixed her hair. (*To the Bishop*). She reminded me so much of our daughter, when she was her age, that I decided to give her one of her old dresses.

THE BAILIFF: When is the Bishop's daughter expected home?

THE BISHOP'S WIFE (*without looking at him*): We expect her any day now.

THE BISHOP (*lovingly*): You are looking forward to seeing her again.

THE BISHOP'S WIFE (*goes to the door*): Yes. This has been a long year, even though I knew she was in good hands. (*They leave.*)

THE BAILIFF (*locking the writing desk*): Do you know if my son has been here?

THE BLIND MAN: He was just here. I was to tell you, if you asked for him, that he was not feeling well and had gone to bed.

THE BAILIFF (*troubled*): The Bishop will notice his absence in church. (*Opens the door quietly and whispers*): Loftur! (*A loving expression lights his face. He leaves the door ajar. Turns to the Blind Man.*) I haven't the heart to wake him. I am sure he must have pored over his books until dawn. (*Smiling.*) He was called "the little bishop" when he was a small boy, because he was so deep in his own thoughts.

(*Goes to the door, stops.*) I'll see you after the service.
(*Exit.*)

(*The Blind Man listens a moment for his footsteps. Pulls out an enormous, flowered handkerchief, with coins tied up in one corner; he unties it, adds the new coin and ties it up again. Remains seated.*)

LOFTUR (*enters with the book in his hand. Sits down in front of the Blind Man, looks sharply at him*): How long have you been blind? (*Puts the book down on the table.*)

THE BLIND MAN: I have wandered in the dark for nigh on forty years.

LOFTUR: You must have wished time and again that you might get your sight back.

THE BLIND MAN (*is silent for a moment*): Do you know the story of the ferryman and St. Thorlak?

LOFTUR: No.

THE BLIND MAN: It was in the dead of winter, with cold and snow storms. The ferryman was to carry the chaplain from Skalholt over the river. When he got across the river, there were ten of God's almsmen who asked him to ferry them back to Skalholt. Out of his goodness he gave them all a ride. The boat was too heavily loaded, and overturned. The ferryman's clothing was soaked with water, and he sank to the bottom. He tried to wade ashore. But when he perceived that he could no longer breathe, he called on St. Thorlak for help. He prayed that at least his corpse might float to land on the Skalholt side. Then he saw a hand sweep away the water from his face. This happened three times, and he reached land, safe and sound.

LOFTUR: Why are you telling me this story?

THE BLIND MAN: I have often wished that a merciful hand might sweep the darkness away from my eyes.

LOFTUR (*his voice fired with excitement*): How can you be sure that your wish had enough strength?

(*The Blind Man is silent.*)

LOFTUR: I know that man's wishes can perform miracles. They have done so in ages past, and they do so to this very day. (*The maid and the girl come in. The girl is in a new dress, the maid is carrying the old one in a bundle.*)

THE GIRL (*running to her grandfather*): Feel, grandfather. I've got a marvelous, beautiful new dress. (*Holds out the cloth.*) There's lace at the neckline.

THE MAID: Yes, isn't she fancy, though? The Bishop's lady dressed her up from head to foot.

THE BLIND MAN: Did you remember to thank the lady?

THE MAID: Yes, she did.

LOFTUR (*has been looking at the girl with astonishment. Walks over to her and strokes her hair*): How silky soft your hair is. Will you be my little sweetheart? (*The girl clings close to her grandfather. Loftur smiles.*) Are you afraid? (*Takes out his wallet.*)

(*The church bells ring.*)

THE MAID (*puts down the bundle*): Now you'll have to look after your things yourself. I'm off to church. (*Exit.*)

THE BLIND MAN (*gets up*): We're leaving too.

LOFTUR (*has found a silver coin*): Keep this in the pocket of your beautiful new dress. (*Thrusts the coin into her pocket.*) (*The girl kisses Loftur.*)

THE BLIND MAN (*on his way to the door. Turns to Loftur*): I wished—until it became a sin. Not until I gave up wishing was my soul finally at peace. (*They leave.*)

(*Loftur stares after them a short while. Opens the book, which is bound in wooden covers. A single initial letter, illuminated in red ink, covers more than half a page. He puts the book down on the table, takes out a key and opens the chest. Gets down on his knees, picks up books from the chest and piles them up around him. He is obviously hunting for a particular book.*)

STEINUNN (*comes in through the door, speaks softly*): Loftur! (*Loftur fails to hear her.*)

STEINUNN (*louder, sadly*): Loftur!

LOFTUR (*looks up. When he sees Steinunn, his face falls*): So it's you.

STEINUNN: Were you expecting someone else?

LOFTUR: I thought you were in church.

STEINUNN: There was a time when you knew my very footstep. Now you don't even know my voice.

LOFTUR: Did you come to scold me?

STEINUNN: No. (*Is silent a moment.*) I put on my Sunday best today. I know you are happy when I look nice. Look at me.

LOFTUR (*gets up*): You are prettiest in your everyday clothes. What do you want?

STEINUNN (*seriously*): I've got to talk to you.

LOFTUR: The workers have started gossiping. I can see it on you.

STEINUNN: No.

LOFTUR: Then what do you want?

(*Steinunn walks silently over to the window.*)

LOFTUR (*follows her, speaks more softly*): Is it about our future?

STEINUNN (*absently drawing patterns on the window with her finger*): One time this summer I felt as if I had committed a great sin. I felt a cold mist in the room, as if there were frost on the windowpanes. But your voice thawed it out.

LOFTUR (*gazing at her*): Would you be unhappy if I were dead?

STEINUNN (*turns sharply toward him*): You know I would.

LOFTUR (*goes back to the chest*): I know that you would be sad the first few months. Maybe until my grave was covered with grass. (*Gets down on his knees again.*) Though most people's wounds heal faster than those of the earth. (*Takes out more books.*)

STEINUNN (*angrily*): I wish I could burn all your books.

LOFTUR: What harm have they done you?

STEINUNN (*concerned*): You look so tired. You overwork

yourself. No man has the strength to work as you do, without rest, night and day. And you don't need to, either. I've heard the headmaster talk admiringly of your learning. I am sure you could take your examinations this winter, even if you never looked at a book again.

LOFTUR: I think so myself.

STEINUNN: But you can't do it if you overstrain yourself and lose your health. At least you shouldn't deny yourself your sleep.

LOFTUR (*in the midst of his books*): The more I read, the less I feel I know.

STEINUNN (*perplexed*): All your father's ambitions have settled on you, because you are his only child. If only his ambition will not be too much for you.

LOFTUR (*gets up*): His ambition is not mine.

STEINUNN (*more harshly*): Well, what do you want then?

LOFTUR: I? I want to stand on the threshold of the unknown, with all the wisdom of man.

STEINUNN (*frightened*): What do you mean by the unknown? (*Loftur is silent, turns the leaves of his book.*)

STEINUNN (*comes closer to him*): The workmen have started to talk about you. They say you are reading godless books. They've been spying on you. They've heard you speaking into the air when you were alone. They think you have been speaking with spirits.

LOFTUR (*walks away a few steps*): People who know nothing believe anything.

STEINUNN: I haven't warned you before, because I know your father has so much power that they don't dare speak out about it. But they are getting bolder. They say they have seen you in the churchyard at night.

LOFTUR (*turns toward her*): Was this what you came to tell me?

STEINUNN (*evades his question, comes close to him*): For your own sake you should rest a while from your reading. You

don't need to be idle even so. You could take part in the
work of the others. Then they would stop talking about
you. And it would be an unspeakable happiness for me to
hear the scythe sing in your hands.

LOFTUR: And you? What do you think about me?

STEINUNN: You have changed so much in the time we have
known each other. You act like a different man, almost like a
stranger. Even your face is changed. When you talked about
death just now, I thought you must be ill.

LOFTUR (*momentarily assumes a cunning expression, thinking
to frighten Steinunn, but forgets it in his excitement*): If I
wished to stretch out my hand into the darkness, I know it
would not be in vain. Have you heard tell of Bishop Gottskalk the Grim and his *Red Book?* I call it "The Book of
Power."

STEINUNN (*frightened*): Yes, I have.

LOFTUR: Anyone who could read everything in that book
would be the mightiest man on earth. Therefore Gottskalk
took it with him to his grave. He would not give anyone so
much power. I have seen that book.

STEINUNN (*in terror*): You!

LOFTUR : The other night I was lying on his grave out in the
churchyard. The thought came to me that perhaps I could
read it in my sleep. The bishop stood right in front of me, in
a red chasuble, and read aloud from the book. He held it up
so high that I could not see his face. But when he read, the
pages shrivelled up and dropped to the ground like ashes.
(*Looks grimly at Steinunn. Speaks as if he were reading
from a book.*) "Anyone who wishes with all his soul that
someone else were dead, let him bow to the ground and
say—" (*He is seized by trembling and breaks off.*) No, I
won't remember those words. (*Goes over to the bench, sits
down and rests his head on his hands.*)

STEINUNN (*stands still for a moment. Then her expression
clears. She goes over to him and falls on her knees*): So this is

why you have been looking so sickly, as if something were eating your vitals. (*Between weeping and laughter.*) I was afraid it was something about me. (*Gets up, strokes his hair.*) I have loved you so very very much. I am ashamed to admit it, but I have wished that you might fall ill, so that I could nurse you. I would have watched over you night and day. (*Raises her hands.*) You won't believe me, but I have cried for joy. (*Lets her hands drop.*) I once saw a patch of meadow that was gray from drought, and it turned green in a single night. The moistened grass cried for joy. (*Falls on her knees again.*) We will struggle together against the forces of evil. When I am alone in the darkness, I am afraid, but two people have nothing to fear. (*Her voice is bright with love.*) I have heard that when you hold a child's hand in yours, all that is evil must vanish. (*Whispers*) Loftur!

LOFTUR (*gets up*): I ought to live far away from people. They distract me. The unknown never whispers to me except when I am alone. Stones strike the brightest sparks in the dark. Loneliness is my darkness. What does it concern the workmen if I wake? I have felt that they hate me. This is only because I am not content with their trivial little wishes. *My* wishes are great and without bounds. In the beginning was the wish. Wishes are the souls of men.

STEINUNN: Didn't you hear anything of what I said?

LOFTUR: I am furious that the workmen should dare to speak ill of me. (*Contemptuously.*) When I think out loud, they believe I am conversing with spirits. (*Changing his tone.*) Yes, I heard what you said.

STEINUNN: Do you remember how long it is since you kissed me? Don't you love me any more?

LOFTUR: I don't know if I have the gift to love anyone. If we both forget what has passed between us, it will never have been.

STEINUNN: *Can* you forget it?

LOFTUR: Why could it not have been a dream?

STEINUNN: The body has its remembrance. (*Scornfully.*) Are you afraid of your father?

LOFTUR (*in growing impatience*): My patience is not unlimited. You know as well as I why we have had to act in secret. My father would disown me if he learned about us. He would force me to leave school. If I could never open a book again, I would feel as if I were blind. In another half year, when I have my degree, I can defy him. You have promised to wait. Recklessness is not the same as courage.

STEINUNN (*on the point of weeping*): If you only showed me some kindness. You haven't so much as kissed me.

LOFTUR: What is a kiss? Just now I kissed a child's mouth.

STEINUNN (*gets up, her voice growing more vehement*): Have I changed, since you don't love me as you did? (*Draws a deep breath, and fingers the silver loops on her dress.*) Once you told me that these loops were alive: each one had a soul of its own. You said that my breathing was what gave them life. I breathe as I always did. I speak and laugh and cry now as I did before. This spring you were on your feet at sunrise whenever I had to light the fire. You said that you loved to see the fire flickering on my face. Now I have to be content to write your name in the ashes. But the flickering of the fire has not changed.

LOFTUR: Don't work yourself up so.

STEINUNN (*goes close up to him*): You shall know that I have not forgotten a single one of your words. I have written my own marriage license, and you have sealed it with your kisses. The burning sealing wax could be no more fiery than your kisses. And I have taken God as my witness. If you just pretended love in order to get your way with me, you made a great mistake. I am poor and I have no friends. (*Laughs.*) But I won't let you go. You have made me strong. (*Embraces him.*) I could burn you to ashes in my arms.

LOFTUR: Someone might come.

STEINUNN: I don't care one bit who might come. Even your

father. I just wish that he might come. You are hiding yourself from me. (*Looks him in the face.*) I wish he would hold a burning candle before your face so that I could see what you really look like. (*Lets him go.*)

LOFTUR (*disturbed*): I don't know if you are the cause of it, but I feel as if I am forever battling with an unfulfilled obligation. You demand that I should be thinking about you and our future, every hour of the day. I feel it even if you only walk through the room. Lately it has become more and more of an accusation. I can't bear it. My thoughts have to be free. (*Touches the books. Again assumes a secretive expression.*) Perhaps I will never find what I am seeking.

STEINUNN: I hate your books.

LOFTUR: Some men can find the hidden veins of water in the earth. They can release their souls from their bodies. So can I. (*Looks at Steinunn.*) The first time I kissed you my soul was outside my body.

STEINUNN (*laughs scornfully*): Your soul was outside your body!

LOFTUR: You laugh. I'll tell you how it happened. (*Leads her over to the bench, where they sit down.*) You had been here for some time before I noticed you. One warm evening I went outdoors to be in peace with my books. Then I heard someone singing. I followed the sound. You did not see me, for I hid behind a large rock. You stood naked in the stream and poured water over yourself. I have never seen anything that gripped me so strongly. I trembled with fear. (*His voice is warm.*) If you had been one of the seal maidens who dance on the seashore on Midsummer Night, I would have stolen your magic guise. I would not have returned it to you even if you had told me that you had a husband and children in the deep. I wanted to possess you for all eternity, even if it was cruel. (*He moves closer to her. Puts his arm around her waist.*)

(*Steinunn gets up.*)

LOFTUR (*quickly rises, holds her by the hand*): No, you must listen to me. (*They sit down again.*) From that moment I could not forget you. One night, when the thought of you kept me awake, I stole outdoors. I lay down on my back. (*Closes his eyes.*) My soul trickled down into the ground. I stood in front of your bed and kissed you. You have told me yourself that this same night you dreamt that I stood by your bedside and kissed you. You saw me vanish through the door when you woke. (*He has again slipped his arm around her waist and bends down to kiss her. Softly.*) Steinunn!

STEINUNN (*rises*): Let me go!

LOFTUR (*laughs*): So you said when I kissed you the first time, too. (*Draws her to him eagerly and kisses her.*) Let's go back up to the green dell, where we were when I hardly knew if it was my blood or the brook that rushed in my ears. (*They are both silent. Footsteps are heard outside.*)

OLAFUR (*enters, stops when he sees Steinunn, turns to Loftur*): I thought you wouldn't be in church. Am I disturbing you?

LOFTUR (*awkwardly*): No no.

OLAFUR (*gloomily*): For me you don't need to make any pretence. I know that you love each other.

(*Loftur is silent. Steinunn looks at Loftur and walks past Olafur to the door.*)

OLAFUR: Do you need to leave just because I come?

(*Steinunn exits.*)

OLAFUR (*comes into the room*): Loftur, I came to talk frankly with you about a matter that has been tormenting me for a long time. (*He sits down on the bench, remains silent.*)

LOFTUR (*moves a chair over and sits down near him*): What is it, Olafur?

OLAFUR: Steinunn had been here for a month or so when I got home from my trip over the mountains. I saw at a glance that she had changed. She avoided me on purpose. Before that she had always been open with me when we met. Do you know how blind a strong wish can make one? Fool that

I was, I thought she was bashful because she had discovered I loved her.

LOFTUR (*on his feet*): Olafur!

OLAFUR: No, you must not interrupt me. (*Loftur sits down again.*) It did not take me long to discover that you were the one she was following with her eyes. Then I stooped to something I never would have believed of myself. I went spying. Early one morning, when you thought you were alone, I saw you kiss her.

LOFTUR (*rising, scornfully*): Was that a crime?

OLAFUR (*also rising*): Ever since, I have been fighting with myself. My mind began to fill with hate. I tried to root it out. But it was like trying to dislodge a heavy rock in loose earth. At every try the stone sank deeper down. (*Falls silent.*)

LOFTUR: What do you mean?

OLAFUR (*over to him*): I won't bear ill will to you. You have been my friend. Make me understand that you could not do otherwise. If I hear that from your own lips, I will try to forgive you.

LOFTUR (*still scornfully*): Do I need your forgiveness?

OLAFUR (*controlling himself with difficulty*): You have a bad conscience yourself. Since I got home, you have avoided being alone with me. Anyone who feels he has wronged another will often begin to hate him.

LOFTUR: What are you accusing me of?

OLAFUR: Don't you remember when we were boys and played wedding? You wanted a foreign princess, and I—(*warmly*) I only wanted little Steinunn, my cousin.

LOFTUR: You can have the foreign princess.

OLAFUR (*barely restraining himself*): You knew I was the one who brought Steinunn here. You teased me about her every time I mentioned her name. (*Angrily.*) You knew that I loved her with all my heart. You can't be so brazen that you will deny it!

LOFTUR (*uncertainly*): I didn't know you loved Steinunn as
much as all that. (*Reprovingly.*) Why didn't you confide to
me that you loved her?

OLAFUR: You knew that she was the only woman I loved.
Wasn't that enough for you? (*Sadly.*) In our childhood,
when either of us found a rare flower or a clump of berries,
he took possession of the spot. We sometimes *gave* each
other a spot, but we never stole it. (*Bitterly.*) In those days
we needed no fences to protect ourselves from each other.

LOFTUR (*in a low voice*): I was not my own master.

OLAFUR: I have tried to excuse you. You are younger than I,
and you have a violent temper. I have tried to place myself
in your shoes. Could I have acted so toward my friend? And
why should your love come just at this time? After all, you
had seen Steinunn before. Were you trying to convince
yourself that she was worthy of me? Or are you like a child
who enjoys a toy more if he knows that someone else
wants it?

LOFTUR: You don't spare me.

OLAFUR: Why don't you defend yourself?

LOFTUR: What do you want me to say?

OLAFUR: I was expecting every day that you would come to
me. But you were not satisfied to rob me of Steinunn. You
also robbed me of your friendship. I did not wish to see you
as a penitent sinner. I wanted to see both of you happy. (*In a
burst of emotion.*) I think I could have clasped your hand as
a brother.

LOFTUR (*moved*): I know I have acted wrongly toward you.
(*Goes over to him, says in a quiet tone*): Can you forgive
me, Olafur?
(*Olafur is silent.*)

LOFTUR (*turning away*): I have suffered from it myself.

OLAFUR (*getting up*): I'll try to go on being your friend. (*Is
silent a moment. Points to the books on the shelf. His voice is
now quite changed.*) Do you have to read so much? You
don't even grant yourself sleep at night.

LOFTUR: I read more books than concern the school.

OLAFUR: You'd laugh and you'd also be vexed if you knew how the workmen are talking about you.

(*Short silence.*)

LOFTUR: What do the workmen say?

OLAFUR: They are afraid of you. They think you are in league with the supernatural.

LOFTUR: This is the second time today I've heard it. Has the Bishop, or my father, got wind of this?

OLAFUR: Not yet.

LOFTUR (*laughs a little noisily*): It amuses me that the workers are afraid of me. (*Kneels down by the books and puts them carefully back in the chest.*)

OLAFUR: I told them to their faces that this was stupid nonsense. Why should you be trying to get into contact with the powers of darkness? You, who have everything you want? In any case, I don't believe in any supernatural powers, whether bad or good.

LOFTUR (*with a tinge of scorn in his voice*): When we boiled falcon's claws and ate them to make us strong, you knew about all my wishes.

OLAFUR: You mean that I don't know about them now?

LOFTUR (*looks up from his books*): Have you ever wished that you knew the secrets that are known only by the dead?

OLAFUR (*coldly*): Dead men know no secrets.

LOFTUR (*getting up*): You are all so wise in your opinions. Good people go to heaven, and bad people land in hellfire. But my books have revealed something quite different to me. Once upon a time a skull was dug up from an old grave. It was dark brown from age, and all the flesh of the face had rotted away. But the eyes were alive and aflame with terror. That man's punishment was that his soul could not fly away from its body.

OLAFUR: Do you believe everything you read in books?

LOFTUR: This is more deeply engraved in my memory than many things I know for sure are true. (*Opens one of the*

books, lovingly caresses the open pages.) To some people
these symbols are as mysterious as the tracks of birds on the
seashore. But to me they speak as if they were alive. They
can gladden me and make me sad. They teach me the lore of
centuries past. The souls of the dead live in books.

OLAFUR (*scornfully*): Yes. Or the lies of the dead.

LOFTUR (*is silent a moment*): You do not believe in supernatural forces. Yet you won't deny that there is fire down in
the earth, below your feet, even though you have never seen
it. (*Chuckling.*) It only reveals itself as a red cat's paw, when
it wants to play with men. Its nature is destructiveness. And
yet it is compelled to serve mankind. Once in the beginnings
of time some wise man must have tamed it with his magic
incantations. (*Mysteriously.*) If I reveal to you that the fire
down in the earth is nothing but the shadow of the devil,
you will perhaps begin to understand me.

OLAFUR: I'm beginning to fear for your sanity.

LOFTUR (*his voice rising to ecstasy*): God created man from
clay. But then the clay was baked in fire. For this reason few
men can master themselves. Imagine what that being is like
who has fire as his shadow! If only a man could tame him as
well. You are a lover of horses. You can master even the
wildest of them. It is my resolve to saddle the darkness!

OLAFUR (*goes over to him, his voice gentle*): I am very much
concerned about you, Loftur. You are not living in the real
world, but in a world of wild dreams. You are overstraining
yourself. You must rest.

LOFTUR (*more quietly*): Who knows how much can be lost in
a single inattentive moment? Perhaps some great truth was
just about to be revealed at that moment, but no one was
ready to receive it. You can't imagine how often I have
fought back sleep when it was about to overcome me. I hate
sleep, because it steals my time away. But you are all living as
if you had eternity to waste.

OLAFUR: Rest and work must go hand in hand. Remember it is
your duty to those you love to take care of yourself.

LOFTUR (*impatiently*): It is useless to waste more words. We will never be agreed. (*Sits down at the table, opens his book.*)

OLAFUR: I only want to warn you. Your father has great authority, but it does have its limits. If the Bishop should hear the chatter of the workmen, it might be dangerous for you.

LOFTUR: You are like a brook that never tires. What evil can the workmen say about me? Nothing. You are seeing ghosts, you and Steinunn. You two bore me. (*Bends over his book.*)

OLAFUR (*is silent a moment. Then his voice hardens and his expression is cold as ice, as he goes over to Loftur*): Does Steinunn bore you?

LOFTUR (*reads without answering. The sound of horses' hoofs is heard outside. Loftur looks up*): Who would be coming to church so late?

OLAFUR (*deeply stirred*): I had expected to see your face lighting up when you spoke her name. (*He seizes Loftur by the shoulder and forces him up from his chair.*) Are you using her as a plaything?

LOFTUR (*astonished*): What's the matter with you, man?

OLAFUR: I don't know your wishes any longer. Perhaps you don't know mine either. (*Lets Loftur go.*)

LOFTUR (*straightening up*): Since when did you become my guardian?

OLAFUR (*picks up the book*): You stole the woman I love. If you are not good to her, you will pay for it. (*He breaks the wooden binding and hurls the book to the floor.*)

LOFTUR: Have you gone out of your mind? (*Bends down and picks up the book.*)

DISA (*in the doorway, laughing*): Here I am!

LOFTUR (*astonished*): Are you back?

DISA: Can't you see? (*Laughs.*) You both look so deathly serious. Aren't you going to welcome me? (*Greets them with kisses.*) Hello, Olafur. Hello, Loftur.

LOFTUR AND OLAFUR: Hello, Disa, welcome home.

DISA (*eagerly*): It's afternoon mass. I heard the singing. Are mother and father in church?

LOFTUR: Yes.

DISA (*laughing*): I think they'll be surprised when they see me. How have you been? Dad and mother and all of you? (*She starts taking off her riding clothes while she speaks.*)

LOFTUR: We have been fine. And you?

DISA: I've had a wonderful time. But it's just marvellous to be back home. I raced away from my party so the wind whizzed past my ears. Are you the only ones who are not in church?

LOFTUR: Yes.

DISA (*laughs*): Oh you heathens!

OLAFUR: My cousin Steinunn isn't in church either.

DISA: Well, I don't know her. (*Excited.*) I almost forgot my horse. (*To Olafur*): Please hurry and take his saddle off, so he can roll over. He's foaming with sweat, the poor dear. (*Olafur leaves.*)

DISA (*prattling without interruption*): Imagine what I dreamed last night. (*Solemnly.*) I saw a big black horse come swimming across the stream. He pulled the whole stream up to the farm by his tail. (*Waves her arm to show this. Walks rapidly over to the window, opens it, leans out, pointing.*) That's where he came from. (*Sound of singing from the church.*) Listen! My old church! (*Listens. The singing stops. Looks at Loftur, bursts out laughing.*) Look at you, how you're gaping!

LOFTUR (*uncertainly*): How you have grown in this one year. When you left, you were only a child.

DISA (*importantly*): Yes, you can bet your life that I am grown-up now. I can't wear a single one of my old dresses any more. (*Walks quickly over to Loftur. Whispers laughingly.*) I have even had a suitor. (*Retreats, half bashfully. Then she smiles again, and points.*) There is that knot in the wood that looks like a wrinkled little face. I'll never forget when you fooled me into sitting a whole hour waiting for a horsefly to sit down on it. Then, you said, he would blink his eyes. (*Makes faces and blinks her eyes. Shakes her clenched hand at him.*) You shameful rascal you! Well, now I'm going in and pay my respects to the rest of the house. Are you coming with me?

LOFTUR (*with assumed indifference*): So the young lady has got herself a suitor?

DISA (*triumphantly*): You hadn't expected that, had you? What would you have done if I had accepted him?

(*Loftur stares at her for a moment.*)

DISA (*impatiently*): Well! Tell me!

LOFTUR: I would have saddled my white charger and ridden with all my men the shortest way over the mountains. I would have challenged him to combat and chosen a barren island in the raging stream as our battlefield. His blood would have stained the gravel like patches of roses.

DISA (*looks attentively at him. Interrupts him with her laughter*): Ha ha! You think you can still stuff me with stories, as you did when we were children? You have no charger, and no men, and the mountains are impassable in winter!

LOFTUR (*suddenly sad*): Oh how I wish that we were children still, both of us!

DISA (*gently*): Why do you say that so sadly? (*Looks at him attentively and fondly.*) But you are so pale, and your face is drawn. Have you been ill?

LOFTUR (*with a determined air*): No, my health is fine. (*Bends over and tosses the books carelessly into the chest.*)

DISA (*looking at him*): Has something gone wrong for you?

(*Loftur makes no reply.*)

DISA (*continuing*): I know that you were anxious to go abroad, like my father, and become a truly learned man. Doesn't your father want you to go any more?

LOFTUR (*straightening out*): I don't know.

DISA (*happy*): You see, I can guess what your worries are.

(*Eagerly.*) I'll take it upon myself to persuade your father. I can't remember that he ever denied me anything I asked him for. If he won't be moved, I'll get my father to help us. In such things I know your father will yield to him. You have nothing to worry about.

LOFTUR (*strained*): Tell me something about your trip. Did you ride over the mountains? Did you have luck with the weather?

DISA (*displeased*): We had splendid weather all the way. We rode over the mountains. (*Eager again.*) There isn't any disagreement between your father and mine, is there?

LOFTUR: Not that I know.

DISA (*fingering her dress*): Mother thinks your father has too much to say around here. I know that very well. But I think it is quite proper that dad should have all his thoughts on the kingdom of God. You won't think much about property and money matters, either, when you've become a really learned man. Will you now?

LOFTUR (*has been looking at her as she speaks. There is a gentle tremor in his voice*): Why haven't I thought oftener of you than I have?

DISA: Why won't you confide in me what is troubling you? We have always been like brother and sister.

LOFTUR: Oh! If only I were a free man and could sail away to foreign lands this very evening. I'm sure I have wished this ever since you came into the room. (*Looks at her.*) Imagine a ship that is riding at anchor and is anxious to set sail.

DISA (*shakes her head*): I don't know what you mean.

LOFTUR (*more quietly*): I have often sailed in my imagination. While I was standing in the lava fields, I sailed with the whole country far, far to the south. The glaciers were white sails that the sun shone on. And the blue peaks rose and fell in the breakers.

DISA (*looking at him wonderingly, suddenly smiles*): This brings back to me our old game, when you flew with me on your magic carpet. (*Points.*) There it is still, our old rug. (*Goes over to it.*)

LOFTUR (*goes to the rug*): Now it's just my father's carpet. Shall we try and see if it can still fly?

DISA: Yes!

(*They lift the rug and put it out on the floor.*)

LOFTUR (*steps on the rug*): Come and fly with me.

DISA (*laughs*): Are you still so silly?

LOFTUR (*nods seriously*): Come.

DISA (*shakes her head*): No, I don't want to.

LOFTUR (*holds out his arms*): Come, Disa.

(*Disa goes over to him, steps on the rug. While Disa and Loftur converse, the setting sun begins to spread its glow across the sky.*)

LOFTUR (*puts his arm around her waist*): Now let's close our eyes so we can see better. (*Disa closes her eyes. Loftur mumbles as if he were chanting a magic formula.*) Fly thou, fly thou, magic carpet—wherever thou wilt in the world! (*Breathes lightly on Disa's eyelids.*) Now the wind is blowing in our eyes. (*Closes his eyes. They rock gently back and forth.*) Look how the earth is gliding away under our feet. Now we are climbing up over all the clouds. Do you hear the roaring far, far below us? That is the sea. (*Mumbles.*) Fly thou, fly thou, magic carpet! (*Opens his eyes, looks at Disa.*) Do you know the wishing well, where the stones dance? That is where we're flying. The stones are constantly leaping out of the water. Incredibly many of them, speckled and plain. Each with its own nature, as manifold as the thoughts of men. (*Through the open window a soft prelude is heard from the church.*) That is the stone of life, red as dripping blood. There is the stone that makes you invisible, blue with streaks of gold. There is the black heart-shaped stone that breaks all chains. (*During the last sentence Loftur has clenched his fist and opened it again.*) But the stone of wishes itself you can't see, for it is lying on the bottom of

the well, and it never takes part in the dance. Only its white
light shines up through the water. (*His voice rises to jubila-
tion.*) When that light falls on a man's face, his wishes are
fulfilled. Now the light is shining on my face! Disa! Disa!
(*Lets go of her. Stands with his arms extended.*) Now kiss
me!
(*Disa opens her eyes and looks at him. Puts her arms around
his neck and kisses him.*)

CURTAIN

Act II

*Next day. Same room. Outdoors driving rain and storm. The
rain is streaming incessantly down the windowpanes. The
Bailiff is sitting at his writing desk. On the table is lying an
open account book. Olafur is sitting nearby.*

THE BAILIFF (*closing the book*): Now I've told you all you
need to know.
(*Olafur gets up.*)
THE BAILIFF: If it should happen that I am away longer than
this week, just put the men to work at anything you feel is
most pressing. I know I can rely on you.
OLAFUR: Do you want the horses at four o'clock tomorrow
morning even if this horrible weather continues?

THE BAILIFF: Yes.

OLAFUR: I'll see to it that they are ready. (*Exit.*)

(*The Bailiff is quiet a moment. Then he opens a drawer and takes out a large key. He rises, walks over to the chest, unlocks it and lifts up the lid.*)

LOFTUR (*enters, stops in the doorway*): You sent for me.

THE BAILIFF (*closes the chest*): Yes. Come to me, my son.

(*Loftur goes to him.*)

THE BAILIFF: Sit down.

(*Loftur sits down.*)

THE BAILIFF: I lay awake last night thinking about you and your future. Are you still just as eager as you were to go abroad when you have graduated here?

LOFTUR: Yes, I am.

THE BAILIFF: I am happy that you are not looking for a minor position right away. I am very happy. You would be young for a pastor, in any case. What goal have you set yourself?

LOFTUR (*stands up*): I want to gain more knowledge.

THE BAILIFF: Please sit down, my boy.

(*Loftur sits down.*)

THE BAILIFF (*after a moment's silence*): I blame no man for amassing wealth without knowing what he will accomplish later with his gold. Neither do I blame you for wanting to arm yourself with such knowledge that you will be prepared when the hour of action comes. But gold gets its true value only if the will transforms it as the hand gathers it. And the ladder that is called learning will grow a thousandfold more attractive if you know where it is leading you. So follow your father's advice and set yourself a certain goal. This will strengthen your thoughts and your deeds. And the goal is straight ahead of you. You have extraordinary gifts, and your father is rich. What should prevent you from some day having the bishop's mantle hung on your shoulders, in the fullness of time?

LOFTUR: I thought that this would be your wish.

THE BAILIFF: There are only two bishoprics in this country, but
there are many ambitious fathers. So you must forge your
weapons in time. Lay the foundation of your fame while
you are abroad. The wind will carry it, so that it will take
root in unsuspected places. Generosity is usually blind, but it
becomes those who tower above the mob. (*He sits down.*)
Let me tell you the story of one of the old bishops. Once
when he was abroad, three of God's almsmen came into his
room. He had no material possessions, except for a precious
silver beaker. He flung the beaker on the floor. The miracle
happened that it fell apart into three equal pieces. This
established his fame in Iceland. Notice that it was all he had
left, yet he was as generous as ever. This teaches you that it
is wise to conceal one's wealth. This gives one's gifts a
greater value. And none of those who benefit by your gifts
will ask where your wealth comes from. If you are ever
granted power, then conceal it in a cloak of humility, and
people will think that your authority is from God. My son! I
still have not spoken of the thing that is most on my mind,
the decisive thing in your life. When the time comes to pick
a wife, then choose her from a wellborn family. For your
wife is a piece of yourself—and her name will fall upon you
either as a light or as a shadow.

LOFTUR (*gets up*): You don't need to worry.

THE BAILIFF (*in a changed tone of voice*): Stories have been
reported to me. They came like an icecold blast through an
open window. You are said to have chosen a bride. I won't
mention her name. You know as well as I that she is not
worthy of you. (*Gets up.*)

LOFTUR: Who told you this?

THE BAILIFF: I only wish that you would listen to me in silence.
For either you will tell me a lie or you will confide in me,
and I won't have either one. I shall speak of it only as an
unconfirmed suspicion. When first I heard it, anger over-
came me. I was going to use force on you. But as I thought

of my own temper, I realized that this might only make you defiant. I decided that I would just let my anger hover over you like a thundercloud. (*Puts his arm around his shoulder.*) But then I thought of your blessed mother whom you lost so early. Many a time, knowingly or unknowingly, you must have missed her love. (*Releases him.*) Your deprivation has made you receptive. I could see that in your passionate attachment to Olafur. In him you found a trustworthy soul. But now you must have misunderstood your feelings, or perhaps the woman has misunderstood them. My son! I do not scold you, but my grief is standing at your door, listening. (*There is a knocking on the door.*)

THE BAILIFF: Come in.

(*A group of workmen enter. Water is running down from their clothes. They stand in a tight cluster.*)

THE BAILIFF (*astonished*): Has there been an accident?

A YOUNG WORKER: We just wanted to say that the river is rising fast.

THE BAILIFF: Did you all come back from the fields just to tell me this?

THE YOUNG WORKER: We thought maybe you hadn't noticed the rain, sir. We've been soaked through to our skins for over an hour. (*Pulls out his shirt.*) It's not even weather for dogs.

VOICE FROM THE GROUP: Show the bailiff that you can wring out your shirt.

THE BAILIFF (*looking them over, sits down*): The women were called home. You are men and are not ashamed? (*To the young worker*): Your father will certainly be proud of you when he learns that you complain about a few raindrops. I remember one evening he came in from a terrible snow storm. Icicles hung from his beard, and his whole face was singed by frost burns. (*Laughs.*) I did not hear him complaining. He laughed and said that now he would like to see the girl that would want to kiss him. (*Points.*) And you, in

the back there, who want to wring out your shirt. I can
remember this about your mother, that she got up from her
bed three days after you were born to help your father with
the haying. (*Is silent a moment.*) What are you waiting for?
Go into your rooms and change your clothes.
(*The workers leave in silence. A puddle of water is left on
the floor after them.*)

THE BAILIFF (*following them with his eyes. Turns to Loftur*):
Will you close the door. There was something more I
wanted to say to you.
(*Loftur gets up and shuts the door.*)

THE BAILIFF (*rises and approaches Loftur*): You have never yet
had much money in your hands. This is wrong, for you can
expect to become a wealthy man. (*Goes to the chest, opens
it, and takes out a purse, which he deposits on the table.*)
Take this for yourself. You can count it later, after I have
left.
(*Loftur kisses his father.*)

THE BAILIFF: Don't thank me for it. Everything I do for you is
a pleasure to me. (*Locks the chest and puts the key back in
its drawer.*) Now I'm going in to talk with the Bishop about
my journey. (*Stops.*) If you want to make your father
happy, try to win the love of a wellborn young girl before
you leave. I leave it to you to guess the one I mean. When
you get back from your stay abroad, it might be too late.
And in foreign countries there will surely be many temptations in your path. There is no better protection than to
know that someone is waiting. This fetters the hands of lust.
And if the same should happen to you as did to Kjartan
Olafsson, that you should be tempted to forget your country, she will draw you back home. Even if you should win
fame and power, if you settled in some foreign country, I
would still feel I had lost you. My son! (*Clasps his wrist.*) I
will confess to you that there are moments when I have
doubts about my childhood faith, since I have never yet met

any man who I felt deserved immortality. But if fate should grant me the fortune to have you standing at my deathbed, then I would feel I was falling asleep under the Tree of Life. (*Momentarily places his hand on Loftur's head. Exit, closing the door behind him.*)

(*Loftur stands still for a moment. Moves toward the door as if he wanted to call his father back. Stops, goes over to the writing desk, opens the purse. When he hears footsteps, he pushes the purse aside. A light knocking at the door.*)

DISA (*enters. Is bashful when she sees that Loftur is alone*): Isn't your father here? I was supposed to call him.

LOFTUR: He just went in to see your father. (*Goes to her and takes her hands.*) Disa! Are you sorry that you went with me to the wishing well yesterday?

DISA: No.

LOFTUR: Are you sure it wasn't just an impulse due to your happiness at being home again?

DISA: Yes, I am. The mountains were lower and the river was narrower than I remembered them. But you were unchanged.

LOFTUR (*taking her face in his hands*): My playmate! My childhood friend! My beloved! (*Kisses her.*)

DISA: I'm bashful with you. As if you were a prince.

LOFTUR (*kneeling*): I am on my knees, in homage to your youth and your innocence. I am not worthy of you. But I know that you can help me. (*Rises.*) It torments me to think that I might soil you with my love. Your eyes have never known doubt. Their pure light is a paean of gratitude to life. But I—I am broken silver—mere fragments of good and evil.

DISA: I love you the way you are. Last night, when I was going to sleep in my old room again, I lay thinking for a long long time. And then my eyelids fell shut just like a heavy door closing behind us.

LOFTUR (*softly*): What were you thinking about?

DISA (*sits down on the bench*): I was thinking about you. The only bad thing I could remember was that once you caught a little bird and locked it up in a shed. You confided to me that this would help you find some rare herb.

LOFTUR: That was a little wagtail. The mother was supposed to find the plant that opens all locks and free her young with it.

DISA: I never dared to tell you. (*Smiles.*) But I was the one who let it out. Now you would never do anything so cruel.

LOFTUR (*sits*): Not when you are with me. (*Takes her hand.*) Do you know, dear hand, that now you are mine? I have seen you flutter so often with needle and colored thread, like a bird flying to build its nest with a long straw in its beak. (*Smiles.*) I forgive you for all the snowballs you threw at me. (*Laughs.*) And the box on the ears you gave me once.

DISA: You teased me.

LOFTUR: I remember how frightened you were. You flew out of the room like a ball of fire, out in the yard and down the length of the meadow. How you did run! I didn't catch you before you were down by the river. (*Suddenly stops at an unwelcome memory.*)

DISA: You were nice then. You didn't scold me at all.

LOFTUR (*gets to his feet*): I wish this day were over.

DISA (*also rises*): Why do you wish that?

LOFTUR (*evades her*): I wish so many things. (*Goes to the window.*) I also wish it were nice weather. It ought not to be raining now, since you are here. Do you hear how it beats against the panes?

DISA: I didn't notice the rain.

LOFTUR (*to her*): Tomorrow there will be sunshine. Then you will go berrying. The crowberries must be ripe now. I'll come later and find you. Then we'll be entirely happy, just because the sun is shining and we're near one another.

DISA (*leans against him and looks up in his face*): Aren't we entirely happy now?

LOFTUR (*is silent a moment*): Yes, we are. (*Kisses her eyes.*) I used to think that love had nothing to do with one's thoughts. I believed it was only an unconscious yearning for sympathy. A violent thirst for joy. But I was wholly mistaken. (*Briefly covers her face with his hand, caressingly.*) My love for you has changed all my thoughts. You probably think that I am the same today as I was yesterday. But I am not. Yesterday I was a very ambitious man. I wanted to find a door to the unknown and step over the threshold of darkness.

DISA (*a little frightened*): I don't understand what you mean.

LOFTUR: You needn't be afraid. (*Sits down.*) You have restored my health. (*Disa is seated.*) The thirst for power that burned in me has been extinguished. Now I feel a deep joy flowing through me, a joy because I am a weak human being, who has to fight with all his strength for every little victory. With my own hands I will build the bridge you have to cross, and I will love every stone that strains my strength.

DISA: Loftur!

LOFTUR (*kisses her hand*): We know of herbs that heal the body. There must also be remedies that heal the soul. Holy men, who could heal both soul and body, must have possessed such remedies. But they must have been unconscious of it, for otherwise they would have taught them to others. Imagine one who could take away from a poor sinner all his lust for power and money, the flame of wrath and the darkness of hate, just by the laying on of his hand. And could teach this to others, so that the art would never be forgotten. (*Falls on his knees before Disa, and bows his head.*)

(*Disa caresses his hair.*)

LOFTUR (*rises, deeply moved, with tears in his eyes*): A great miracle has been performed in my soul. Love can make the hand of man sacred.

(*Disa gets up. Loftur takes her hand and kisses it.*)

DISA: I love you. (*She kisses his hair.*)

(*Knocking on the door.*)

(*Steinunn enters. She is carrying a pail and a floor mop. She is dressed in working clothes. Her face is sad. Looks at them a moment. Gets down on her knees and starts mopping up the puddle of water.*)

DISA: Mother must be wondering what happened to me. (*Smiles.*) She would like it best if I sat with her all day. (*Goes to the door.*)

LOFTUR: Are you leaving?

DISA: Yes. (*Stops in the doorway and looks at Loftur, her eyes shining.*)

(*Loftur returns her glance, then looks down. Disa leaves.*)

LOFTUR (*looks at Steinunn, with obvious distress. To avoid it he goes over to the window. Stands a moment with his back to Steinunn, then to her*): Steinunn! I need to talk with you.

STEINUNN (*gets up*): If I were only as pretty as the Bishop's daughter.

LOFTUR (*paces the floor*): Yes, she is pretty. (*Catching himself.*) You're pretty, too.

STEINUNN: What do you want to say?

LOFTUR: I had decided to talk with you today. If you hadn't come in here, I would have gone to find you.

(*Steinunn puts aside the pail and sits down.*)

LOFTUR (*sadly*): You have had reason to believe that I loved you. You staked everything on me. It makes me sad, Steinunn. But I have to tell you the truth. I don't love you.

STEINUNN (*in a low tone*): I knew it.

LOFTUR: You have never demanded anything. You trusted me. If trust alone were enough to inspire love, I would have had to love you.

STEINUNN: Yesterday I came to realize that you did not love me. But I hoped that you wouldn't tell me so.

LOFTUR: This morning it didn't seem so difficult. But when you came into the room and I saw your face, I realized how great my guilt was. (*Again goes back to the window, stands there.*)

STEINUNN (*gets up*): I should have hidden my love from you.

LOFTUR (*turns to her*): Whatever you think about me, you must never doubt that I was sincere.

STEINUNN (*coldly*): Are you in love with the Bishop's daughter?

LOFTUR: Can't we two part without bitterness? Be generous, Steinunn, and forget what has passed between us.

STEINUNN (*supporting herself on the back of a chair*): What has passed between us? You have taught me the joys of sin. My fear was like a mist around me—that made you and my happiness seem greater. All your caresses were powerful enemies of my conscience. When I thought of my mother, I blushed for shame. But in the same breath I could weep for joy. And now you ask me to forget!

LOFTUR (*unhappily*): I never wished you any harm. I thought I loved you.

STEINUNN: You thought you loved me? Didn't you know it?

LOFTUR: What could I know except what I thought? A man is not master of his feelings.

STEINUNN: There are actions that strengthen one's feelings. You demanded everything of me without giving in return all that you could. Why didn't you tell your father about me? If you had ventured that for my sake, you would have behaved differently toward me now.

LOFTUR: You just won't understand that I was compelled to be silent with my father.

STEINUNN: Don't fail me, Loftur. I'll be a good wife to you. If poverty and sorrow assail you, I'll share them with you as gladly as if they were wealth and happiness. I'm so afraid that you are ashamed of me, and that this is the reason you don't love me. But you'll see that you won't need to be ashamed. If I can be yours in the eyes of all men, you will not find a woman anywhere who will bear herself more proudly than I. (*Takes a step.*) Every step I take will be a hymn of praise in your honor.

LOFTUR: You think I'm ashamed of you. And still you can love me.

STEINUNN: I have given you so much that I can't let you go. You have to be good to me, Loftur. Everyone in my family is prone to brooding. I don't know how I could bear it if you should fail me. I think the malicious and hypocritical sympathy of the others would kill me.

LOFTUR: People can't feel sympathy for something they know nothing about.

STEINUNN: They know much more than you think. Servants and envy have a thousand eyes. I have tried to make friends with all of them, but no one has returned my friendship. They hate me.

LOFTUR: Does their opinion really mean so much to you? I thought you were different from the rest.

STEINUNN: God is sometimes so far away, but the opinions of men are always present. Have pity on me!

LOFTUR (*greatly troubled*): I have done you a wrong. I beg you to forgive me, if this is possible. But you can't wish that I should marry you for pity. That would bring you no happiness.

STEINUNN: Does it look as if I am thinking of happiness?

LOFTUR (*in a toneless voice*): I'll be quite frank with you. Then you can judge me any way you please. You asked me if I loved the Bishop's daughter. A poor little girl whom I saw in her castoff clothes made my heart throb with joy! Yesterday when she herself came into the room, I was like a blind man who has suddenly become seeing.

STEINUNN (*bitterly*): The Bishop's daughter is wealthier and of higher birth than I.

LOFTUR: Is your opinion of me as low as that?

STEINUNN: How am I supposed to know what you are hiding behind the words you carry like a shield? If you were noble enough in spirit to regard us as equal, because we are both human beings, there could be no doubt in your mind as to

how you should act. Your feelings are like drifting sands—
one thing today and something else tomorrow. You should
build your house on your duty and on your honor.

LOFTUR (*in a low voice*): Would you live with me if I should
become an evil and ambitious man? If I should risk my soul
to gain power over darkness?

STEINUNN: What do you mean?

LOFTUR (*with a fanatical fire in his expression*): We are nothing but a shadow of reality. Reality consists of the two
eternal powers, Good and Evil, and the souls they have
created together. The Evil is closest to men, in the same way
that the fire of earth is closer to us than the sun. Evil can
reach its perfection. But the most sacred passion of man must
be his passion for the Good. (*Moodily.*) Ever since I felt
myself bound to you, my thoughts inclined more and more
to darkness.

STEINUNN: So now I'm to blame for your evil thoughts?

LOFTUR: No, you are not to blame. (*Walks restlessly back and
forth.*) I let myself be bewitched by an image in running
water.

STEINUNN: Am I that image?

LOFTUR: It was not the memory of your soul that kept me
awake at night.

STEINUNN (*sadly*): Did you ever ask about my soul?

LOFTUR: You will have to believe me, Steinunn. If we should
live together, we would torment each other. We would
make each other evil.

STEINUNN (*a suspicion dawns on her*): Have you told the
Bishop's daughter that you love her?

LOFTUR (*after a moment's silence*): Yes, I have.

STEINUNN (*hatefully*): Did you ask her to be your mistress?
(*Loftur turns away from her and starts toward the door.*)

STEINUNN (*runs to the door to block his path*): Are you trying
to run away?

LOFTUR: Go away!

STEINUNN: Why don't you force me aside?

LOFTUR (*his face turning dark and strange. His eyes flash with evil, half-conscious wishes*): I wish that you were dead! (*But then his expression turns to terror. He goes into the room again, sits down on the bench. Hides his face in his hands.*)

STEINUNN (*stands by the door a moment, goes over to him*): You told me once that I was proud. Do you think it is on your account that I have thrown my pride overboard? (*Her lips tremble and tears start running down her face.*) You have seen the mountain grouse sweep the dust from the road to protect her young. I am going to have a child. (*Falls on her knees and begins to sob.*)

LOFTUR (*rises*): God help me! (*Steinunn's sobbing is quiet, but desperate. The rain is heard beating on the windowpanes.*)

LOFTUR (*moving away from Steinunn. A touch of pity on his face*): If only you were a stranger to me, so I could comfort you.

STEINUNN (*sobbing*): I have known it for more than a month. But I couldn't bring myself to tell you. I was waiting for a day when you would love me so much that I could believe this would be a joy to both of us.

LOFTUR: We will have to be strong. We can't allow fate to overpower us. (*Suddenly, in uncontrollable impatience*): Stop this crying!

(*Steinunn rises to her feet. Forces herself to stop crying. Her expression is cold and observant.*)

LOFTUR: Does anyone but us know about this?

STEINUNN: No.

LOFTUR (*pacing about the floor, stopping now and then in the midst of his speaking. The decisive ring of his voice is reminiscent of his father's*): You will have to leave this place. There is no other way of keeping it secret. I'll speak to my father later today and ask for his help. He will have to find some place where you can take refuge. No one but the three of us needs to know about it. When the child is born, I'll see that it gets into good hands. My father has given me money, so I can take care of it without his help. I promise you that you will never need to have any worries about the child. The hardest part of it will be how you can leave without causing any attention.

STEINUNN: Is that the hardest part of it?

LOFTUR (*harshly*): Yes, that's the hardest part of it. But we can manage that too. When father comes home from his trip, he will say that one of his friends has asked him to find a maid for the winter. He will ask for you.

STEINUNN (*with a sly expression*): Is it very important to you that I leave?

LOFTUR: You have to leave, both for my sake and your own.

STEINUNN: Let's leave me out of it. If I speak out, you will be mercilessly driven out of the school, even if you are the son of the Bailiff. The Bishop makes no distinction between rich and poor. And his wife will be zealous against you, I'm sure. All your hopes for the future will be dashed. This will be a great disappointment to your father. Old people are so ridiculously sensitive to disappointments. (*Laughs.*) They can catch their death from them. You are his only son, and you will dishonor his name. And then there's the Bishop's daughter, who thinks you are an honorable man. Nothing is so bitter as to discover that the person you love is a scoundrel. If I speak out, you will not only lose her. You will also poison her whole life.

LOFTUR: You hate me.

STEINUNN (*unable to restrain herself*): Your own unborn child hates you through my soul.

LOFTUR (*after a moment's silence*): What do you gain by destroying me? You will be destroying yourself at the same time. Is it just to avenge yourself?

STEINUNN (*more quietly*): I don't wish to destroy you. You or your father just see to it that a minister marries us secretly.

When I am your wife, I'll go away immediately anywhere you wish.

LOFTUR: You are trying to frighten me into marrying you.

STEINUNN: It is written that a wife shall be obedient to her husband. It is not written anywhere that his mistress has to be so.

LOFTUR: Up till now I have felt pity for you. Now I have no feelings left at all.

STEINUNN: Your feelings make no difference to me any more. I lay the matter before your judgment. Remember that I am wealthier now than I was before. Your honor and your future are my dowry.

LOFTUR: Even though all the wealth of the Bishop's see were your dowry, you would never become my wife. (*Turns away from her.*)

STEINUNN (*after him*): I don't want my firstborn child to be a fatherless thing. I rather think that your father will be of the same opinion. I think he will consider it your duty to acknowledge your child. For you surely won't deny that you are the father. (*Holding her breath.*)

LOFTUR: No, I don't deny it. (*Sits down.*)

STEINUNN (*draws a deep breath*): I'll wait for you for as many years as you wish. Some day, when you return from abroad, people will admire you for marrying the love of your youth—a poor woman.

LOFTUR (*recovering his composure*): My conscience tells me that I ought to cast away all hopes of happiness and do my duty. (*Gets up.*) But I can't do it! I won't do it! Besides, I'm not sure that my conscience is right. You called me a scoundrel. All the others will probably agree. I'm not afraid of that. If you had told me at once that you were with child, so that no angry words had passed between us, I might have been so weak-willed that I would have done what is called my duty. I don't know. I don't even care to know. You can destroy my future. You can make my father unhappy. You can take away from me the woman I love. But you have no power to keep me from living and working in solitude, with those memories that are the purest and most beautiful thing I possess.

STEINUNN: Have you quite forgotten your child?

LOFTUR: I promised you I would see that it got into the hands of good people—people who perhaps would give it more love than I ever could.

STEINUNN: Do you know how much love strangers show a child that they accept for a handful of money? Suppose they were bad people. Suppose they give your child an upbringing which will make it a criminal.

LOFTUR: Then the responsibility would be theirs who had given it that upbringing, not mine. Unless perhaps responsibility rests outside mankind.

STEINUNN (*moves away from him*): Even though you reject me, even though you wipe me out of your memory, you can't take my child away from me. (*Turns towards him.*) I shall bring it up in hate. Perhaps I can't disturb your solitude—but I can enrich you with an ugly dream. On the day of judgment you will meet a face which is exactly like yours, except that it is distorted by sin and suffering. That face will demand its soul back from you!

LOFTUR (*in a hoarse voice*): If you are such a monster that you can bring up your child in hate—then go ahead and do so. Not one of your threats will make me bind myself for life to a woman I hate!

STEINUNN: A woman you hate! (*In her desperation turning to a last resort.*) You said yesterday that I looked best in my everyday clothes. You probably meant that a simple stone should have a cheap setting. (*Opening her bodice.*) When you saw me in the river, I had no setting at all!

LOFTUR (*staring at her*): What are you doing?

STEINUNN: From now on I'll accept every man who might wish to have me—everyone! Everyone except you! (*Tears off her bodice and throws it aside. She is wearing a white slip under the bodice.*)

LOFTUR (*excitedly*): You're lying! (*Seizes her wrist.*) You belong only to me.

(*Steinunn stands perfectly still. Loftur lets go her wrist, turns away and walks out of the room, his head bowed.*)

STEINUNN (*stands paralyzed for a moment. Picks up the bodice and puts it on. Throws herself on the bench, puts her hands to her head, rocks back and forth, moaning*): Oh, oh, oh!

OLAFUR (*enters. When he sees Steinunn, he stops in the doorway. Goes over to her. His voice is loving and sympathetic*): Are you ill?

STEINUNN (*looks up, lets her hands fall*): Leave me alone. Yes, I'm ill. (*Sits dully.*)

OLAFUR (*looks at her, understands her grief. Sits down near her. Takes her hand*): Give me leave to talk with you as your friend.

STEINUNN (*quietly withdraws her hand*): I have no friends.

OLAFUR (*hunting for words*): One is often lonely even where there are many people. It was my doing that you came here. You knew few people before that, but those you knew were your friends. (*Suddenly gets up.*) I can't endure seeing how unhappy you are. (*Walks a few steps away from her.*) Can't you live without him?

(*Steinunn looks up. Her face gets a distant attentive look. Short silence.*)

OLAFUR (*goes back to her, leans down over her*): I know despair myself, otherwise I would not dare to disturb your sorrow. (*Again sits down beside her.*) Give me leave to be a brother to you. Anyone who is as unhappy as you, needs to confide in someone. Otherwise life is too heavy to bear. I knew one who lost her faith in God and men. That was my mother. She confided in me, an ignorant child. (*Quietly.*) I know why you are so upset.

STEINUNN (*attentively*): What do you know?

OLAFUR (*gets up, unwilling to look at her*): I have loved a woman for many years. She chose another. I think it is impossible that you can have loved Loftur more than I love her. (*Looks at her.*)

STEINUNN (*suspiciously*): Has Loftur told you anything about me?

OLAFUR (*disappointed, sadly takes a step away from her. In a colder tone*): I asked him. I had the right to ask. (*Moves still farther away.*)

STEINUNN (*eyes blazing with feeling, her voice restrained*): Did he tell you when and where he first noticed me?

OLAFUR: I don't know. I don't remember that.

STEINUNN (*breathing a sigh of relief. Gets up. Walks over to the window, stands still a moment. Unconsciously whispers out loud*): "Can't you live without him?" (*Turns to Olafur.*) Why do you ask me that question over again?

OLAFUR (*frightened and astonished*): What have I asked?

STEINUNN (*realizes that Olafur's question, "Can't you live without him?", is echoing in her own mind. Goes over to him*): Please be patient with me a little while. (*Goes to the bench.*) Don't go away from me. (*Sits down.*)

OLAFUR: I won't go away. (*Goes over to her.*)

STEINUNN (*mournfully*): I know that from now on he will think of me only with contempt. I couldn't bear to lose him. I threatened him that I would become an evil person.

OLAFUR (*angrily*): Loftur doesn't deserve either your love or your despair. He plunges himself into useless fancies and forgets the realities of life.

STEINUNN (*still mournful*): Why couldn't I have been his sister? A sister loves her brother unselfishly. I would have watched over his health. I would have filled his room with flowers. Now I am nothing but a burden to him. (*Gets up. Her words sound like a vehement answer to someone.*) No, I can't do it.

OLAFUR: What can't you do?

STEINUNN (*is silent a moment*): I can't talk to him again, for I know that either hate or love will blind me. (*Is silent again.*)

OLAFUR (*looks at Steinunn. Struggles with himself. Approaches her, wants to speak out*): Steinunn! Little Steinunn!

STEINUNN (*faces him. Her voice and expression are changed*): When the falcon tears at the heart of the grouse, he screams, because then he understands that the grouse is his sister. He shall scream!

OLAFUR: What do you mean?

STEINUNN (*more quietly*): Surely people can do each other so much harm that they understand they are brothers and sisters. (*Walks quietly over to the door.*)

OLAFUR (*follows her. He has made up his mind*): Don't go right away.

(*Steinunn stops.*)

OLAFUR: I beg you again: let me be a brother to you. Let me speak to Loftur. You say you can't speak to him yourself. What should I tell him?

STEINUNN (*is silent a moment. A transfigured stillness comes over her face and her voice*): Tell him that all my bitterness has left my heart. Tell him I have forgiven him. Will you do that?

OLAFUR: Anything you wish.

(*Steinunn takes his hand, bends over and kisses it. Walks quietly out. Olafur remains standing briefly; looks at his hand, which he has not moved. Lifts it with his left hand and touches it to his lips. Exit. The stage is empty.*)

LOFTUR (*enters, visibly excited. Walks over to the chest, opens it, tosses the purse carelessly down into the chest and locks it. Goes to the bookshelf, takes out one of his schoolbooks. Sits down. Opens the book, hits upon the eleventh song of the Odyssey. Puts his hands to his ears and reads out loud to shut out his thoughts*):

Then left I the place where I stood, till anigh me my
mother drew,
And drank of the dark-hued blood: then straightway her
son she knew;
And she wailed at the sight, and the winged word-flight
from her pale lips flew.*

(*Gets up.*) No! (*Flings the book aside. Walks around the
room, wringing his hands. His expression turns evil and men-
acing. Stops. Says in a low voice*): He who with all his soul
wishes the death of another person— (*Is silent. Paces the floor,
stops. A fearful strength comes over his face. In a loud, strong
voice*): He who with all his soul wishes the death of another
person, let him bow his head towards earth. (*Tilts his head
slowly, first up, then down—falls on his knees.*) And let him
say: "Thou who dwellest in everlasting darkness! Make my
will into Thy will! Kill Thou this person! —and I swear, in
the name of the great trinity: in the name of the sun, which is
the shadow of the Lord; in the name of the earth-fire, which
is Thy shadow; and in the name of my body, which is my
shadow, that my soul is Thine, from everlasting unto everlasting." (*While reciting these words, he has concentrated
his entire will on his burning hate. But as he repeats the last
words, his strength fails him. An unspeakable terror is
reflected on his face. He repeats with trembling lips as he
rises to his feet*): "—that my soul is Thine, from everlasting
unto everlasting." (*He is overcome by sobbing. He throws
himself into a chair, bends over the table and buries his face
in his arms. His body is shaken by vehement sobbing.*)

CURTAIN

---

* *Odyssey* 11:151–53, tr. Arthur S. Way.

Act III

Interior of the Holar Cathedral at night. Outer pews facing the spectators. Flagstones in the aisle, some of which are well-worn inscribed gravestones. The church is empty. Deathly stillness. Moonlight shines in through the windows on the right. Shadows of drifting clouds play on the gravestones of the floor, touching the high tops of the pews on either side of the center aisle and the great figure of Christ. They fill the church with a mysterious life.

A key is turned. A heavy door creaks on its hinges. The pulpit shades the door.

Disa enters. Curtsies and crosses herself before the small figure of Christ over the altar.

Loftur enters. His face is furrowed by sleeplessness and suffering.

DISA (*walks down the steps. Curtsies again before the large figure of Christ*): Merciful Savior, forgive me my sins.

LOFTUR (*follows her down the steps*): Do *you* speak of sins?

DISA: I was just a little girl when my father let me carry the church key for the first time. He wanted to show me his trust. Now I have taken the key without his knowledge. I feel as if I had stolen it.

LOFTUR: You did it for my sake.

DISA: I promised to do what you asked without knowing what

you wanted. I never dreamt that you would ask me for something dishonorable.

LOFTUR (*growing more and more disturbed. His voice is trembling*): The moonlight makes everything so strangely alive. (*Points to the floor.*) Look! Isn't this like an ice floe in a dark river? It must be cold to drown.

DISA: Poor Steinunn!

LOFTUR (*suspicious*): Why do you mention her name?

DISA: Aren't you concerned about her soul? Olafur says he saw the storm drive her out into the river. But we don't know whether he saw it as it really was.

(*Loftur is silent.*)

DISA: Father says it is not for men to judge. But mother thinks she killed herself. Isn't that horrible? (*Looking at Loftur.*) And no one knows the reason.

LOFTUR (*pointing*): There, where the shadow is blackest, there her coffin stood this morning. (*Points.*) What's that over there? Is it blood?

DISA: Blood? It's heather that fell from the coffin.

LOFTUR (*looking up at the image of Christ*): He only suffered for the sins of others. He should have sinned himself. (*Sinks down wearily on one of the steps.*)

DISA: You still have not told me why you wanted to come here at midnight. Have you come to say your prayers?

(*Loftur is silent.*)

DISA: Why don't you answer me?

LOFTUR (*looking up*): Would you commit a sin for my sake?

DISA: Something terrible has happened to you which I don't understand. (*Comes closer to him.*) You do love me, Loftur?

LOFTUR: Your innocence is the rainbow that can lead me up to heaven.

DISA: Just say yes.

LOFTUR: Yes, of course. You know that. (*Gets to his feet.*)

DISA: If you love me, you will tell me what is troubling you.

LOFTUR: You are so good. (*He takes her hands.*) Once this summer I came down to the shore the day after a storm. A soft breeze blew rainbow colors over the spray, as if it were trying to quiet it down. Your voice is soft like that breeze. (*Lets go her hands.*) But the summer breeze cannot still the breakers that roll in from the open sea.

DISA: You're treating me like a child. I'm not a child any longer. (*Sits down.*)

LOFTUR: I can't tell you what is troubling me because it is best for you not to know it. Knowledge and innocence do not go together.

DISA: Did she love you?

LOFTUR (*after a moment's hesitation*): How can I know that?

DISA: You are afraid that you are guilty of her death.

LOFTUR: Who has made you believe that?

DISA (*gets up*): You yourself. (*Her question is direct and inescapable.*) Were you engaged to her and did you abandon her for me?

LOFTUR (*angrily*): No, I was not.

DISA: Why have you been so completely changed since she drowned?

LOFTUR: I have told you that I can't confide in you what is troubling me. Please leave me, beloved, and let me be alone here. (*Kisses her forehead.*) Tonight my greatest wish will be fulfilled.

DISA: What are you going to do? (*In sudden fear.*) Some kind of evil power has won mastery over you. I can see it in your face.

LOFTUR: Go, Disa!

DISA (*looking at the image of Christ*): We shall both get down on our knees before the image of the Savior and pray that He will help us.

LOFTUR: I can't pray.

DISA: I will not leave you in your despair. We must do as Jacob

did and not let the Lord go until He has answered our
prayer.

LOFTUR: My will is prepared to break open the door that leads
to the unknown. My soul's salvation is at stake. Don't try to
stop me.

DISA: You won't listen to me. You're driving me away from
you. I know a voice that is stronger than mine. (*She walks
quickly up the church aisle, disappears among the pews.*)

LOFTUR: Where are you going? (*Takes a few steps after her.
Stops. The beautiful melody of Luther's "A Mighty Fortress
is our God" sounds softly and sweetly through the
church.*)

LOFTUR (*looks up, makes a deprecatory gesture with his hand*):
No, no. (*The playing continues.*)

LOFTUR (*standing still for a while. He trembles. Falls on his
knees, folds his hands. His sentences come at long intervals,
but the words are clearly heard through the soft music*):
Hast Thou forsaken forever the most miserable of all Thy
creatures? The fragrance of Thy Holy Spirit no longer
touches my eyelids so that I can gain rest in my sleep. All my
cries return to me with the echo of scorn, as if Thy heaven
were a vault of stone. Didst Thou not give me the power to
sin because Thou didst intend to forgive me? From whom
did I get the power that makes my sin greater than Thy
grace? Lord, lord! Give me Thy peace if only for a moment! (*Lifts his face, with his eyes closed and his hands
clasped. Lies still on his knees.*)

(*The music stops.*)

DISA (*comes quickly down between the pews. Her face shines
with peace and joy. Hurries to Loftur and falls on her knees
beside him*): I knew it! I knew it!

LOFTUR (*bows his head*): God has deserted me. He will not
hear my prayers. (*Rises.*)

DISA (*gets to her feet. Helpless for a moment*): What have you
done, Loftur, that makes you so desperate?

LOFTUR (*turns to her. Speaks half to himself*): I understand. He does not have the power to forgive me. In the everlasting struggle between Good and Evil there are moments when the will of man has to stand alone.

DISA: Even if you have committed a sin that weighs on your conscience, you must not despair. I have heard my father say that despair is the greatest of all sins. To despair is to doubt God's omnipotence. Whoever repents with all his heart will get forgiveness for his sins.

LOFTUR: I can't repent. If I could, I would already be standing in the shadow of forgiveness. Only one path is open to me. I have to go on into darkness. I have to gain so much knowledge that I can win power over Evil. If I can then abstain from ever wanting anything for myself, I will be forgiven in the hour of my death.

DISA: You frighten me more and more.

LOFTUR (*with a touch of madness in his expression*): When I make use of Evil to promote the Good—what is then Good and what is Evil?

DISA: My own, beloved Loftur!

LOFTUR: I have ventured too far to be able to turn back. Tonight I must win my victory. I will cry until the dead one rises from his grave and gives me the power.

DISA: You are ill.

LOFTUR (*suddenly seized by overwhelming terror*): You must not fail me. (*On his knees, holding her hand.*) Without you I have no hope of salvation. If I lost you, I would be entirely evil.

DISA: Can you imagine that I would ever fail you? Even if I should have to leave my father and my mother, I would be at your side. Loftur! (*Caresses his head.*) I felt so lonely this year when I was among strangers. They were seldom happy about the same things as I. I was never happier than when I found one of the flowers you had taught me to know. Then I felt that I had a piece of your soul with me even though the mountains were between us. And when I brought the flowers into my room, I always longed to be home.

LOFTUR (*rises, caresses her hands*): Water from a clouded well would turn pure in your hands. If you stand beside me, I can resist the temptations of power. (*Lets go of her.*) And if we should lose our footing, we two will live in Good and Evil, as our hearts command us. I shall attain unlimited power. I can then extend life. And I can change our shapes. If you wish, we can live as long as the earth itself, in the shape of men, or animals, or flowers. (*Draws her to him.*) We will be two white anemones growing in a lonely place near the glaciers, where the long kisses of the sun will not leave the reddened leaves before the autumn storms blow them down on the gravel. (*Kisses her forehead, they unconsciously assume the same poses as when they stood on the flying carpet.*) And then we will both fly anywhere we wish, we two birds, with human souls in our eyes.

DISA: Loftur dear, come home with me now.

LOFTUR (*heedless*): Perhaps I can win peace in that way too. Perhaps Good and Evil sprang from the same source in the beginning of time. Perhaps they will again unite.

DISA (*helpless*): I'm going to call father and tell him that we love each other. Please come with me.

LOFTUR: Just you go, never fear. (*His voice grows stronger.*) I have to be alone. I shall come when victory is won.

(*Steps are heard. Disa and Loftur listen involuntarily.*)

DISA: It's father.

OLAFUR (*enters*): So here you are. I looked for you in your room. (*Looks intensely at Loftur.*)

LOFTUR: What do you want?

DISA: Ask Loftur to come home with us.

OLAFUR (*to Disa*): Why are you out here so late? Are you practicing music at midnight?

DISA: No.

LOFTUR: What do you want?

OLAFUR: You had better go home, Disa. You are only a child yet. I don't want to cast a shadow on your soul. You must be here without your father's knowledge.

DISA (*closer to Loftur*): We have decided to tell father that we are engaged.

OLAFUR (*starts. Turns to Loftur*): When were you engaged?

LOFTUR: Is it any of your business?

DISA (*troubled*): Why do you speak so angrily to one another? You, who are old friends? (*Tries to smile.*) Aren't you going to wish us happiness?

OLAFUR: It distresses me deeply, Disa, both for you and for your innocence. But you will have to hear the truth. Loftur has been my best friend. Now I have only one wish, to erase him from my memory. I will not stay one day longer under the same roof with him. Tomorrow, when the Bailiff comes home, I will take my leave for good. I will not breathe the same air as he. I will not look at the same mountains. (*To Loftur.*) May fortune grant that you never again cross my path.

DISA: What harm has Loftur done you?

OLAFUR (*to Loftur, more quietly*): I have a message to you from Steinunn, which I promised her I would bring you. I met her in your father's living room the same day she drowned. I have never seen more tragic despair. After she had spoken to me, I thought she had calmed down. Fool that I was, I didn't understand her calm.

LOFTUR: Save your message till tomorrow. Then I will be ready to hear it. Not now.

OLAFUR: You shall hear the message now. (*Continues.*) Right after she had left the room, I saw her run down the meadow, bareheaded, with a shawl on her shoulders. Then I understood her. I ran after her. I called to her. (*Sadly.*) Perhaps my cries helped to drive her to her death, for she threw away her shawl and ran even faster when she heard me call. She didn't hesitate even a moment at the river's edge. When

I got down to the river, the current had taken her and no human power could save her life. (*Looks with hatred at Loftur.*) It was your fault that she drowned herself.

DISA (*to Loftur, her voice failing from fear*): Is this true?

LOFTUR: Don't be frightened, Disa. (*His voice is strong.*) Steinunn didn't drown herself. Olafur hates me because he loved her, and now he is trying to disturb my conscience. He said himself that she forgot her shawl out in the meadow and went out to look for it, and he saw how the storm caught her and made her lose her footing on the riverbank.

OLAFUR: Do you think I would let the woman I loved be buried outside the churchyard? And think of her mother! Wasn't it enough that she should lose her daughter? Should she also have to worry about her salvation? When I ran home to get help, I was overcome by sorrow and hate. But on my way I came to myself. And when I saw her shawl, it occurred to me how I could conceal her desperate act. Now that she has come to rest in her grave, I can say it.

DISA: You told me you were not engaged to Steinunn.

OLAFUR (*to Loftur*): Then you lied.

LOFTUR: I forbid you to talk!

OLAFUR: Can you also silence your conscience?

LOFTUR: Don't listen to him, Disa. I would rather tell you myself. Yes, it is true, I was engaged to Steinunn. (*Approaches Disa.*)

DISA (*retreating*): You had so little confidence in me then that you would lie to me.

LOFTUR: No, you mustn't leave me. You alone have all my love. I will lose my footing and fall into the abyss if I lose you.

DISA (*deeply saddened*): How can I know whether you are telling the truth or lying?

LOFTUR: Can't you love me even though I am a sinner? He who never sins is not human. (*Madness seizes him. His speeches are a mixture of sly persuasion and defiance.*) Disa! There is a mysterious joy in sin. All good deeds are only irresponsible imitations. Only in sin does a man become himself. Sin is the beginning of all that is new. One is born anew of oneself in unspeakable terror.

DISA: I have already realized that you are ill. Olafur—now I'm going to get father. (*Walks quickly out of the church.*)

LOFTUR (*takes one step after her*): Disa!

(*Disa leaves, without looking back.*)

LOFTUR (*turns to Olafur*): The Devil sent you here. Her innocence was the only thing that could have saved me.

OLAFUR: You didn't think twice about abandoning the girl you had seduced into loving you. Maybe now you will get some drops from the same chalice.

LOFTUR: Go away!

OLAFUR: Yes, I'll go. But first I mean to keep my promise to Steinunn to bring you her last words, even though you are not worthy to hear them. She asked me to tell you that all bitterness had left her heart. She asked me to tell you that she had forgiven you.

LOFTUR: She has no power to forgive me.

OLAFUR: Is your conscience coming to life again?

LOFTUR: You think that Steinunn killed herself? No, I was the one who killed her! My wish was in the storm. My wish was in her feet when she was running and when she lost her footing on the riverbank. My wish was in the stream that took her. I have sold my soul.

OLAFUR (*looks at Loftur and realizes that he is ill. Puts his hand reassuringly on his shoulder*): Disa will soon be back with her father.

LOFTUR (*is suddenly joyful, puts his hands on Olafur's cheeks*): You are the one who went with me up to the glacier when I found the anemones. I can confide everything to you. In this night I will be made the ruler! My conjurations will drive Bishop Gottskalk the Grim out of his grave and force him to give me the Book of Power. (*Fearfully.*) I know that the good bishops will come too. They can't bear to hear the evil words in the house of God.

OLAFUR: Try to be quiet. Remember that Steinunn has forgiven you.

LOFTUR (*turns away from him*): Even almighty God does not have the power to forgive me.

OLAFUR (*follows him*): You can't pray to God for forgiveness because you know nothing about God except what you have heard and dreamt. You will have to forgive yourself. Or if that is impossible, you will have to wait for death. Loftur! I have heard death speak. It was not Steinunn who forgave you. It was death itself.

LOFTUR: Forgiveness of the Good is peace. (*In a loud voice.*) But forgiveness of the Evil is a hardening. Why should I not be evil? When I gain power, I shall use it as a scourge. I'll tempt and force men to sin, so that they can suffer some of the same torments as I. (*Walks up the steps, stops. Looks slowly at the door.*)

OLAFUR (*follows him up the steps*): Poor man! (*Stops.*) I know that you no longer understand my words—but now I forgive you. I forgive you in the name of that ray of light which once grazed my hand.

LOFTUR (*turns towards him. His looks are dark and threatening*): Now leave!

OLAFUR: Yes, now we'll both leave.

(*Loftur seizes Olafur by the shoulder with all the strength of a madman, propelling him towards the door. The pulpit shades them. The noise of scuffling is heard. The door creaks on its hinges.*)

LOFTUR (*comes in. His jacket is torn. He goes up to the altar, turns his back to it, bows deeply*): Thou who livest in everlasting darkness. I call to Thee through the earth. (*The church grows dark. He has become entirely mad.*) Grant me Thy power. Clothe me in Thy strength. Purify me of all good deeds. And make my heart strong in Evil.

(*A gleam of lightning flashes through the church. The tapers light. Bishop Gottskalk the Grim stands in the pulpit, dressed in a red chasuble, a little bent, holding the red Book*

*of Power in his outstretched hands. The coldness and maj-
esty of death is in his face. On both sides of the pews are
lined up rows of bishops in full vestments. They all wear
miters and dark purple chasubles with golden crosses. Each
one is holding a Bible before his breast in both hands. They
stand perfectly still, like statues, and speak in turn. They are
the Voices of Conscience.*

Loftur starts back.)

FIRST VOICE OF CONSCIENCE: Who art thou that defilest this holy
place with thy mad lust?

SECOND VOICE OF CONSCIENCE: Thou risest up against the Almighty. He is sending the least of His servants, the worms,
to meet you!

THIRD VOICE OF CONSCIENCE: In the hour when the river of
death breaks into your house, the dress of arrogance will fall
away like dust.

LOFTUR (*going quickly towards the last voice*): I am a spark of
the Almighty.

FOURTH VOICE OF CONSCIENCE: The lights love the darkness, so
that they may shine themselves.

FIFTH VOICE OF CONSCIENCE: Thou art no nearer to heaven,
though thou goest up in the mountains. But the stars are
reflected in humble waters.

LOFTUR (*goes in the direction of the voices*): The bow that
sends the arrow knows no humility.

SIXTH VOICE OF CONSCIENCE: The fire dies in the ashes, and
dreams betray the arrogant.

SEVENTH VOICE OF CONSCIENCE: Even the seed that is borne by
the wind knows its God.

LOFTUR: God knows the seed and the wind, and He answers
the prayer of the grass under the snow. (*Bitterly.*) What
concern is that of mine? He does not hear *my* complaints!

EIGHTH VOICE OF CONSCIENCE: Darkness and shadows live by the
grace of light, until the gold-embroidered tents of heaven are
swept aside.

LOFTUR: Be quiet! Be quiet! (*Again bows to the ground.*) Grant me Thy power. Clothe me in Thy strength. Purify me of all good deeds.

VOICES OF CONSCIENCE (ALL): Woe! Woe! Woe!

BISHOP GOTTSKALK THE GRIM (*without expression*): In the darkness—

(*Loftur stops his incantations when he becomes aware of Gottskalk. Looks at him.*)

BISHOP GOTTSKALK THE GRIM (*continuing*): —before thou wert born—Evil cleft thy will.

LOFTUR (*joyfully reaches out for the book*): Now! (*Falls to the floor and dies.*)

(*The lights go out. The vision vanishes. The church is empty and desolate, as before. The moonlight and the clouds fill it again with their mysterious life.*

A little later the door is opened quickly.)

DISA (*is heard*): Loftur! Loftur! (*Runs to Loftur, kneels beside him. The Bishop and Olafur follow her quickly.*)

DISA (*in despair*): Loftur! (*Lifts up his face; looks at it in silent terror.*)

OLAFUR (*quietly*): He is dead.

DISA: Loftur! (*Throws herself upon him, sobbing.*)

THE BISHOP: Is he dead? (*Goes over to him and bows his head over him and Disa.*) Peace be with thy soul. (*Puts his hand on Disa's head.*) My child! My child! How deeply you must have loved him.

OLAFUR (*standing motionless*): Death has forgiven him.

CURTAIN

THE
GOLDEN
GATE

A Play in Four Acts

Gullna Hliðið by Davið Stefánsson

Translated from Icelandic by G. M. Gathorne-Hardy

First published in Icelandic 1941

Introduction

The second play in our collection, *The Golden Gate* (*Gullna hliðið*, 1941), is also built upon an Icelandic folktale, but the treatment is vastly different. Davið Stefánsson, who was fond of adding the designation "frá Fagraskógi" (from Fairwoods) to his name, was one of the foremost representatives of the national romanticism that dominated Icelandic literature in the interwar years. In Iceland these were the years of home rule, granted by Denmark in 1918, crowned in 1944 by a complete independence which was only briefly marred by the wartime presence of English and American troops after 1940. Icelandic authors no longer looked to Denmark for their audience, and writers like Davið Stefánsson won themselves a great reputation as exponents of this first blossoming of a free nation. Even would-be realists and radicals like Thórbergur Thórðarson and Halldór Laxness, who scourged their countrymen, did so in the name of a passionate love for their country. Both of them delved deeply into the folk life of Iceland, and Laxness in his *Íslandsklukkan* (*Bell of Iceland*, 1943) produced a truly national saga.

Davið Stefánsson's patriotism was of an entirely different but no less real sort. In words and forms of the utmost simplicity he succeeded in giving voice to a lyricism which struck a new note in the often harsh atmosphere of Icelandic literature. His first collection of poems, *Svartar fjaðrir* (*Black Feathers*, 1919), expressed a tenderness, a warmth, and a humor which immediately won him tremendous popularity. His love poems

are memorable, with a lilting quality reminiscent of the ballad,
and at the same time a jesting tone that keeps them from
becoming sentimental. He is particularly successful in his lulla-
bies, melodious poems written for children and adults alike.
His poetry deals with people and is close to people, appealing
to their emotions through a combination of sound and mood.
In many of his poems there is a deep symbolic concern with
the great problems of human life, love and hate, life and
death.

In a series of collections he established himself as the "national poet" of his generation. His lyric descriptions of Icelandic scenery, his espousal of the simple virtues of life, and his
whimsical drolleries endeared him to a public which was rapidly moving off the farms and into the cities. He expressed
perfectly their nostalgia for the old and simple virtues, the
faith and the hope of the past, while also suggesting a new and
romantic view of life that gave hope for the future. His political views were mildly socialistic, but he always preserved a
deep sense of solidarity with the soil from which his ancestors
had sprung. His father was a farmer in the northern region of
Eyjafjör$\eth$ur, able and prominent enough to be elected to the
Althing; his uncle, Ólafur Davi$\eth$sson, was a folklorist from
whom he learned a great deal, and to whose memory he was
later to pen a vigorous tribute.[1] Born at Fagraskógur in 1895, a
graduate of the gymnasium in Reykjavík in 1919, a great
traveler and lover of books, Davi$\eth$ was librarian at Akureyri
from 1925–52. He remained unmarried to his death in 1964.

The Golden Gate was not his only venture into the dramatic field. In *Munkarnir á Mö$\eth$ruvöllum* (*The Monks at
Mö$\eth$ruvöllum*, 1926) he tried his hand quite unsuccessfully at
recreating the Middle Ages. After his success with *The Golden*

---

[1] His uncle published a collection of folklore entitled *Íslenzkar gátur,
skemmtanir, vikivakar og þular* (Reykjavík, 1887–1903); the article by
Davi$\eth$ Stefánsson appeared in his book *Mælt mál* (Reykjavík: Helgafell,
1963), 108–18.

Gate in 1941 he tried again in *Vopn guðanna* (*The Weapons of the Gods*, 1944), based on the oriental tale of Josaphat and Barlaam, and in *Landið gleymda* (*The Forgotten Land*, 1953), on the rediscovery of Greenland by the Norwegian missionary, Hans Egede. Somehow neither of these had the dramatic qualities that would ensure them life on the stage. His one novel was more successful, *Sólon Islandus* (1940), the symbolic narrative of a nineteenth-century Icelandic vagabond. In the words of Stefán Einarsson, "it is a truly Icelandic tragedy, the life of an ambitious, artistic dreamer with no means to realize his ambition, or to develop his talents which might have borne fruit in a bigger nation."[2] It is understandable that Davið, with all his own success, nevertheless could feel a deep kinship with this Icelandic Peer Gynt. He was basically a dreamer, and most of his writing builds on dreams.

The folktale on which *The Golden Gate* is based was written down by the nineteenth century national poet of Iceland, Matthías Jochumsson, in his student days, and printed in the previously mentioned collection by Jón Arnason.[3] The title of it is "Sálin hans Jóns mins," a phrase weakly translated as "The Soul of My Own John." It is a short and salty tale about a woman who is married to a good-for-nothing husband, but who nevertheless loves him enough to make a quite extraordinary effort to save his soul. Just as he dies, she holds a leather bag to his mouth and ties the soul up in the bag before it can escape. She hides the bag under her apron and starts off for heaven. On her knock, Saint Peter comes out and she begs him to admit her husband; when he rather curtly dismisses her, she reminds him of the time he denied his master, and he bangs the

---

[2] Einarsson, *History of Icelandic Literature*, p. 307.

[3] Arnason, *Íslenzkar Þjóðsögur*, vol. 2, 39–40 (1954 edition, vol. 2, 42–43); English translation in *Icelandic Legends* (Collected by Jón Arnason), tr. by George E. J. Powell and Eiríkr Magnússon, Second Series (London, 1866), pp. 45–48.

door in her face. She knocks again, and has a similar encounter with Saint Paul; she reminds him that he had persecuted Christians. The third person to come is the Virgin Mary, and she has the nerve to remind her that she had had an illegitimate child. When finally Christ himself comes out, she sees her chance and throws the bag into heaven before he can close the door. Similar stories are known from other countries, but the Icelandic one has its special twist in the woman's outspokenness.[4]

The story amused Daviδ sufficiently for him to make a narrative poem out of it, with the same title as the folktale, which appeared in his collection *Í Byggδum (In the Valleys*, 1933).[5] The spirit of his poem is far removed from that of the folktale, in spite of the common plot. The angry dialogue with celestial persons is dropped: the only one she meets is St. Peter, and their conversation is quite harmonious. The body of the poem consists of the long journey from her home to the door of heaven, described in great detail as a laborious mountain climbing operation. Once she has reached the top, however, the descriptions of heaven are a whimsical reflection of the peasant's conception of bliss: tall grass, fat cows, sleek horses, woolly sheep. This is just the place for her John, though she is not quite sure he is the man to manage such glorious possessions.

In a conversation reported by his journalist brother, Valtýr Stefánsson, Daviδ said that he was not satisfied with his treatment of the theme in the poem.[6] So he delved into the religious world of his own past, studying the hymnbooks, devotional

[4] For parallels see Stith Thompson, *Motif-Index of Folk-literature.* (Bloomington: Indiana Univ. Press, 1955–58), under motif K 2371.1.3 Heaven entered by trick: "wishing sack" thrown in.

[5] Reprinted in his collected poems, *Að norδan* (Reykjavík: Helgafell, 1952), vol. 2, 340–45.

[6] *Morgunblaδið*, December 24, 1941. Here cited from Matthías Johannessen's Introduction (p. 7) to the 1966 edition of *Gullna hliδiδ* (Reykjavík: Helgafell, 1966), to which the following discussion owes a great deal.

writings, and sermons of preceding centuries, steeping himself in the conceptions of the hereafter which had been entertained by the common people of his country. He found that these conceptions were of a singularly robust and tangible quality, sometimes so precisely expressed that an architect could have built the hall of heaven and a housewife prepared the meals described! In an essay *Á leið til Gullna hliðsins* (*On the Way to the Golden Gate*), Davið wrote, "In heaven there was never frost, never storm nor hail, now and then a gentle rain for pleasure's sake, otherwise fair weather, eternal Icelandic summer. . . . There were neither taxes nor Danish merchants; all were masters of their own labor and their lives, and yet united in the spirit of God's love and wisdom. No one doubted the omnipotence of the Lord, but His mercy was so great and His views so noble that He reminded one rather of a graybearded, respected parish official and father than of the King's representatives."[7]

If we are entitled to regard *The Wish* as an Icelandic *Faust*, this play qualifies as an Icelandic *Divine Comedy*. *Mutatis mutandis*, Dante's conception of the hereafter was not greatly different from that which the Old Woman of Davið's play harbors. In both works we find the conception of the other world as a high mountain up which mankind must struggle, at the risk of losing his footing and falling into a bottomless pit. While these views have ample scriptural basis, they come with special appropriateness in mountainous and volcanic Italy and Iceland. In the play Davið spun this theme even further than in his poem, and got a chance to introduce the Devil and his followers, among whom were some of his favorite antipathies (as in Dante's poem). The authorities of this world, the rich and the rulers, even the ministers, do not come off well. Only the simple of heart are destined for heaven, and all of Jón's sins are not sufficient to outweigh the love of his wife. He goes to heaven in spite of himself.

[7] Davið Stefánsson, *Mælt mál* (Reykjavík: Helgafell, 1963), p. 221.

The most important innovation in the play is the author's introduction of Jón as a major character. In the tale and the poem his chief function had been to die and be transported to heaven. In the play he furnishes dramatic contrast to his patient, long-suffering wife, and his blustering, colorful speech offers a welcome relief from her pious, loving manner. As the wife grows more saintly, Jón gets testier and more unwilling to be raised to glory. He retains his earthiness, even his hellishness, almost to the end. Matthías Johannessen, in a study of the play, points out that while her world has virtually vanished from Icelandic folk life, her husband's is still alive: "I feel as if I have often spoken with this fellow, chatted with him on the kelp-covered beach, while he takes his snuff sitting on the moss-grown rocks, or under a tumble-down farm wall."[8] Jón has taken over from the folktale some of the woman's saucy answers to the celestial authorities, here seen as the underdog's privilege of barking at the Almighty and carrying on the peasant's grumble at his circumstances in this life.

The play was first performed by the Reykjavík Dramatic Society on December 26, 1941 under the direction of Lárus Pálsson assisted by the author. The main roles were played by the well-known actors Brynjolf Jóhannesson and Arndís Björnsdóttir, while the author read the prologue. The performance was a tremendous hit; it attracted full houses throughout the season and received ecstatic reviews. Music composed for the four songs by Páll Ísólfsson added notably to the performance, wrought as they were in the spirit of old hymns and folktunes.[9] Immediately after the war the play was produced in Norwegian at Det Norske Teatret in Oslo (March 5, 1946) and in Finnish in Finland, with great success. The present translation by G. M. Gathorne-Hardy, which we are privileged to include, was performed in the Christmas season,

[8] *Gullna hliðið* (1966 ed.), p. 10.
[9] *Gullna hliðið*. Fjögur sönglög eftir Pál Ísólfsson. Reykjavík: Víkingsprent, 1942.

1948, in Edinburgh, and again at the Edinburgh Festival, August 20–25, 1949. Students mounted a performance at Oxford University in 1949. The Icelandic troupe has presented guest performances in Denmark, Finland, and Norway.[10]

Everywhere audiences were impressed by the spirit of religious humanism which breathes through the play. Davið Stefánsson has here preached a powerful sermon against all forms of hypocrisy, while exalting the power of love to overcome evil. His folk parable is a charming and ingenious picture of an Iceland that will soon be gone.

E. H.

Davið Stefánsson: Bibliography

IN ICELANDIC

Svartar fjaðrir (*Black Feathers*). Poems. Reykjavík: Bókaverzlun Á. Árnasonar, 1919.

Kvæði (*Poems*). Reykjavík: Prentsmiðjan Acta, 1922.

Kveðjur (Greetings). Poems. Reykjavík: Prentsmiðjan Acta, 1924.

Munkarnir á Möðruvöllum (*The Monks at Möðruvellir*). Play in three acts. Reykjavík: Prentsmiðjan Acta, 1926.

Ný kvæði (*New Poems*). Reykjavík: Prentsmiðjan Acta, 1929.

Kvæðasafn (*Collected Poems*). 2 vols. Akureyri: T. M. Jónsson, 1930.

Í byggðum (*In the Valleys*). Poems. Akureyri: T. M. Jónsson, 1933.

[10] All of this information comes from M. Jóhannessen's Introduction to the 1966 edition of *Gullna hliðið*.

Að norðan (*From the North*). Poems. Akureyri: T. M.
Jónsson, 1936.
Sólon Islandus. Novel. 2 vols. Akureyri: T. M. Jónsson, 1940.
Gullna hliðið (*The Golden Gate*). Play in four acts. Akureyri:
T. M. Jónsson, 1941. New ed., with introduction by Matth-
ías Johannessen (Reykjavík: Helgafell, 1966).
Kvæðasafn (*Collected Poems*). 3 vols. Akureyri: T. M.
Jónsson, 1943.
Vopn guðanna (*Weapons of the Gods*). Play. Akureyri: T. M.
Jónsson, 1944.
Ný kvæðabók (*New Book of Poems*). Akureyri: T. M.
Jónsson, 1947.
[Collected Works]. 4 vols. Reykjavík: Helgafell, 1952.
Ávarp fjallkonunnar (*Address to Iceland*). Poems. Reykjavík:
Helgafell, 1954.
Landið gleymda (*The Forgotten Land*). Play in four acts.
Reykjavík: Helgafell, 1956.
Ljóð frá liðnu sumri (*Songs from Summer Past*). Poems.
Reykjavík: Helgafell, 1956.
Í dögun (*At dawn*). Poems. Reykjavík: Helgafell, 1960.
Mælt mál (*Spoken Matters*). Essays. Reykjavík: Helgafell,
1963.
Skáldið á Sigurhæðum (*The Poet at Sigurhæðir*). Essays, ed-
ited. Akureyri: Odd Björnsson, 1963.

IN ENGLISH

"I Sail in the Fall," in Watson Kirkconnell, *The North Ameri-
can Book of Icelandic Verse* (New York: L. Carrier & A.
Isles, 1930), pp. 220–22.
"The Parson's Confession," in Paul Bjarnason, *Odes and
Echoes* (Vancouver, Canada, 1954), pp. 92–95.
"Mother Wants to Sleep," "I Sail in the Fall," and "The
Shadow" in Martin S. Allwood, *20th Century Scandinavian
Poetry* (Mullsjö, Sweden, 1950), pp. 13–15.

"Fairy Hill," "Oft Flames amid Ashes Lie Hidden," "The Bride's Slippers," and "The Shadow" in Richard Beck, *Icelandic Lyrics, Originals and Translations* (Reykjavík: Thórhallur Bjarnason, 1930), pp. 208–11.

"Elfinhill" in *American Scandinavian Review*, vol. 40 (1952), 321; "The Guest," *ibid.*, vol. 46 (1958), 334.

Characters

Jon, a cotter*
An old woman, his wife
Vilborg, a wise-woman
A sheriff's officer
A man and woman, Jon's former employers
A thief
A jailer
A drunkard
A woman, Jon's mistress
A rich man
A sheriff
Parents of the old woman
Helga, her friend
A priest
A farmer
A fiddler
Saint Peter
Saint Paul
The Virgin Mary
Michael the Archangel
The Enemy
Four imps
Angels and the elect

Sources: Popular folk-tale and old hymns.

* Occupant of a cottage on a farm, paying with labor in lieu of rent.

Prologue

Much by the veil of time is hidden yet
To which our creeds and customs are in debt.
Deserted crofts in glens remote and bleak
Tell much to those to whom their stones can speak.
Gold may be found in many a ruined hall,
And hearths long cold their former fires recall.
Here, long ago, a folk in rags and tatters
Groaned 'neath the weight of sacerdotal fetters:
Men prayed—but used in age their childhood's prayer;
Witchcraft and spells spread darkness everywhere;
Spectres and goblins danced around the hall,
Brought death to men—and horses in the stall.
In crags was found the troll, in mounds the elf,
While down in hell lived the arch-fiend himself:
Each hamlet he with sin and evil filled,
Appearing there in any shape he willed.

Dark was the age. What sanctuary more
From ghosts and devils knocking at the door?
With ice the seas were barred, the springs were sealed;
Mountains spewed flame, the land with earthquake reeled;
The neighbourhood with shameful lust was cursed;
Some men were tortured with a quenchless thirst,
Some lived a beggar's life on moss and leaves,
Others were turned by famine into thieves.
Men slew their brethren, maddened by disaster,
And recognised the Devil as their master,

His realm from hell extending to the sky.
In such a wolf-age, whither could they fly?

Yet some there were who sought to save themselves,
Pored over ancient volumes on their shelves,
Turned o'er the pages, blew the dust away,
And much would read, and fervently would pray.
In books, as many fancied, they could find
God's purpose, and his promise to mankind,
Seeking to point the road their souls to save,
In hope of better things—beyond the grave.

The pilgrim soul from each man's corpse was driven
To climb a mighty mountain—up to heaven.
Rocky and steep the slope, and hard to climb,
Bowed with the load of sins, through snow and rime;
While, as the rustic sages would declare,
Old Nick lurks in ambush everywhere.
Many a crippled soul climbs upward late,
But reaches in the end the Golden Gate.
After confession and beseeching prayer,
Some find eternal bliss awaits them there;
While others learn at last themselves to blame,
Hurled down to burn in everlasting flame.
Such was their faith of old—this race of ours,
A strengthless striving—'twixt two mighty powers!

Here we would sweep the stony path once more,
And resurrect our ancestors of yore,
That thus the young may gain the power to feel
That inner strife which bygone times conceal;
Since buried in those secret depths, indeed,
Lie the main roots of custom and of creed.
The generations change. Age yields to age.
And what is now our children's heritage?

Take not offense, though our design be crude,
And dead men talk, with earthly speech endued.
Far be it from us to wound the trustful soul;
To bridge the gulf that sunders is our goal.
We breathe new life in hymns and peasant tale,
And show you thus the world behind the veil!

Act I

A small cottage in a remote valley. Turf walls, earth floor. A pallet bed under a weatherboard roof, and above it a small window closed with a membrane. Opposite is a door, and a hearth with a pot on it. Firewood and cooking utensils. Against the gable wall is an old chest, and on it a carved wooden bowl and a couple of devotional books. Above the chest is a lighted train-oil lamp, fastened to the wall. There is a glimmer of firelight from the hearth. An evening in early winter.

Jon lies dying on the bed. He is in a red homespun shirt, and is old and bearded. His breathing is labored. The old woman (his wife) is sitting by him, knitting. Vilborg is busy at the hearth.

OLD WOMAN: Jon dear, Jon. (*Looks up.*) It's a fair caution how he can sleep.

VILBORG: Aye, 'twas real strong, the last dose he had. It's no use giving that Jon of yours extract of yarrow or thyme tea. I know the stuff for him. He's not the first I've treated when they're mortal bad with sickness.

OLD WOMAN: That's something to thank God for—being able to ease the sufferings of others.

VILBORG: There's all sorts of herbs. I've learnt by experience to tell them apart and know what's best in each case.

OLD WOMAN: No one doubts your knowledge, Vilborg, or people wouldn't come to you when it matters most.

VILBORG: There's some herbs as does away with unwholesome fluids and poisons in the body; others strengthens the blood and does good to the nerves as well. And then there's herbs just helps to get rid of wind from the belly. Some you have to boil on a slow fire, others over a roaring flame. And often a lot depends on your using the proper sort of fuel. One herb you must allus cook just with scrub or heather, others with bits of mahogany that drives ashore at spring tide, and a third sort with droppings of well-fatted ewe lambs. And then there's mixing the brew, with a drop of all sorts in one and the same dose.

OLD WOMAN: You want godfearing honest folk to handle these blessed herbs.

VILBORG: Ah, but 'tain't allus enough to say prayers right, seemingly. You have to suit your thoughts according to the nature and badness of the illness. Those herbs I gave your Jon a brew of just now is rare and hard to find, and they only grows where there's fire in the soil, close to hot springs and brimstone pools.

OLD WOMAN: Lord 'a mercy on us!

VILBORG: What's bad takes bad to drive it out. Supposing anything's to save him, it'll be that last dose, or another a trifle stronger.

OLD WOMAN: Seems to me he's terrible low.

VILBORG: Seemed to me he could use his tongue all right just now.

OLD WOMAN: Ah, that's only old habits from when he was a boy, God bless him! I'm ashamed to say I scarcely notices his bad language; you get used to that sort of thing quicker than in forty years of wedlock. At first I did all I could to wean him from this continual nastiness, but there as in other things I didn't get very far.

VILBORG: You're not the only one that tries and fails.

OLD WOMAN: Many's the time it's been difficult, living with him, and yet it allus seems to me there's something fine about my Jon. But he might at times have been harder working at home, bless his heart!

VILBORG: Those as is lazy and idle has got seven devils in their lap, and is scratching the back of the eighth.

OLD WOMAN: That's why it went as it did. It wasn't the way he was brought up as a lad, either. You might put it that he came into this sinful world without father or mother, so you needn't ask about his upbringing. Thrashed he was, plenty of that, and starved into the bargain. So was it to be wondered at if the lad couldn't keep his hands still?

VILBORG: It's a wicked world.

OLD WOMAN: I think there's other folk to be blamed for the way things went with him. But God in heaven above us knows I tried everything I could to keep him out of mischief.

VILBORG: No one as knows about it can doubt that!

OLD WOMAN: It may well be that I've grown as bad as him, but I had to try to share his burdens as long as I could. But God knows all the same that I refused for a long time to cook what he brought into the house, when I knew it was come by wrong and dishonestly.

VILBORG: Such ways didn't come to him by nature.

OLD WOMAN: Many's the one as has said that.

VILBORG: Many's the wiles of the Devil.

OLD WOMAN: And my Jon gives way, like lots of others. What was I to do? Of course I shielded him. Wasn't I his wife, as had sworn before God's holy altar to be true to him for ever?

VILBORG: Some people has a heavy cross to bear.

OLD WOMAN: And then we lost the children. God called three of them to him the same week, the others have flown off to the ends of the earth. It's often I've missed them, specially when I was left alone in the cottage.

VILBORG: It's a marvel what's left of you. You can't have been badly put together at the start.

OLD WOMAN: What do you think ought to be said of my Jon, then? Life's treated him harder still. Up to now his heart's never been known to fail, though I know he's never had his full health since they pinched him. It wasn't human, the way they treated him.

VILBORG: What else could you expect?

OLD WOMAN: He was mocked and scourged like our blessed Saviour. And it was as if each trouble seemed to harden him more. When I wanted to scold him, or opened the scriptures, he told me to shut my mouth, and at times he'd snatch the book from me and throw it into the corner.

VILBORG: It's as sure as anything that some folks are possessed by evil spirits. Didn't you ever look up someone who knew a thing or two?

OLD WOMAN: O no, Vilborg, dear. I've set my trust in the Lord and his word, and so I do still.

VILBORG: I don't know as it would have done any harm to read one of those exorcisms over him, if those had done it as understood about it.

OLD WOMAN: Oh, do you think so? (*Jon groans and tosses.*)

OLD WOMAN (*attending to him*): God help you, Jon dear.—He's dropped off again, same as before.

VILBORG: I'm inclined to think something foul is after him.

OLD WOMAN: I should think it might be the old lot, the sheriff or his underlings. They've been here before, and always on the same errand. God knows if they haven't got something fresh on my Jon. It's as if he couldn't leave that sort of thing alone. But they'd never take him away from me, sick to death as he is.

VILBORG: It's to be hoped not.

OLD WOMAN: Perhaps God'll release him from human punishment. And if he'd got rest coming to him, I'd be easy. But God is just as stern a judge.

(*Vilborg rakes the fire.*)

OLD WOMAN: My last hope is that Jon will repent his sins before he goes, whenever that may be.

VILBORG: I'm inclined to think that sickness and pain of body may sometimes purge a hard heart, same as fire clears the dross from gold.

OLD WOMAN: Don't mention fire or brimstone, Vilborg dear!

(*Jon stirs, with a deep groan.*)

OLD WOMAN (*attending to him*): Are you feeling terrible bad, Jon dear? (*Jon is silent.*) Do you want to go on sleeping? Better try to wake up and pray, though there mayn't be much time.—There, he's dropped off again as usual.

VILBORG (*goes to the bed and lays her hands on the sick man's forehead*): It's easy to see he's had the proper dose. It's a good thing he's sweating, 'cause sweat's nothing but poisonous fluids in the blood, as have got to find their way out, if things are to be better.

OLD WOMAN: It looks as if he was a scrap easier just now. Don't you think so, dear?

VILBORG: I don't like his breathing. Even if the dose was strong and good, it's a question how it'll turn out. He's an old man, and worn out.

OLD WOMAN: I'm ready for anything, Vilborg dear.

VILBORG: Well, there's nothing else to do but to bide and see how things go. (*Sits by the hearth, takes a tobacco pouch out of her pocket, rubs it a good while, and takes a pinch of snuff.*)

OLD WOMAN: I asked him this morning if he wouldn't like the priest to come and give him the holy sacrament, but that didn't suit him. He's never been wishful to go to God's table. (*Sits on the chest, knitting. A pause.*)

VILBORG: Last communion Sunday, two ravens were seen flying in a cross over the church.

OLD WOMAN: That's always been held a bad sign.

VILBORG: At the north end of the churchyard was an open grave. While the service was going on, there was rain fell on the soil.

OLD WOMAN: After that, I can expect anything!

VILBORG: Well, it's the way of life! You're too reasonable and steady a woman not to take things quietly as they come.

OLD WOMAN: We've all got to die. But, as you know, there's lots of places in God's holy word where it says that them as dies in their sins, without repenting, are in for a bad time.

VILBORG: I understand.

OLD WOMAN: My Jon, worse luck, has always been careless and hasn't got ready for death as a Christian should. That's why he mustn't just slip away in his sleep. He must repent, 'cause all his salvation depends on it. (*Jon stirs. She gets up and goes to the bed.*) Jon, Jon darling! (*Jon is silent.*)

OLD WOMAN (*takes up one of the devotional books and turns over the pages. Goes up to Vilborg*): Sing this hymn with me, Vilborg dear. He must wake up, if it's possible.

VILBORG (*looking at the print*): Don't you need to see the words too?

OLD WOMAN: I should think I knew this hymn by heart—"Lord be thou mine only peace." And the tune as well.

BOTH (*sing*): Lord, be thou mine only peace,
And take me in when life shall cease;

In through Heaven's glorious door,
Where none are hungry, none are poor;
And all thy flock sing words of cheer,
Most wonderfully pure and clear.

But then their chastisement begins
Who unrepentant die in sins:
Who lied and stole and falsely swore,
And likewise those that played the whore.
All those who covet earthly show
Into the flames of Hell must go.

JON: What's all this howling?

(*The Old Woman nudges Vilborg; they go on singing.*)

BOTH: Repent, my soul, from mockery flee,
And call on Him who died on tree.
Call thou on God and all his state,
And then shall ope the Golden Gate,
Where all enjoy eternal bliss
With angel hosts in Paradise.

JON (*who has turned round during the singing*): What a devilish row!

OLD WOMAN: God forgive you. We were singing a hymn.

JON: No peace to sleep as usual. Suppose you want me to suffer as much as possible?

VILBORG (*gets up and goes to the bed*): I think you're an abominable brute to your wife. I suppose she ought to have slaved for you a bit more! You should be ashamed of the way you've behaved to her before, sooner than chuck abuse at her!

OLD WOMAN: There, there, Vilborg dear. He can't help it.

VILBORG: I know what I'm doing. This isn't the first time I've stood by a sickbed.

JON: Each of you's as crazy as the other.

VLBORG: He's not fast asleep this time. (*Goes to the hearth and stirs the pot.*)

OLD WOMAN: Confess your sins to God, Jon darling, and pray
the blessed Saviour of souls to have mercy on you. That's
the only true remedy.
(*Jon groans heavily.*)
VILBORG (*taking up the bowl*): He needs a fresh dose.
JON: Brandy!
OLD WOMAN: You know there ain't any. Try now to forget all
earthly pleasures, and turn your thoughts on high. We're all
sinful creatures. If you confess and make amends, you'll
share the glory of the angels.
(*Jon gives a cry.*)
OLD WOMAN (*to Vilborg*): He's in dreadful pain.
VILBORG: I know what's wrong with him. It's not always the
one that cries loudest that's the most hurt. (*Pours into the
pot and stirs it.*) He'll soon get his dose. It's no good hur-
rying in a matter of life or death. (*Mumbles to herself.*)
OLD WOMAN: Eh, what are you muttering, Vilborg dear?
VILBORG: Leave that to me.
OLD WOMAN (*to Jon*): Wouldn't you rather I sent for the
priest, so that you could receive the last unction and the
bread and wine, like a repentant Christian child of God? It'll
give you peace.
JON: Baccy—brandy!
(*Wife looks at Vilborg in despair.*)
VILBORG: What's up? (*Goes to the bed with the bowl.*) Here
now, Jon, it's best for you to swallow this down. (*To the
Old Woman.*) He's done for, anyhow. (*Helps Jon to drink.
The dose goes down the wrong way.*) Get it all down.
That's real stuff. It's got a kick in it.
JON: Damned muck!
OLD WOMAN: I'm beginning to think there's something unnatu-
ral about his illness.
VILBORG: I saw at once, from the way the first dose acted on
him, that the sickness was more than a bit queer. Don't you
notice an odd smell in here?
OLD WOMAN: Like rancid butter?

VILBORG: I'm not so sure it ain't the smell of coming death. It's the stink of brimstone, no less!

OLD WOMAN: God help my Jon!

VILBORG: The air's stiff with foul spirits.

(*The light grows dim.*)

JON: Hey! Devils!

VILBORG: He's calling them.

OLD WOMAN: He's out of his senses.

VILBORG: Why? Why is he out of his senses? . . . They've drunk the oil out of the lamp.

(*The light goes out. The Old Woman screams, grabs the lamp in panic and goes with it into the corner to attend to it. In the glow from the hearth four imps are seen dancing round the bed.*)

FIRST IMP (*fat and fiery red, holding out a keg of brandy to Jon, hisses*): Drunkard!

(*Jon laughs, rises half up and reaches for the keg, but falls back screaming on the pillow. His wife strides to the bed, takes one of the religious books from the chest, lays it on Jon's breast and bends over him.*)

SECOND IMP (*grey and woolly, with a sheep's head, bleats*): Sheep-stealer!

THIRD IMP (*with fat white woman's breasts and red lips, waving a red rag*): Adulterer!

FOURTH IMP (*coal black with red horns on his head, waves a rune-stick*): Heathen! (*Jon screams.*)

OLD WOMAN: God have mercy on you!

VILBORG: Lie quiet as the grave and still as a stone. The croft's full of devils. Let me talk to them. (*Strides to the door and opens it, seizes a blazing brand from the hearth and makes the sign of the cross with it in the air. The imps howl.*) With the burning torch of light I make the blessed sign of the cross over this sick man. In the name of Holy Trinity, in the name of the archangels of heaven, the blessed Michael, Gabriel, and Raphael, I conjure from him venomous vermin and evil spirits, who have been sent out by the Devil to possess his soul and drag him to the abode of the damned.

THE IMPS (*beckon to Jon, leaping about the floor and hissing*):
Come, come, come, come! (*Jon moans.*)

VILBORG: In the name of the Crucified, who gave sight to the
blind and healed those possessed of devils, in the name of all
healing herbs that grow on the earth, I conjure away venomous snakes and the generation of vipers which gnaw the life
and lungs of this sick man, fill his blood with poisonous fluids
and thus would destroy his heart and bowels, his gall, spleen,
and all his entrails. (*Advances towards the imps, who retreat
across the floor.*) Yield to the holy and almighty sign of the
cross; depart to the confines of the realm of your black
master, who awaits you in the lowest depths of fiery rain,
with his glowing trident, ready to strike it into your coal-
black bellies and plunge you in the seething brimstone caul-
dron of hell. (*The imps vanish through the door.*)

VILBORG: To the sick man let help come from the earth, victory
from the sun, sustenance from the stars, and strength from
the angels of God! (*Goes out after the imps. Wife looks
up.*)

VILBORG (*off*): *In nomine Patris et Filii et Spiritus Sancti.
Amen.*

OLD WOMAN: In His blessed name, Amen. Aren't you feeling
better now, Jon? (*Jon is silent. His wife takes the lamp and
lights it from the hearth. Vilborg enters, shuts the door and
crosses it.*) You've crossed the outer doors too, Vilborg
dear?

VILBORG: I should think so! I know what suits them. We'll say
no more about that.

OLD WOMAN: Blessing be with you, wherever you go! (*They
go to the bed.*)

VILBORG: Ain't you a bit easier now? Everything's quite pure
around you now.

OLD WOMAN: Don't you notice it, Jon dear? (*Throws the light
on his face.*)

(*Jon is silent, his eyes staring. His wife looks questioningly at Vilborg.*)

VILBORG: It's easy to see the way things are going. (*Jon unconsciously strikes his hand on the book lying on him, so that it falls to the ground.*) That's likely to be his last act this side of the grave.

OLD WOMAN (*picking up the book*): Perhaps he wants me to read him something. (*Sticks the lamp up on the wall, sits down and reads*):

Judge me, O God, and plead my cause against an ungodly nation;

O deliver me from the deceitful and unjust man.

For thou art the God of my strength; why dost thou cast me off?

Why go I mourning because of the oppression of the enemy?

O send out thy light and thy truth; let them lead me; let them

Bring me unto thy holy hill, and to thy tabernacles.

Then will I go unto the altar of God, unto God my exceeding joy;

Yea, upon the harp will I praise thee, O God my God.*

VILBORG: Are you going to go on reading? He's unconscious, and his time's coming very quick. Oughtn't I to open the window?

OLD WOMAN (*standing up*): No, for God's sake don't do that! (*She pulls out a leather bag from the foot of the bed.*) I'll not leave go of Jon's soul before it's in heaven!

VILBORG: Are you gone clean crazy, woman?

OLD WOMAN (*in a whisper*): I durstn't be sure St. Peter'll open the door for him, if he comes by himself. (*Aloud.*) And Jon's got nobody but me.

* Forty-third Psalm

VILBORG: So—your faithfulness won't stop at nothing! You've got a bit of string to tie up the bag, when it's wanted?

OLD WOMAN (*takes off one of her garters and holds it up*): That ain't none too good for him, though it's woven in checks and with my initials. (*Short pause.*)

VILBORG: There doesn't happen to be any ptarmigan feathers in his bedding?

OLD WOMAN: No, none, Vilborg.

VILBORG: Then he should be all right this way. Didn't he often put his socks under the pillow at night?

OLD WOMAN: Yes, often.

VILBORG: As I thought. Put his socks at the head of the bed. That'll do no harm.

(*Wife takes a pair of blue woolen socks from the chest and puts them under the pillow.*)

OLD WOMAN: These are his best pair.

VILBORG: Seems to me he's taking a rare long time to breathe his last. Stick the psalter right under the pillow—since we haven't a priest's vestment handy, or the names of the Seven Sleepers on a bit of writing.

OLD WOMAN: With God's help, that ought to do. There's power in the psalter.

VILBORG: We'll see. (*Takes Jon's hand.*) I think that ought to do the trick. The ends of his limbs has got cold.

OLD WOMAN (*stroking his hands*): God forgive your hands, Jon dear.

VILBORG: Now his soul's being released from the bonds of ungodly clay. Come here with the bag. (*The wife puts the bag over Jon's nostrils.*) That was the first!

OLD WOMAN: In the name of God the Father—

VILBORG: That was the second!

OLD WOMAN: And the Son—. Ready with the garter.

VILBORG (*taking hold of the garter*): Third! and the last.

OLD WOMAN: And God's Holy Ghost. (*Pulls together the mouth of the bag. They tie it up and cross it.*)

VILBORG: His earthly strife is over.

OLD WOMAN (*lays the bag at the head of the bed, falls on her knees at the foot, and prays silently*): God give your soul peace. Amen. (*Performs the last offices for Jon, kisses him, and signs him with the cross. Weeps.*)

VILBORG: "Dew falls at last, when day is past."

OLD WOMAN: I'd sacrifice my own salvation, if that'd give him a share in the bliss of God's children. (*Dries her eyes on the corner of her apron. Three knocks on the door.*) That'll be them, no doubt.

SHERIFF'S OFFICER (*entering*): I make so bold as to step in. Good evening all.

VILBORG: Good day, officer.

OFFICER: Isn't Jon at home? Ah yes, he's on the bed. I have come here by the sheriff's orders. You have been charged, Jon, with a fresh theft, and the sheriff has instructed me to take you in custody and remove you to the place of trial. I have to obey his orders.

OLD WOMAN: Who doubts it? Everyone knows the way you do your duty.

VILBORG: Won't you sit down, officer?

OFFICER: I mustn't sit. Jon, you heard what I said. Show a leg, I've no time to wait. Are you deaf and dumb, or pretending to be asleep? Do you think that'll do your case any good?

OLD WOMAN: You might try shaking him.

OFFICER (*does so*): There then, dress yourself at once, Jon, and come along.

OLD WOMAN: He's not got much to say for himself. But this time he's got a lawful excuse.

OFFICER: Lawful excuse?

VILBORG: He's dead.

OFFICER: Dead?

OLD WOMAN: Aye, he's taken the liberty, though it might interfere with the sheriff's arrangements.

OFFICER: And you let me address a dead man, and summon him to court!

OLD WOMAN: It never struck me that the servants of the law

wouldn't be sharp-sighted enough to tell a live man from a corpse.

OFFICER (*makes sign of cross over Jon*): Peace be with you.

OLD WOMAN: You can punish his body, but his soul you'll never get!

OFFICER (*makes a move to go*) I'll report Jon's death to the sheriff.

OLD WOMAN: I've no doubt you'll both pray for him. But if you think he's for the bad place, that hope of yours'll never come off. In at the Golden Gate he shall go!

OFFICER: Good-bye.

VILBORG: Good-bye. (*Exit Officer.*)

OLD WOMAN: Waking or sleeping, my prayers and thoughts shall carry him there—since I trust in thy mercy, O Lord, to lead me and remove me to thy holy mountain and to thy dwelling.

CURTAIN

Act II

A rocky, precipitous slope, veiled in mist. A yellow gleam on the rim of the mountain.

OLD WOMAN (*enters, in her Sunday clothes, holding the bag*): Now I must sit down at once and take a breather. I'm fagged out. (*Sits down.*)

JON (*or rather his soul in the bag*): You're not getting on, woman. Do you think I want to lie for all eternity in this damned bag?

OLD WOMAN: Now, you must have a scrap of patience, Jon dear. As if I wasn't doing all I could to struggle on, and it's no good my breaking down half way. This ain't no highway, far from it. It's even steeper than the slope at home, and you probably remember what that's like. And you know too that I'm only an old worn-out creature that's been mother to ten kids; you ought to know something about that, Jon dear.

JON: I've a dim recollection of it.

OLD WOMAN: And then you ask me to run up hill! Do you think I can keep it up for ever, same as a fox? And it's not as if I could be quite free and limber with your soul to drag along. It doesn't take much to burden the traveller.

JON: Well, you shouldn't have been in such a hurry to start on this trip—I'm stifled.

OLD WOMAN: It says in God's holy scripture—the body's mortal, but the soul lives for ever. You must have known before we set off that the road to heaven is long and hard.

JON: Anyhow, I'm sure most of what's in the scriptures is nothing but a pack of lies.

OLD WOMAN: I might have known it! It's a sin to listen to you. Surely you forget you're dead and on the way to the great judge. Try now to mend your ways a bit, or all this trouble will have been taken for nothing.

JON: If you grudge taking this bit of a stroll with me, I bloody well won't accept your help. Do you hear?

OLD WOMAN: Just like you! You're always the same.

JON: You'd much better open the bag, so I can go my own way.

OLD WOMAN: Let me settle that. If you want to shorten the trip, then say what few prayers you know and call your misdeeds to mind. The bag'll get lighter for every sin you repent. (*Jon laughs sarcastically.*) God help you, Jon.

JON: No fear! When has he ever helped me?

OLD WOMAN: You're never tired of blaspheming. Where do you think you'd be without the Lord's help and assistance? And then you mean to cap your shame by blaming him for the trouble you've brought on yourself. You took up with dishonest folks and let yourself be caught by the wiles of the Devil. I know there's forgiveness for them as is born weak. But you've gone on and despised the strength that's given by trust in God and by praying.

JON: Oh, dry up!

OLD WOMAN: All the same you might bear in mind the difference between living with angels and the chosen in heaven and wading breast high in fire and smoke with the hardened sinners.

JON: I'm stone-dead of thirst.

OLD WOMAN: What do you think then you'll be later on, if you've got to lie up to the waist in flame?

JON: Don't you see a brook or a spring?

OLD WOMAN: No. There's nothing here but mist and stone, stone everywhere, hoarfrost on the rocks and slippery at every step.

JON: Open the bag at once, so I can lick the frost. It'll cool me.

OLD WOMAN: I can't do that. You must put off cooling yourself while we're on the road. Say your prayers. They're the cooling water of life. Try that, Jon dear.

JON: I'll get nothing by that. That's no good.

OLD WOMAN: God Almighty hears in heaven, as soon as you pray hard enough.

JON: Maybe. But wouldn't it be a good idea to get a trifle higher first? In fact, are you sure you're on the right track? It's likely you're quite astray.

OLD WOMAN: Leave that to me.

JON: You was always a damn fool in mist. You'd better have let me get out of the window.

OLD WOMAN: Oh, I'm sick of your grumbling! Nice reception you'd have out there in the dark, to be sure.

JON: I wish my soul was back in my body.

OLD WOMAN: Yes, so you say now, Jon my boy. But that can't
be done now, till the last day, when the dead rise.

JON: Don't you think my carcass will get pretty high by then?
Don't you see any tracks in the frost?

OLD WOMAN: You needn't worry. I'm on the right track. It says
in the hymn—
"The way for all must upwards climb,
O'er crag and stone, through frost and rime."
No one goes astray, who follows God's holy word.

JON: The worst of it is—you can't be sure. Well then, try to
get a move on.

OLD WOMAN: Yes, yes. Don't behave as if you was out of your
senses. Just let me tuck up my skirts. It won't mend matters,
to get to heaven with my petticoat all ragged and torn.

JON: Don't you see any signs of people?

OLD WOMAN: The hymn says—
"Through mist and cloud the way goes by,
Till verdant meadows greet the eye."
But I shouldn't be surprised if we happened to meet some old
acquaintances from our country. (*Noise from the rocks.*)
God be with us!

JON: What was that?

OLD WOMAN: Somebody falling.
"The damned who up the mountain go
Must fall lamenting down below."

JON: Hold the bag tight, so they don't take me with them in
their fall.

OLD WOMAN: Oh, so that's it! You can trust me, Jon dear. But
don't let on to anybody.

JON: Do I generally talk out of fun? . . . But we might just ask
them the way, even if they are damned.

(*A Man and Woman fall onto the stage, and lie moaning.*)

OLD WOMAN (*attending to them*): You must have hurt yourselves, poor things!

MAN: We're all black and blue.

OLD WOMAN: Why, you're the couple that starved and thrashed my Jon when he was a boy.

WOMAN (*half rising*): It may be my man gave him a belting now and then, but he always got enough to eat, the young rascal.

JON: That's a lie.

WOMAN: What was that?

OLD WOMAN (*trying to keep Jon quiet by beating the bag*): The voice of truth, I fancy. You're the last people I expected to meet here. If I rightly recollect, it's a good thirty years since you passed away.

MAN: Thirty thousand years, more like, I should think.

OLD WOMAN: What, wouldn't they open the Golden Gate? But I suppose you counted up all your good deeds?

WOMAN: We wouldn't have been here otherwise.

OLD WOMAN: So I should have thought.

MAN: We were driven away like curs. (*Jon laughs.*)

WOMAN: What devil's laughter is that?

OLD WOMAN: Oh, it came from somewhere down below.

MAN: That laugh sounded to me like your Jon's. He can't be far off.

OLD WOMAN: Why, whenever did you hear him laugh? It's likely he'd think of laughing, when he came home with the milking ewes, with his face all blue with the cold, and then got hard words and beating for his pains.

WOMAN: There was a mean streak in that good-for-nothing puppy.

MAN: We meant him nothing but good.

OLD WOMAN: So you think thrashings and starvation gave the child a better disposition? They generally does! The blessed heavenly Father don't treat nobody more severe than them as mishandles defenseless kids. And nobody does it but rogues, my good woman. But now the bruises on the child's body have got onto your own carcasses. (*Jon laughs.*) As you sow, so must you reap. But it ain't no pleasure to me to see you treated like this. I'd willingly help you if I could.

WOMAN: We must be getting on.

MAN: Down the hill. There's no other lodging to turn to.

OLD WOMAN: "Great is the misery of man."

(*The Enemy peeps out from behind a rock, sneering. He is black and scorched, with two horns projecting from a shining skull. He waves his hand, pointing downward. He appears, without the Old Woman being aware of him, each time when new arrivals leave her and continue their journey. The Man, the Woman, and the Enemy disappear.*)

JON: They've got the punishment they deserve.

OLD WOMAN: Can you laugh at those poor creatures of another world, who've got nothing before them but suffering? You should be ashamed of yourself, Jon. You'll sing a different tune if the gate ain't opened for you.

JON: We'll take things as they come. Now then, are you going to make a move?

OLD WOMAN: I'm sure it's all the same, even if the journey takes a long time. You're none too quick at mending your ways.

(*The Thief falls onto the stage, screaming.*)

OLD WOMAN: "They try to cling, but down they go,
Like as the walls of Jericho."
So it's you, you swine, the chap who got Jon to pinch his first leg of mutton?

THIEF: I never heard but that you liked the taste of it all right.

OLD WOMAN: There wasn't a morsel of it passed my lips, nor the children's either, I can tell you, though it was a tight fit at home. I knew how it was come by. You'd have done better to have warned him of the risk, sooner than shove him over the brink.

THIEF: 'Twasn't me taught him to steal. It came more by nature than by schooling.

OLD WOMAN: After the first mishap, it was as if all my Jon's finer feelings had given way.

THIEF: Finer feelings, ha, ha! I reckon folks don't care much about that sort of thing on earth, they mostly tries to look after themselves and their belongings as best they can. Is it better to die of hunger and poverty? All proper chaps is thieves. They pinches each other's time and job, their food, their characters, their money, their sheep, horses, and women.

JON: *And* women! (*Laughs.*) Dead right, dead right, old man!

THIEF: Hullo! Is Jon here?

OLD WOMAN: I can't see him.

THIEF: There's plenty worse than me gets off all punishment in their lifetime, and yet slips into heaven after death. I think the same damned injustice applies there as on earth. The weaker gets turned away. Others is received with open arms.

OLD WOMAN: It's most likely you've read your lesson upside down and backwards—same as the Devil reads the Bible.

THIEF: But it never was so bloody bad where I came from that folks had to hunt over hill and dale to find a lodging.

OLD WOMAN: Ah, but there's a bit of difference between putting a chap up for one night and taking him in for ever and ever, amen. No, you scallywag. You've deserved to be shown out. Worse luck!

THIEF (*angrily*): That's a lie!

OLD WOMAN: You've no call to quarrel with me about it. I've got no say in what happens to you. You settled it yourself, while you was alive, by your own faults. You paid no heed to God's word and the advice of good men.

THIEF: Blast the whole lot!

OLD WOMAN: You was always out of luck. It's awful to see you. Brand of a thief on your cheeks and both your ears bleeding.

THIEF (*feeling his ears*): They've been cut to bits on the sharp rocks.

OLD WOMAN: It's the right marking. "Cropped and punched through." That was the mark on the first sheep my Jon pinched. (*Jon laughs.*) There's a queer echo among these rocks. What do you think me and the kids had to put up with, on account of what you whispered in Jon's ear, when you was showing him the way to thieve and rob? But all the same, I'd pray God to help you, if I thought it'd do a bit of good.

(*The Jailer falls onto the stage; stops by the Thief, groans.*)

THIEF: You had no pity on me nor Jon neither, when you was giving us the cat, you damned hangman! (*Jon laughs.*)

OLD WOMAN: "One mourns his suffering with tears,
One curses, and another jeers."
That's straight out of the hymnbook.

JAILER: Who was that speaking?

OLD WOMAN: Oh, it was only old Jon's wife.

JAILER: I'm in agony. I'm smarting all over.

OLD WOMAN: You're being paid for what you did on earth.

JAILER: Just look at my hands!

OLD WOMAN: That's how it is with everyone that uses the cat.

JAILER: I caught them in a crack in the rocks, and couldn't get them free except by tearing off three fingers from each hand. (*Jon laughs.*) Was that Jon? Lucky for him I can't get at him!

OLD WOMAN: Don't you think that may have been an echo of your own brutal laugh. You didn't think it enough—thirty or forty stripes on the bare flesh, for quite a small offense.

JAILER: It was the sheriff's orders.

OLD WOMAN: Who asked you to take on the job, but your own hard heart? Why, no one could stop you from laying it on. You could have stopped, though, without losing your job. This was no way to treat my Jon.

JAILER: He bloody well deserved it!

JON: You're a liar!

JAILER (*clutching the Thief*): What was that?

OLD WOMAN: A spirit, giving evidence against you.

THIEF: Let me go, blast you. (*They struggle with one another, shouting.*)

OLD WOMAN: Ah, you're poor wretched creatures. But there's no saving you.

(*Jailer and Thief disappear.*)

JON: Pleasant journey. Happy homecoming!

OLD WOMAN: I'm ashamed to listen to you. As if it was any good to you, those curs getting a bad time.—We may meet more before it's over. If you want to get to heaven, you'll have to forgive them all, and pray for them with all your heart.

JON: Those blackguards? Not much!

OLD WOMAN: No one can tell whether they're a bit worse than you.

JON: It's just as it always was. You excuse me in one sentence, and abuse me in the next.

OLD WOMAN: That's quite true. But it's a bit of an uphill job trying to find excuses for you. That'll be proved when the time comes, Jon.

JON: Well, start toddling on now.

(*A noise from the rocks.*)

OLD WOMAN: "Great is the misery of man."

(*The Drunkard falls onto the stage, moaning.*)

OLD WOMAN: "So must they too as outlaws pine
Who are destroyed by ale and wine."

DRUNKARD: My head's done for. My head's quite done for!

OLD WOMAN: Well, no wonder. The brandy you've took down is more than a drop.

DRUNKARD: I'm blind and muzzy, but I do know that voice.

OLD WOMAN: That didn't hinder you, when you was giving my Jon the taste for it. You both drank yourselves to damnation.

DRUNKARD: 'Twasn't me as beat you and pulled your hair.

JON (*in a low voice*): Oh, shut up!

OLD WOMAN: We won't quarrel about that. You've got a pretty heavy load anyhow.

DRUNKARD: It's the devil to have no brandy.

JON: Same here.

DRUNKARD: Have I started to hear things?

OLD WOMAN: You may have a little glimmer of conscience left.

DRUNKARD: I'm just dying of thirst.

JON: Me too.

OLD WOMAN: Poor chap. Wouldn't they open the Golden Gate to you?

DRUNKARD: The truth is I didn't exactly grovel to them. I was never given to licking the boots of the gentry.

OLD WOMAN: No one's without some saving grace.

DRUNKARD: It's all the same to me where I am, if only I've got enough liquor.

(*Jon laughs.*)

OLD WOMAN: How did the blessed St. Peter take it?

DRUNKARD: Oh, he started some drivel about reason and intelligence and the behavior of God's Christian children. Maybe the old billygoat was afraid I would tweak the apostles' beards or seduce one of those angel hermaphrodites. (*He and Jon laugh.*)

OLD WOMAN: What an expression! There ain't much risk of the blessed little angel bodies being like that.

A WOMAN (*on the rocks above*): Wait for me. I'm coming.

OLD WOMAN: You know the voice. And unless I'm much mistaken, so does Jon.

DRUNKARD: That's the wife of that—that—. How should I remember, with my head splitting?

WOMAN (*falling on the stage*): Where's Jon?

OLD WOMAN: "All are reputed beasts untamed
Who are by fleshly lusts inflamed."

WOMAN: Where's Jon? I heard him laughing.

OLD WOMAN: It's an echo of him still in your ears. Time was when it wasn't only your ears he tickled. (*Jon and the Woman laugh.*)

OLD WOMAN: It's hardly a laughing matter. Suppose you're laughing at your own sin?

WOMAN: I'm sure that was my Jon's laugh.

OLD WOMAN: Not a scrap of him was ever yours, you creature. But everyone knows you didn't mind being false to your own husband on the sly, and setting your traps for Jon, even though he was mine in the sight of God and man, and the father of my children.

WOMAN: He was the father of a couple of my children too.

JON: Oh?

WOMAN: What was that?

DRUNKARD: You're hearing things. Echo. Nothing else.

OLD WOMAN: And you dare say that to my face! Do you glory in your kids being bastards? Then why didn't you get Jon to acknowledge them?

WOMAN: Because of you and the law. But up at the Golden Gate they knew it all.

OLD WOMAN: Was that why they wouldn't let you in?

WOMAN: I was called a kept woman, a whore, a barefaced sinner—and so they slammed the gate.

OLD WOMAN: You had only yourself to blame. That was no way to live.

WOMAN: I liked forbidden fruit best. The greater the sin, the greater the pleasure.

OLD WOMAN: And the greater the suffering. I think there was some poison in your body, poor thing. We're all weak, but some of us controls ourselves better than others. You was loose in everything.

WOMAN: Yes, I was a sinner.

OLD WOMAN: And couldn't repent before you died?

WOMAN: No, I couldn't repent. (*Pause.*)

OLD WOMAN: My Jon would never have been led astray, if his will hadn't been crippled by drink and trouble of all sorts. Drink makes beasts of everyone.

(*The Drunkard laughs.*)

WOMAN: Jon was a lovely man—a lovely beast.

OLD WOMAN: Yes, he certainly could be that—the darling. But all the same you did wrong to tempt him.

WOMAN: I couldn't help it.

OLD WOMAN: No, you couldn't. I quite believe that. My Jon could be quite irresistible.

WOMAN: I love—love—

OLD WOMAN: But they wouldn't open the gate to you?

WOMAN: I love my sin.

DRUNKARD: Come along.

OLD WOMAN (*as they disappear*): Even if sinless Almighty God can't forgive you, I can all the same.

JON: So do I.

OLD WOMAN (*sighing*): They knows everything in heaven. They can even tell from the looks of the children who was their father.

JON: I'd nothing to do with them, not a drop of blood.

OLD WOMAN: Do you mean now to tell lies to the Father of Heaven him—self. You're a dreadful creature. It's surely not worth our carrying on any further.

JON: Are you losing your courage?

OLD WOMAN: Small wonder if I did. Hush, hush! (*Listens.*) Wait now, and keep quiet as a stone.

(*The Rich Man falls on the stage.*)

OLD WOMAN: "A spirit greedy and depraved
By great possessions is not saved."
It says so in the blessed hymn.

RICH MAN: What are you mumbling, woman? Who are you?

OLD WOMAN: We've only lived a generation in the same parish, so it's hardly to be hoped as you'd know me. But perhaps you remember my Jon?

RICH MAN: Yes, yes. Now I remember you. Where are you going?

OLD WOMAN: I'm on my way up to the Golden Gate.

RICH MAN: You can save yourself that trouble.

OLD WOMAN: I trust in the mercy of the Heavenly Father. It says in the Bible that in his house them as was poorest on earth will find refuge and shelter.

RICH MAN: Nice people there must be then inside the gate! Tramps, paupers, thieves, and other criminal riffraff. Now I begin to see why I wasn't welcomed.

OLD WOMAN: They can hardly have turned you away without a reason. And of course you had your pockets stuffed full of gold and silver. Didn't they ask how you came by the money?

RICH MAN: How I came by it? What do you mean? All doors were open to me before, even the house of the sheriff himself, and he wasn't generally free with invitations.

OLD WOMAN: Of course the sheriff and the Heavenly Father would be likely to have the same standards on human beings. Couldn't you soften the people that looked after the gate?

RICH MAN: I offered them handfuls of silver.

OLD WOMAN: And what did they do then?

RICH MAN: Do? Why, they spat on my hand.

(*Jon gives a low laugh.*)

OLD WOMAN: I thought you might have tried to bribe the servants of the Heavenly Father. But they're not that sort, I'm told. I wonder though if they didn't find one or two of Judas's pieces of silver in your fist.

RICH MAN (*angrily*): Why do you think so?

OLD WOMAN: They're said to be still in steady circulation on earth, so it struck me in my simplicity that they might have got into your pocket some time or other. Wealth goes where wealth is.

RICH MAN: How dare you make such insinuations against a gentleman, you old hag?

OLD WOMAN: "Inasmuch as ye did it to one of the least of these my brethren, ye did it unto me." You remember who said that? And perhaps you remember too how the richest gentleman in the country charged the poorest of the cotters with stealing three of his sheep?

RICH MAN: That was my duty. Sheep thieves are outlaws.

JON: What was you yourself? A skinflint, a criminal, a rascal.

RICH MAN: Wha—what was that?

OLD WOMAN: This is where the stones cry out. It's not for me to judge if you or Jon was the bigger thief. But I know this—that he never took anything from the poor. He never grabbed the holdings of cotters and turned them into penni-less slaves. And he never had your riches, nor your blood money. But what good is all your wealth to you now?

RICH MAN: What business is that of yours?

OLD WOMAN: Bitter is the tears of a woman, whose husband's in jail, with ten kids to feed and clothe at home. But now things have changed, so that you, my fine gentleman, are more to be pitied than she is. I'd help you if I could, though you'd probably be ashamed to receive my help.

RICH MAN: Your help!

(*Laughs. A noise from the cliff. The Sheriff falls on the stage.*) Why, it's the sheriff. (*Goes to attend to him.*)

OLD WOMAN: "The land of light as lowly rates
The quirks and pomp of magistrates."

RICH MAN: How are you, Mr. Sheriff?

SHERIFF: How d'ye do? Did you wish to speak to me? If I remember rightly, there was a small matter of an unsettled tax assessment. We can discuss that later.

RICH MAN: I'm afraid your memory has managed to play you false, Mr. Sheriff.

SHERIFF: We can go into that later, I said. Was there anything else—a complaint, a boundary dispute, or a case of larceny?

RICH MAN: Excuse me, Mr. Sheriff—

SHERIFF (*interrupting*): Yes, yes, yes, yes—. Good day. (*Tries to hurry away, but collides with the Old Woman.*) What are you doing, wandering here?

OLD WOMAN: Is this place in thy jurisdiction?

RICH MAN: A cotter's wife doesn't say "thou" to the Sheriff.

OLD WOMAN: O well, I've never learned fine manners, and if I can say "thou" to God Almighty, the Sheriff oughtn't to be more particular.*

SHERIFF: Who is this woman?

---

* Translator's Note: The use of "thou" is a disrespectful familiarity. As this is not so in English, and it would be unnatural to use the second person singular where it occurs in the original, this passage might have to be changed or omitted in acting.

RICH MAN: She's the wife of that Jon Jonsson.

SHERIFF: I never served her with any summons to report here. What do you want? You should have applied to the Sheriff's Officer.

OLD WOMAN: You seem to think your authority extends beyond death and the grave.

SHERIFF: What do you mean?

RICH MAN: Excuse me, Mr. Sheriff, but—

SHERIFF: But what?

OLD WOMAN: You're both dead as mutton.

SHERIFF: Yes but—yes but—

RICH MAN: That's quite correct, Mr. Sheriff.

SHERIFF: But am I not bound to maintain law and order everywhere?

OLD WOMAN: You might think a man of your sort would be wanted in heaven. But I think the laws there is different.

SHERIFF: Those laws which are not signed and ratified by His Majesty the King are neither law nor justice. Do you realize that? Do you know who I am?

OLD WOMAN: It'd take less to make me see that.

SHERIFF: Do you think it is seemly to insult a royal officer and a judge, who has spent a full thirty years in the public service? What sort of justice is this?

OLD WOMAN: It's the judgment of God.

SHERIFF: This is a penal offense, under the law of Christian V.

RICH MAN: I entirely agree with you, Mr. Sheriff.

SHERIFF: Much obliged! *Vox regis, vox legis.*

OLD WOMAN: And all the same they must have been able to see you was in gold braid and gold buttons.

SHERIFF: Do you suppose that they were all stone-blind? They might as well have been.

OLD WOMAN: No doubt they'd have opened the gate to you if they had been. But they'll have seen something through the uniform, as wasn't to their liking. What about that sentence you passed on Jon?

SHERIFF: Wasn't that sentence pronounced in accordance with the appropriate section of the relevant law? Do you mean to teach me law and jurisprudence? Do you know to what you are liable for insulting a judge by royal warrant, a person in authority?

OLD WOMAN: If my Jon had been rich, you'd have stopped the case. But that wasn't the way of it, so you sentenced him without mercy.

RICH MAN: Do you dare to bandy words with the Sheriff?

SHERIFF: Do you consider that I do not know how to deal with a delinquent of that kind? Are you taking the liberty of impugning my judgments?

OLD WOMAN: I'm not afraid of either of you any more, now.

(*Jon laughs.*)

SHERIFF: I summon you for contempt of court. (*To the Rich Man*): You are a witness. Such persons should be arrested.

OLD WOMAN: But you're not a royal official anymore, only a lost soul what falls down the great mountain, lonely and despised. Even them as suffered worst from the rod of your authority pities you, and is sorry for you.

SHERIFF: Do you know whom you are addressing? (*He stumbles.*)

RICH MAN (*approaches the Sheriff and gives him a hand*): May I accompany you, Mr. Sheriff?

SHERIFF: As you please. But come at once then. I am very busy.

RICH MAN: It is certain, Mr. Sheriff, that I was absolutely free from liability at my death.

OLD WOMAN (*as they move off*): I know that the King's law is not God's law, nor the judgments of men the judgments of God.

(*The Devil has peeped out from the rock.*)

JON: There's a rush of them down at the Old Boy's place today. But what's become now of the blood of the Lamb, and all this salvation they preach about?

OLD WOMAN: There's some folks is past saving, and it's likely

you're one of them. The soul can be so black that it mayn't
be easy to wash it clean, not even in the blood of the Lamb.
It'd be a sight better for you to cry over your wretchedness
and the misery of mankind, than to laugh and please the
Devil. (*Sees the Enemy, recoils and gives a cry of terror.*)
JON: What's up now?
OLD WOMAN (*crossing the bag and herself*):
Lord, support me in strife and woe,
Staunch the misery here below.
My soul, my heart and what else may be
Bow before thee and call to thee—
Drive the devils away from me!
ENEMY: I hear your squalling, but feel no qualms
At the caterwauling of ancient psalms;
In me is a power too strong to be vexed
By the use fools make of a musty text.
I still need service about my throne,
For this I have made a man of Jon.
I saw from each inward and outward sign
The proper stuff for a rogue's design.
I moulded from childhood his condition,
In poverty, rancour, and superstition.
From pilfering crumbs and scraps he passed
To earn the name of a thief at last;
His conscience started to rot and perish,
And his rascal nature to grow and flourish;
His character turned to blackened ashes;
Then I gave him a taste of the jailer's lashes.
With fleshly passions I seared him first,
Then breathed in his spirit a drunkard's thirst,
Till his dross was purged of its precious metal,
And heaven and he could accord but little.
OLD WOMAN: That's God's to settle. (*She crosses the bag.*)
ENEMY: Who crosses thee, Jon? 'Twas a woman's hand:
The cross will fail, but the sin shall stand.

Thy soul, though small, is a useful chattel,
And 'tis mine to fight and to win the battle.
Thou hast served me in life and in death as well,
And shalt have thy pay—in the flames of Hell.
Nor prayer nor law can avoid the evil
That waits thy soul.

JON: That's the very devil!

OLD WOMAN: Be quiet, Jon.

ENEMY: Nay, for both 'tis best
No wise to vary from my behest.
Come then to me, nor clamber and crawl
On crags where all who attempt them fall.
Thou knowest, Jon, that thy dirty poke
Is a short-lived shelter for foolish folk.
Thy soul I have roasted far too well
To let it escape to heaven from hell.
And how can the Lord my power defy?
I am stronger than He.

OLD WOMAN: That is hell's own lie!

ENEMY (*While he speaks, the sky darkens.*):
Full half of the world for mine I claim,
Its depths, its darkness and all its flame:
So shuffling subterfuge profits nought;
Gainst rebels my craft and my might are brought.
For the recreant soul that declines my hell
I will fashion a new and a potent spell.
I darken the sky with my mighty power:
I charm the clouds, and the lightnings shower.
(*Thunder and lightning.*)
The road of the thunder is my call;
I pound the mountains to atoms small,
And then my potency bursts its chain,
Which the Lord of Light would dare restrain.
His host shall break, as resistance ceases,
His heaven be cloven and dashed to pieces,

And down to the bottomless pit be driven—
(*Laughs.*)

OLD WOMAN: Save and defend us, God in Heaven!

ENEMY: Think you to 'scape my hand's control,
You damned, bag-skulking, shrimp of a soul?

OLD WOMAN: Pray hard, Jon dear.

JON: Then open the bag, so as I can get a look at him.

OLD WOMAN: You're a damned good-for-nothing rascal, but I'll
never let you fall into his clutches. God be with us!
(*Michael, the Archangel, appears on a high crag. Beams of
light from him shine on the Old Woman, who falls on her
knees.*)

JON: What's up now?

OLD WOMAN (*in a whisper*): The Archangel Michael.

MICHAEL: Praise to the Lord of Hosts,
Maker of heaven and earth,
The Lord of life and death.
Though heavy be your loads,
Yet climb the steep ascent
Up to the Golden Gate.
Wayfarers, undismayed,
Pass on, with me your guard,
Against the Fiend's assaults,
Till sentence is pronounced.
Heaven's messenger am I,
Sent from the source of light,
Where only justice rules,
And peace for ever reigns.

OLD WOMAN: Amen. (*Michael the Archangel disappears.*)

JON: Well, I thought that stuff of his was pretty feeble.

OLD WOMAN: How can you say such things, Jon, about our
escort and guardian, the blessed messenger of light! (*Flash of
lightning. The Old Woman leaps to her feet.*)

ENEMY (*who has been standing on the watch*):

O slaves of light, I have known you too long
To lend my ears to your tuneless song;
The burden of all your bellowing seems
A feeble echo of ancient hymns;
I prefer the blast of a belly windy,
Or the literal version of hell's own shindy;
And sooner to stocks and stones I'd kneel
Than the drone of your star-crazed spinning wheel.
I know no angel ninny to equal
For empty-headedness that same Michael,
That sexless envoy of Heaven. No wonder
My sneer is lightning, my laughter—thunder.
(*Thunder and lightning. Howling from the depths below.*)

JON: Now I'm really enjoying myself.

OLD WOMAN: Are you losing the glimmer of sense that God gave you? It's a fearful disgrace to listen to you. If the lightning was to strike me, where'd you be then? Don't you hear the howling from down below?

JON: It shall never be said that Jon Jonsson went to heaven with his mouth shut and without a word to say for himself.

ENEMY: Well, go your ways, you will learn ere long
What doom awaits you, whose laws are strong.
Then you may pack in a smaller poke.

OLD WOMAN: That was a meaner devil who spoke!

JON: Do you mean to stick here forever, or what?

OLD WOMAN: Do you think it's weather for climbing slippery cliffs?

JON: Well, didn't he say he was going to look after you in front and behind, that there ambassador of heaven?

OLD WOMAN: Well, all right then, in God's name! (*Climbs on a ledge of rock, and throws herself against the mountain side to shelter from the lightning.*)

ENEMY: E'en though the rocky ascent be passed,
My power is the same to the very last.

The prettiest souls have been oft my prey,
When once in the scales of truth they lay.
So let them the question of guilt dissect,
You'll see what wages Jon can expect.
On then, old woman, before much longer
We'll see and prove which is the stronger,
He who reigns in the fiends' abyss,
Or the Lord of Light in Paradise.
(*Laughs.*)

JON: The gall of the man!

OLD WOMAN: It wouldn't hurt if I was to say the old traveller's prayer that my poor old granny taught me, blessed be her memory! That prayer's always brought a lucky trip.

JON: Then be quick and cough it up.

OLD WOMAN (*kneeling*):
Show me the light of your guiding star,
Melchior, Kaspar, and Balthasar:
Abraham, Isaac, and Jacob too
Follow me all my journey through.
Holy Spirit, thy comfort lend,
Angel Michael, my head defend.
Gentle Saviour, with me abide,
Blessed Mary, be by my side.
Guard the heart of me, Peter and Paul,
Then am I safe, whate'er befall.
Blissful then shall my journey be
And home and flock I again shall see. Amen.

JON: Amen and hallelujah. And let's be getting on.
(*The Old Woman gets up and starts climbing.*)

ENEMY (*looks out from the rocks in the flashes of lightning, and stares menacingly up the hill*)
I follow the laggards who go astray,
And show them their path—

JON: Till then, good day!

CURTAIN

Act III

Woodland trees with green foliage on both sides. In the center is a view across green meadows. In the distance are rays of light from heaven and the Golden Gate. Sunshine and clear blue sky.

OLD WOMAN (*entering with the bag*): Lord God and Heavenly Father! How glorious! I must say, Jon, this is a land of plenty.

JON: So?

OLD WOMAN: Yes, don't you know we've crossed the border of the Heavenly Father's estate in heaven?

JON: Oh, have we?

OLD WOMAN: This is what I can see—and more: trees in full leaf on both sides, green fields stretching on and away, pasture for I dunno how many hundreds of horses, and far away the light from the Heavenly Jerusalem and the Golden Gate.

JON: Oh, really?

OLD WOMAN: It's as if you didn't care about it. You're so dull and sluggish.

JON: It's not as if I could see anything.

OLD WOMAN: No, poor boy, I know. But you must feel that there's perfect calm and sunshine here, none of them storms and lightning we had going up the mountain.

JON: Blowed if I notice a bit of change.

OLD WOMAN: You just doze away in your bag, and if you open your mouth it's only to curse and swear—just as if you really wanted to get into trouble.

JON: Ain't you pitching it pretty strong?

OLD WOMAN: Well, is it strange if I'm hurt? Why do you think I took on this trip?

JON: You wanted it. I never asked you.

OLD WOMAN: I might have known it. You get more and more ungrateful as time goes on. How do you think you'd be now, if I'd let you go into the monster's open jaws, as you wanted yourself?

JON: Do you think I'd have been any worse off?

OLD WOMAN: Ain't you afeared for your soul's salvation, Jon?

JON: I've never been afeared of anything.

OLD WOMAN: Maybe. You get cheekier and cheekier as we get near the gate. Do you think that's the best way to save your soul? No, Jon, now you must look to yourself. Now or never. And in this heavenly spot. How lovely all round!

JON: Open the bag.

OLD WOMAN: No, I daren't. The Enemy may very well be close by—you're never tired of harping on his name. He can change himself into the shape of every living thing, the wretch, beasts or men or even angels. Are you feeling bad?

JON: Need you ask?

OLD WOMAN: You'd better call to mind your schooling a bit, before we get to the gate. You'll have to confess there, and there's no hope if St. Peter doesn't feel that everything you say is steeped in burning remorse and penitence.

JON: I think I can do quite well without confessing to him, the old billy goat.

OLD WOMAN: You can't get out of it. Anyhow he knows all about every mortal thing folks have done on earth.

JON: You don't say! I'll bet he knows!

OLD WOMAN: You'll find out before the end. I mean to tidy myself up a bit, before we come to meet anyone.

JON: Are you expecting all the hosts of heaven to come and meet you?

OLD WOMAN: Who knows but that the blessed Archangel Michael may have told them I'm on the way. I may be of little account on earth and still less up here in heaven, but it don't follow that everyone will have forgotten me. (*Goes a few steps from the bag.*) I'm going to wash off most of the sweat in this here spring.

JON: Hi! Shove the bag down into the spring in the meantime, to cool me a bit.

OLD WOMAN: Are you dreadfully hot?

JON: Hot? What do you think?

OLD WOMAN: All right, then. (*Puts the bag into the spring.*) Are you more comfy now?

JON: Ah-h, that was good!

OLD WOMAN: There you have a foretaste of heaven. Say your prayers now, Jon dear.

JON: I'll say them quietly to myself. That will do just as well.

OLD WOMAN: Do so, dear. (*Unfastens her dress, and washes and dries herself.*) I see myself in the spring as if it was the finest looking glass.

JON: Must be a sight to see your ugly mug.

OLD WOMAN: Is that how you says your prayers?

JON: Don't interrupt me. (*Pause.*)

OLD WOMAN: I feel I've grown many years younger by washing myself in this holy well of heaven.

JON: That's quite likely. You haven't got your virginity back?

OLD WOMAN: There's someone moving in the woods. If they was to come here, then mind and don't say a single word unless you're spoke to.

JON: Anything that comes from you will be clever enough.

OLD WOMAN: You're not funny.

(*Enter the Priest and the Old Woman's Parents. They are dressed in white and hold palm branches, with their hands crossed on their breasts—very solemn.*)

PRIEST: We greet thee in the name of the Eternal Trinity.

OLD WOMAN: God be with you.

MOTHER (*aside*): She doesn't recognize us.

PRIEST (*speaks all the time in his pulpit manner*): It is not to be hoped that thou shouldst perceive from our countenances who we are, seeing that it is long since we, by the Lord's mercy, were called forth from the great vale of sorrow, where men walk clad in curses as with a garment, and the teeth of sin are as the teeth of lions whose bite is mortal. I am a servant of God and thine ancient spiritual counsellor, and these are thine earthly parents.

(*The Mother takes a step nearer to the Old Woman and spreads out her arms. The Old Woman kisses her.*)

MOTHER: A hearty welcome to you, my child.

FATHER (*as the Old Woman kisses him*): The Lord bless your coming.

OLD WOMAN (*drying her eyes on a corner of her apron*): I knowed you at once—but you've grown so white and fine. But how nice of you to come and meet me.

PRIEST: Submit thyself in all things to God's will, and thank, above all, thine intercessors, thy Redeemer and Comforter, who offered Himself to death and paid with His precious blood for the sins of mankind.

OLD WOMAN: Oh, you're still the same blessed light.

PRIEST: I rejoice unspeakably to see once more the children of my former congregation, within the bounds of eternal life.

OLD WOMAN: Well, what can you tell me about my boys?

MOTHER: They were given wings at once, like everyone who dies in childhood, and now they flutter round the sky, singing with the angel children.

FATHER: You needn't be the least uneasy about them, my daughter.

OLD WOMAN: Bless their little hearts. I'm terribly anxious to see them. (*Sobs.*) But no doubt I don't deserve that mercy.

PRIEST: As it is necessary for thee to comprehend, and as I have ofttimes declared unto thee aforetime in the house of God, it is here, in the land of the living, that the scriptures are fulfilled, which declare that the mortal children of earth shall meet again and be welcomed by their beloved ones, so soon as they are called away from the realm of the world, provided that they have been pure and devout and submissive to the power of the Lord in their daily lives, and behaved themselves prudently and in accordance with his word, as is purely and clearly set down in his holy book. If thou hast so done, here is neither room nor occasion for sorrow, seeing that thou shalt then shortly be allotted a lasting dwelling place within the Golden Portal and partake of the habitation of the angels and the elect.

JON: He talks just like a prayer-book. (*Laughs.*)

FATHER: What was that?

OLD WOMAN: The rejoicing of the redeemed can be heard all the way here. They must be wonderful happy.

FATHER: You should know that quite well, my daughter. We, who live in the heavenly Jerusalem, have received the highest prize of victory.

PRIEST: Even as thou seest, we have put off the earthly rags of our sin, washed in the regenerating fountains of the Holy Spirit, put on the white robes of innocence, and thus, bearing branches of palm, we sing and dance around the throne of the Lamb in an ever-shining choir of glory. There is no poverty there, nor wrath nor adversity, but absolute plenty and health, thoughts of peace and a most blessed welcome. There we are satisfied with the love and mercy of the Lord.

OLD WOMAN: That's just what it said in the revival hymns you gave me.

FATHER: We believed God's word and acted accordingly. It's always been our one wish and prayer that you'd do the same.

MOTHER: As if our daughter hadn't done that! Hasn't she shown the fullest faith, and Christian patience in word and deed?

FATHER: Obedience to parents is one of the highest duties of God's children. You broke that obligation, my daughter, when you went and married Jon, who by his ungodly life disgraced the word of the Lord, you yourself, your parents, and all the family.

JON: You'd have been more at home in the place down below, old man.

(*The Mother catches hold of her husband.*)

FATHER: We are saved. No harm can come to us.

OLD WOMAN: I won't argue with you, father. But I thought that you and everyone else that lives in heaven ought to be able to forgive my Jon his trespasses. Isn't it written somewhere—love your enemies, bless them that curse you?

FATHER: Justice will judge him, when the time comes.

PRIEST: Though Jon has too long hearkened to the ungodly, whose fellowship is as fuel of fire, and thus by his behavior and course of life and pride run the way of destruction, even as bloodthirsty and false traitors, who betray their Lord and Master, as did the traitor Judas, yet may he be enabled mercifully to excape from the claws of the Enemy, but only if tears run down his cheeks, and his prayers are even as those of the penitent robber on the cross.

FATHER: Whatever's in store for him, we wish with all our hearts that you may not have to pay for your fault, since you must have repented it bitterly.

OLD WOMAN: No, father, I haven't.

MOTHER: God help you, my dear child.

OLD WOMAN: I loved my Jon. And it says in God's word that those who love a lot shall be forgiven a lot.

PRIEST: In the last moments before a human creature comes to the great portal, it serves him best to tarry alone and confer with his God and his conscience. Wherefore we will walk a

little longer in the wood, but soon after return. God be
merciful to us all. Amen.

MOTHER: I will pray the holy mother of God to pity you.

OLD WOMAN (*as they move away*): Nay, I'd rather you prayed
for my Jon.

JON: Damned if I care for their prayers. It's like you to demean
yourself to these spirits out of the hymnbook, this precious
trio!

OLD WOMAN: It's a shame to listen to you.

JON: Have you no self-respect—or what is it?

(*The Enemy, disguised as an angel, peeps out from among
the trees close to the spring, and reaches for the bag. He has
a fiery red shock of hair, which hides his horns.*)

JON: Pick me out at once from this poisonous hole. Do you
want me to catch my death of cold?

(*The Old Woman sees the Enemy, and snatches the bag in
a panic.*)

ENEMY (*mimicking the Archangel Michael*):
Praise to the Mighty, him alone,
From him have I been sent
To guard you, wayfarers, upon your road.
Put not your trust in any word of those
Who swell with overweening arrogance,
Born of their own success.
Entrust to me your load,
And I will bear it on,
Home to the Golden Gate.
Since Might has sent me as his messenger.

OLD WOMAN: Get thee behind me, Satan!

JON: That's a nice way to address him.

(*The Enemy disappears.*)

OLD WOMAN: Oh, his looks suits his talk, even if he is got up as
an angel. Trust me to spot him!

JON (*laughing*): But what are you dawdling here for? Ain't
you done titivating yourself enough?

(*Enter the Farmer and Helga, dressed in white. He is elderly, she is young and sprightly.*)

OLD WOMAN (*welcoming*): Can I believe my eyes? Is it you,
darling?

(*They kiss one another repeatedly, pat one another on the
shoulders, and both talk at the same time, while greeting one
another.*)

HELGA: How are you, darling. Welcome, welcome!

OLD WOMAN: Bless you, bless you, and thanks from my heart
for all the good old times.

HELGA: And thank you ever so much more. (*They finish
kissing.*) But what fun to see you again!

OLD WOMAN: What ought I to say, then? (*Shakes hands with
the Farmer.*) How do you do, old friend.

FARMER: Good day and welcome. So you know me, even
though I'm not in my old duds?

OLD WOMAN: Do you think I don't know your face?

HELGA: I wanted to be the very first to meet you on this side.
But I came after your parents and the priest, after all.

OLD WOMAN: Yes, they were with me for a little while and have
just gone off into the wood. But I couldn't help it: I felt
somehow so unworthy compared with them.

HELGA: I think they've been much too godfearing while they
were on earth. But aren't you tired after your journey? I
should almost think so. But now it's pretty well over.

OLD WOMAN: Just like you. You're just as young and pretty as
ever, and your nature's not altered. But what a pretty dress
you've got, and how it suits you!

HELGA: That's the sort they weave now in Heaven.

OLD WOMAN: I'm sure that not even the storekeeper's wife ever
had such a fine frock, nor of course the priest's wife when
she was alive, neither. (*Feels the dress.*) I should think this
was good wearing stuff—even though it may be thin—and
stands washing? But does it give you any cover, dear?

HELGA (*laughing*): Here you could easily go stark naked all the
year round.

OLD WOMAN: Now you're at your old jokes. But ain't they terrible strict here—about morals and such?

HELGA (*laughing*): Bless you, don't ask me that! Here they're all saints—much too saintly. At least the lads at home in our parish had some life in them.

OLD WOMAN: Yes. Reckon they was not too good to kick over the traces a bit.

HELGA: Some folks are shocked at everything. But a lot of what men call sin is no more than fun, innocent fun.

OLD WOMAN: That's what I've always said too.

FARMER: Was the cattle in middling good condition down there, when you left home?

HELGA: He was bound to get onto that. He'll never talk about anything but cattle.

OLD WOMAN: Thanks. I should say they'd done pretty moderate. It turned wintry early in the autumn, and though really there wasn't much snow, the frost as you might say killed all the grazing for the sheep.

FARMER: Any losses from disease?

OLD WOMAN: Well, it hit them here and there.

FARMER: That's bad. Folks must have started folding them at the first gathering. But the horses are still at grass?

OLD WOMAN: Oh yes, they're left to God and the frost.

HELGA: I remember when the village lads used to saddle the ponies and gallop about the farm, like princes in a fairytale. Many's the horse whose flanks I've patted. I gave some of them milk to drink, when I left them.

FARMER: Blessed creatures. It was always a poor soil at home, the hay crop was scrappy and the grazing mostly bad.

HELGA: But I feel at times I'd almost like to swap heaven for my old parish.

OLD WOMAN: Lord, fancy that now! Why the soil there is nothing like what it is here.

FARMER: It was wonderful what the lambs was like this autumn. But how did the farmers do on the whole?

OLD WOMAN: Oh, it seems as if some can't never make ends

meet, even though they scrapes every penny and breaks their backs.

FARMER: That's true as day, but still farming's the best way to live. How was your Jon, when you passed on?

JON: Damn bad! (*They look at one another.*)

OLD WOMAN: Did you hear anything?

FARMER: I wouldn't say no.

OLD WOMAN: You was the best and truest friends to Jon and me, while you was on earth. Private-like to you, I've got a little something with me on the trip.

HELGA: Now I'm getting curious.

OLD WOMAN: You see that bag there. What do you think's in it?

JON: Me.

HELGA: How in the world—?

OLD WOMAN: Say howdyedo to the folks, Jon dear. You know that namesake of yours, that was always so helpful and kind to us?

JON: Good day, namesake.

FARMER: That's his voice.

OLD WOMAN: Now the lady too. You know who she is.

JON: Good day to you.

HELGA: Am I to believe it's you, Jon?

JON: Oh yes, it's me all right, worse luck.

OLD WOMAN: It's his soul, bless it.

FARMER: Well, I'm clean flummoxed. How are you, namesake?

JON: I suppose you've grown so proud from living in heaven that you didn't mean to speak to me, you damned old scoundrel.

OLD WOMAN: Don't he sound still like his old self?

HELGA: It's refreshing to hear old Jon talking our blessed mother tongue. How did you manage to pack your husband into this bag?

JON: She shoved it in front of my lips just as I popped off, and so I spat my rotten soul into the bag.

HELGA (*to Old Woman*): However did you think of it?

OLD WOMAN: Oh, don't ask me that.

JON: She thought I'd have to go to hell, like all the great sinners.

HELGA: But you're not a great sinner, Jon.

JON: Listen to that now, old gal.

OLD WOMAN: Of course you're a sin-afflicted soul.

JON: That's a whopping lie. Open the bag directly, and let me out of this hell. I'm not a great sinner.

OLD WOMAN: Have a little patience, dearie. It won't be long now.

JON (*in a rage*): I'm not a great sinner!

OLD WOMAN: Well, it don't matter. I'll not let you out of my hands till we're at the gate.

FARMER: I can't make head nor tail of all this.

OLD WOMAN: That's what I'd expect you to say. I hardly know myself whether I'm dead or alive, but I do know that that's my Jon's soul, in that there bag. However things go, I intends to bring it safe to the gate.

FARMER: I always knew, namesake, that you had a good wife.

JON: Rot!

FARMER: You mustn't talk like that, namesake.

OLD WOMAN (*in tears*): I had ought to be used to them kind words of his.

FARMER: In Heaven we have to mind our speech, like steady respectable farmers, and keep up the reputation of our old parishes.

JON: This is a damned dog-kennel!

HELGA: Well, in spite of everything, it was often good to be on the earth. When do you think you've enjoyed yourself most, Jon dear?

JON: When I had enough booze and baccy.

FARMER: And I, when I carried the fresh hay to my sheep.

OLD WOMAN: Though I'm ashamed to say so, I never enjoyed myself better than in the arms of my Jon.

JON: Ah, it's something that you should think that!

HELGA (*sighing dreamily*): Happiness came to me like a lovely song that you can't ever forget. (*Pause.*)

JON: Well, it wasn't altogether such a damn bad place—our dirty old world! And to tell you the truth, I've never had a slavish belief in this everlasting bliss of the hymnbook.

FARMER: You'd talk different if you saw what we see.

JON: Oh, do you think so?

FARMER: Here there's unlimited land and masses of grass.

JON: You get a tidy crop of hay, then?

FARMER: No, we never puts a scythe to the ground here.

OLD WOMAN: What's that you say? Don't you never make no hay?

JON: What, are you all so bone-lazy, or haven't you any livestock?

OLD WOMAN: Need you ask that? Don't you remember how I told you on the way, when I was passing the blessed cattle: first the flocks of sheep with silver fleeces, and then the stud of horses—but you must have managed to hear them whinnying, they neighed quite a lot—and then the herds of cows, and they was something like cows, Jon. And the bulls, sleek as a mass-cope.

JON: All this stock must take a tidy bit of feeding.

FARMER: All the stock finds its own grazing here, all the year round.

JON: Now you're pulling my leg, namesake.

HELGA: No, he's telling nothing but the truth, Jon dear. All the same, at first folks can get bored with all these joys of Heaven. Never a storm, always flat calm—as you might say.

OLD WOMAN: Aye, it was always refreshing to come from the fire out into the cold.

HELGA: That's why I sometimes feel too well off, and long to be back on earth, with all its toiling and moiling.

OLD WOMAN (*patting her shoulder*): Oh, my dear!

HELGA: I miss most of all never seeing snow. I never forget how lovely the mountains were, with their white peaks gleaming in the sunshine. At times I've even wished to be out in an Iceland blizzard.

OLD WOMAN: I can easy believe it may be dreadful wearisome, this eternal mild calm, this never-ending heavenly weather.

HELGA: To say nothing of the dark. What fun it was, and often how handy! (*Jon laughs.*) But here we have sunshine all the year round—glaring bright, everlasting day.

JON: Damned if I believe what you say. But, tell me, namesake, are there any cattle that live out all the time?

FARMER: I'd never have believed there were any such sheep. They never falls off. It's a sheer pleasure to take a look at them.

JON: Them fat-bellied ones can't be bad eating?

OLD WOMAN: But the cows—I suppose they don't stay dry long? Ain't they all wonderful milkers?

FARMER: They're first rate.

JON: But the horses? Do they ride them?

FARMER: It's just like sitting on your bed—it feels just like a bird in flight. And as to the build of them—there's simply no describing it in words.

JON: I can hardly believe that you can't describe them in Icelandic.

OLD WOMAN: These are heavenly animals. You have to mind that, Jon dear.

JON: Even if they are heavenly, as far as I remember, folks used sometimes to describe the Lord himself. So I should think it ought to be easy to describe his cattle. But tell me, namesake, do you own many sheep?

FARMER: I can't exactly answer that.

JON: Eh?

HELGA: He owns all the livestock in heaven—and so do I. And soon you'll own them all—every single one.

JON: Now I can't understand anymore.

HELGA: In heaven no one is poor and no one is rich. Everyone owns everything there.

JON: Now you're at your jokes again (*Laughs.*)

OLD WOMAN: Are you laughing at it, Jon dear?

JON: You must think that I'll believe everything you stuff me with. Hasn't each farmer got his own house?

FARMER: Nobody cares about that.

JON: Indeed. Then don't people marry up here, in this heavenly village?

HELGA: No. No one marries here.

JON (*laughing*): I like that! What do the women say to those regulations? Can the men take them altogether without ceremony, so to speak?

HELGA: It's you that's joking now, Jon dear.

JON: Perhaps it's not quite as mad an arrangement here in some ways as I thought.

OLD WOMAN: Mayn't Jon and I be together, if both of us is allowed to get in?

HELGA: Yes, yes, bless your innocence, if you want to yourself.

JON: Oh, but mightn't a man now get himself someone younger and slimmer than you, old gal?

OLD WOMAN: You'll be glad to have your old grievance, if I knows you right.

JON: Then do people lie out of doors at night on all the crofts?

HELGA: It's nice to sleep in the grass.

JON: In the grass? No thanks! But since all the stock fends for itself—what do you really do? Nothing?

FARMER: I can hardly tell about that.

JON: Now you're telling me a lie, namesake.

FARMER: There's some goes round the stock for pleasure.

HELGA: Some pick fruit from the trees, others make garlands of flowers.

JON (*contemptuously*): Make garlands of flowers? Is that a job, now? No one can live on that damned nonsense.

HELGA: Some play with little birds.

(*Jon shrieks with laughter.*)

OLD WOMAN: Pretty thoughts you've got now!

HELGA: Some listen to the singing of the heavenly choir.

JON: I shouldn't think that howling would be edifying. Do you eat at all, namesake? You surely don't live on garlands and the songs of angels.

FARMER: We're fed on heavenly food.

OLD WOMAN: The Lord's everlasting love and mercy, as the priest used to say.

JON: He can eat his eternal love himself, the poisonous old glutton. I want something more solid.

OLD WOMAN: You remember what it says in the hymn—"clear wine, with marrow and fatness too shall there be freely given."

JON: Is that true, namesake?

FARMER: Here there is all that the heart can desire.

OLD WOMAN: Do you hear that, Jon dear?

JON: I believe you're all lying about this, but I believe my namesake more than the priest.

OLD WOMAN: Wouldn't you like to ask now how you ought to behave to get into all this happiness?

JON: Do you think you won't be able to save me?

OLD WOMAN (*to Helga*): Please tell me, dear, how I ought to behave at the gate.

HELGA: That's quite simple. You knock three times. St. Peter comes out, and you tell him all the truth.

OLD WOMAN: I know he must be quite straightforward and simple. But—I suppose no one needs to try hiding anything?

FARMER: It's best to make a clean breast of everything.

JON: Oh, is it?

OLD WOMAN: And oughtn't the soul to be full of remorse and penitence?

FARMER: Yes, there's no denying that.

OLD WOMAN: You hear, Jon. And if now he should get in, which is quite uncertain, what happens then?

HELGA: Then he's washed in the water of regeneration, and dressed in white robes. It's all done in a flash.

JON: Really? They must be damned spry.

OLD WOMAN (*whispering*): Do I have to tell my parents about Jon?

FARMER: That makes no difference.

(*Enter Priest and Parents.*)

PRIEST: Now the great hour is swiftly approaching when thou shalt stand trembling before thy Lord and Judge, and beseech Him with prayers and humble supplications; since it is my hope that thou hast gained that blessed humility, likewise that gracious state of penitence, as also the one true faith: for thou hast been taught as a child of God and frequented constantly his Holy Church.

OLD WOMAN: Certainly I couldn't count the times I've been to church. But it did me good—no stones for bread. Oh them sermons of yours, what a help and consolation!

PRIEST: Ofttimes didst thou make thy way thither by hard roads and in foul weather, whilst others rested at home in their sins, who had a shorter road and were in every wise stronger in body and constitution.

FARMER: Some of us couldn't leave home. If I knew the beasts was short of food, I paid no attention to nothing, not even to God's word.

HELGA: You certainly had your sheep as much to thank for your salvation as our blessed priest.

PRIEST: It is good for us to be here. And I can still pray my old prayer for the children of my congregation, both those who are here and those who are dwelling yet in the world below, in the weakness of the flesh and the hurts and perils of the temptations of the Devil. (*Sacred singing in the distance. The Priest clasps his hands on his breast.*)

O thou most mighty Lord of Glory, thou who alone art crowned, spotless and innocent, bless thou all our counsel and condition, our aspirations and intentions, our going out and our coming in, and make all thy handiwork to prosper. Grant good fortune to our fishermen, and fruitfulness to our cattle, protect us from pestilence and famine, flood and tempest, lightning and thunderstorms, and impending perils of the elements. Defend us from spirits of the air, wild beasts, venomous serpents, and all the assaults of the Devil, from mortal peril and from extinction. Grant us that we may make ready in time and fill our lamps with olive oil and, endued with the breastplate of faith and the helm of hope and the sword of charity, may meet our beloved bridegroom and go in unto thy wedding feast, before the door of mercy has been shut. And when thou dividest the sheep from the goats, let thy blessed right hand lead us, thy spirit control us, thy seraphim guard us—and sweeten all our adversity with a foretaste of the heavenly joy. (*Jon makes a sound to show that he has grown bored.*) Amen.

THE OLD WOMAN'S PARENTS: Amen.

JON: Amen.

OLD WOMAN: If the precious gift of mercy is vouchsafed me, it'll be thanks not least to my old minister.

HELGA: While I was on earth, I never thought about death, I very often forgot to say my prayers, and very seldom went to church—and yet they let me in. If I've managed to deserve that, in spite of everything, I think everyone ought to deserve it straight away.

FARMER: I think so too.

OLD WOMAN: If you had your way, my Jon wouldn't need to worry.

HELGA: Your Jon? (*The Parents look at one another.*) God knows, he's deserved many times over to live in heaven for all eternity. If I had my way, I'd forgive everybody everything.

OLD WOMAN: It's always been a sort of heavenly joy to be in your company.

PRIEST: As one having the cure of souls, I take leave to ask: Has your Jon done anything wrong since last time?

OLD WOMAN: That's not for me to judge.

FATHER: Is he still in the cottage?

OLD WOMAN: If he ain't on his way up to the Golden Gate.

FATHER: On the way here?

JON: Oh yes. Did you think I was immortal? Put that in your pipe and smoke it!

(*The Parents look at one another.*)

PRIEST: We will all accompany you home, but at the Golden Gate you, like others, are obliged to stand alone. We will also pray for you fervently in the meantime, and when you enter into glory we will sing Hosanna in our hearts.

OLD WOMAN: Oh, I'd rather you prayed for my Jon.

PRIEST: We will do that also.

JON: I suppose the Lamb's food has made you keen on praying.

(*Violin music and singing of angels.*)

PRIEST: What was that?

OLD WOMAN: The angels—oh, how prettily they sing!

PRIEST: You cannot really have heard them.

FATHER: I heard too.

JON: You're just the same damned bootlicker. (*The Old Woman hides the bag under her apron. Enter the Fiddler and Three Child-Angels. They are all dressed in shining garments. The fiddler is playing his fiddle, and the angels on small violins. They dance round the Old Woman, singing "Eia, eia!"*)

OLD WOMAN: My darling boys!

ANGELS: Yes, that's who we are, mummy. (*They kiss her on the cheeks.*)

OLD WOMAN (*in tears*): I can't hardly believe them's the sons of Jon and me—such divine creatures! And yet I recognize them, my blessed little goldilocks.

FIDDLER (*Plays and sings. The Angels join in.*):
>   Horsehair on catgut,
>   And hollow wooden frame;
>   That was all the fortune
>   To the fiddler's name.
>
>   He sang in the cottage,
>   And the goodwife soon

Gave him his supper
And some nice new shoon.

The fiddler was a lover
Of beauty and of song;
So now he lives for ever
In the ages long.

Horsehair on catgut,
And hollow wooden frame;
That was all the fortune
To the fiddler's name.

OLD WOMAN: I reckon he hadn't much to be grateful to me for, poor lad.

HELGA: You remember him, then?

OLD WOMAN: I've never forgotten. I told you you two would meet again, and yet he was only a bird of passage, same as a wild swan from the hills.

(*The Fiddler and Helga look into each other's faces with sparkling eyes.*)

HELGA: Sing some more, my dear. Sing that old song of yours about love.

FIDDLER (*Addresses his song to her. The Angels accompany and dance. Before the end of the song, all except the Old Woman start dancing.*)

Long was the time I tarried,
My lily fair, for thee:
My tuneful strings I carried
When wintry storms blew free;
I trysted neath the birches
That grow by Greenwood Lea.

Through shady groves I wandered,
My lily fair, with thee;
While livelong summer squandered

Its sunlight on the sea,
And zephyrs stirred the birches
That grow by Greenwood Lea.

Now, heart with heart combining,
My lily fair, we see
A flaming radiance shining
Across the welkin free;
And blithe 'tis neath the birches
That grow by Greenwood Lea.

(*Helga throws herself upon the Fiddler's neck and kisses
him. Dance with music.*)

OLD WOMAN (*fascinated*): Oh the blessed angels! (*Aside to
Jon.*) Do you hear, darling?

JON: Do you think I've gone deaf? Have the kids got wings?

OLD WOMAN (*trying to keep Jon quiet, whispers*): Angels'
wings.

FIDDLER AND ANGELS (*show themselves about to go away, sing*):
Eia, eia!

ALL (*draw up in file and sing as they move off*):
To the Golden Gate we go,
—Eia, eia!
Bright the heavenly legions show;
—Eia, eia!
Mary maid, and Savior high
Pity those who live and die.
—Eia, eia!

CURTAIN

Act IV

At the Golden Gate. Music and wordless songs are heard in the distance. The three angels enter, take their places, and point to the gate. The Old Woman comes after them, crosses herself, falls on her knees and prays in silence.

ANGELS: We await you inside the gate. (*Exeunt.*)

OLD WOMAN: Amen. In his blessed name, amen. (*The song stops. Old Woman looks up.*) Then the time has come. (*Sees that the angels have gone, and rises to her feet.*) So we two are alone outside the Golden Gate.

JON: At last!

OLD WOMAN: Have you repented your sins now, as humble sinners should?

JON: I'll hardly change for the better from this.

OLD WOMAN: Remember then to mind your speech like a Christian.

JON: Haven't I always?

OLD WOMAN: If you're asked to speak, then tell the truth honestly. St. Peter knows everything.

JON: You think so?

OLD WOMAN: And try now to talk a bit gentler like, Jon dear. That'll make a better impression on strangers than this continual offhandedness.

JON: Oh?

OLD WOMAN: If, by God's help, you should be let in, then you must give my best love to our boys. And so I wish you everlasting—

JON: Look here, just go and knock.

OLD WOMAN: Are you ready now to meet your judge.

JON: Oh yes, just as I've always been.

OLD WOMAN: Then I'll knock in the Lord's name. (*Knocks three times.*)

JON: Looks as if they wasn't in any hurry to come to the door.

OLD WOMAN: In the realm of heavenly peace, there ain't no hurry about anything.

JON: Perhaps they thinks it's good manners to keep folks waiting. Knock again, woman.

OLD WOMAN: Take it easy, Jon dear, and mind you don't speak till you're spoke to. (*The gate opens, showing a vision of glory inside. Enter St. Peter. He is in a long blue gown, with a bunch of keys at his belt and a big ledger under his arm. In face and appearance he suggests an old church deacon.*) God bless you, holy guardian of heaven, servant of the Lord and blessed apostle.

PETER: So you are from Iceland? Peace be with you, my good woman. (*Shuts the gate.*)

OLD WOMAN: I'd humbly beg your pardon for giving you this trouble, poor wretched creature that I am.

PETER: It's never been exactly restful, having charge of the keys here in heaven. But so far I've tried to do my duty, and as far as I know the Holy Trinity haven't yet wanted to find anyone else for the job.

OLD WOMAN: Well, and it's certainly most unlikely that they'd hit on anyone else who was better and more trustworthy. I knows that much about you from my reading of the holy scripture. But what a grace it is—to stand face to face with you.

PETER: No one who has read the scriptures wonders who I am.

But isn't there a widespread neglect of that study? So I have gathered anyhow, from some of those who have come here.

OLD WOMAN: I've often seen pictures of you in religious books and on altar-pieces, and I must say that you looks and behaves even grander in reality. But in the pictures there was always a ring of light round your head—of course you only wears that on special occasions, though. But it suits you uncommon well, blessed man of God.

PETER: That's enough now, my good woman.

OLD WOMAN: Oh naturally you've got other things to attend to but listening to me. But, as you see, I've come here, and it's a long way from Iceland to heaven. I must say it's a long and weary way. And in fact, I hardly knows myself whether I've got here awake or asleep, alive or dead. But I've trusted all the time that you'd have mercy on me when I came.

PETER: Everyone trusts Peter, old as he may be. And it may not seem much, at first glance, to turn a key in a lock, but when it's this one (*lifting up the key*) it's not all the same who holds it. It looks as if some people thought it was no more than a trifling favor to open the door for them, but it's really no small matter to grant men everlasting happiness.

OLD WOMAN: Well, it wasn't really on my own account that I came to take this on. I just wanted to have a talk with you and find out if it'd be quite impossible for you to have pity on my Jon.

PETER: I like nothing better than to take in those who have deserved it, and it was never my habit to turn innocent folks away. On the other hand people must understand that heaven is an old and respectable establishment, which will not have a stain put on its reputation. It ought to be enough if we settle about your husband when he gets here.

OLD WOMAN: He died a little while back, and isn't far off. He's had his share of trouble—plenty of it—on earth, poor chap, and seeing as how I'm his wedded wife and have had ten children by him, it was my duty to come with him from our cottage, since he hadn't many to lend him a hand, barring me and the children. But you see it'd be a great relief to me to know Jon was comfortably housed, with kind and real quality people.

PETER: Well, we shouldn't think of lodging him just in a shack here in heaven.

OLD WOMAN: If I know anything of my Jon, he'd be ready to take on a job of work to pay for his board and some old rags to wear. He was always a bit demanding, but they surely won't skimp the daily bread here in heaven. I can safely say that he was clever with his hands and especially good with animals.

PETER: That won't hurt any. But it often seems as if people don't realize till too late what is agreeable to God. Men rush through life and trust to mercy, but things can sometimes turn out differently from what they expected. We make a practice of examining all their papers here at the gate.

OLD WOMAN: I know that heaven won't be mocked. But no one expects anything special for my Jon; he'd do better in some job like minding cattle, or looking after a dairy in the summer pastures, than making up wreaths of flowers, or fiddly little chores like that.

PETER: We've never had any trouble with our folks, once they were inside the gate.

OLD WOMAN: I've no doubt Jon would get on all right with sensible folk, even though he may have had his little faults, same as all us children of men. I've had no reason to complain of him, that much is sure. And our kids wasn't no weaklings. Three of them came to meet me just now—my little lads. They've been well treated with you, and we their parents can be very thankful to you and the Heavenly Father.

PETER: Yes, they're in the best of health, the young things.

OLD WOMAN: If Jon could be father to such nice children, it's hardly likely but he was good himself at bottom. Oh, he could be a real gentleman, if it comes to that, and that was exactly his real true nature.

PETER: If that's so, there oughtn't to be any difficulty about him. But sometimes things turn up when I look at this. (*Lifting the ledger.*) It's not everyone who takes care to guard against it.

OLD WOMAN: Well, you couldn't really say that my Jon was a regular churchgoer, if I'm to be quite honest, but he often read his Bible, so it didn't make much difference. He wasn't the sort of man to show off before others.

PETER (*opens the ledger*): I'll have to take a look at his record. Oh, dear, dear, I remember. It isn't good.

OLD WOMAN: But he was a godfearing man all the same, in his own way.

PETER: You wish Jon well. That is nice of you and will be borne in mind. But I have to answer for all I do to the Holy Trinity.

OLD WOMAN: I once read that there would be more joy here over one sinner that repented than over ninety and nine just persons.

PETER: Quite correct. But always provided he repents.

OLD WOMAN: I hope too that my Jon has done that—with God's help.

JON: I've never been a great sinner.

OLD WOMAN (*looks imploringly at Peter*): You mustn't imagine that I meant to keep it from you that I'd got Jon's soul with me. It's for his sake I've come here. (*Pulls out the bag.*)

PETER: Best that I talk to the lad himself.

JON: Of course. And no offense.

OLD WOMAN: It'd be awful nice of you if you'd be lenient with his faults. Isn't it best for him to stay in the bag meanwhile, or should I untie it?

JON: Untie it, untie it directly!

PETER: The soul must appear naked before its judge.

OLD WOMAN (*sits down and bends to untie the bag. Looks up*):
But the soul is perhaps just a mere vapor, drifting out in the
wind?

PETER: In your eyes it will have the appearance of Jon, just as
he was in his lifetime.

OLD WOMAN: Oh then you'll let him keep his shirt and under-
pants. They're snow-white homespun, white as ivory. I'm so
afraid he'll catch cold, if he's stripped for long. Well, I don't
think I shall ever get this untied. I don't like cutting my
garter.

PETER (*stretching out his hand*): Rise up, farmer Jon, and give
an account of your deeds.

JON (*rises gradually till he breaks out and shakes himself*): I'm
glad of this. How d'ye do, Peter, old boy.

PETER: Good day, my man.

JON: That's the worst that has ever happened to me—to be
rolled up in that rotten bag. But it's all owing to my old
woman.

OLD WOMAN: Talk like a Christian, Jon dear.

JON: I should think I can talk exactly as I please—just like
every other Icelander. I've never heard they had occasion to
be ashamed of their mother tongue, so far. The clergy thinks
that prayerbook language is what you talk here in the heavenly village, but—

PETER: By their fruits ye shall know them.

JON (*laughing*): You talk pretty good Icelandic yourself.

OLD WOMAN: What do you suppose, man? Him, what speaks
with the tongues of men and angels. But he knows, bless him,
that we're simple common folks what only knows their
mother tongue.

JON: Hold your tongue, woman. Of course Icelandic is spoke
in heaven—and nothing else. Do you think they talk some
kind of Latin up here?

PETER: I speak the languages of all Christian peoples.

JON: Have you talked to Luther?

PETER: Why do you ask?

JON: Have you talked to the Pope? You'd hardly care to waste words on that old scoundrel. Are there any Danes here in Heaven?

PETER: Why shouldn't I take them in?

JON: Are they here too, then? Well, it's all the same.

PETER: You're plainspoken people, you Icelanders.

JON: Yes, Peter old boy, we're used to speaking plain, so it can be heard through the roar of surf and the rumble of volcanoes. You know that Iceland's way out at sea, and that it's powered by fire and glaciers. It hasn't its like in the wide world.

PETER: True, it's a beautiful country. But somebody who came here told me that the people very soon lost their freedom, because of the quarrels and tricks of the inhabitants.

JON: Don't speak of it, it's a sad story. Such a thing would never have happened, if I'd been alive in those days.

PETER: It might have been expected that the men would have changed for the better, when the church was encouraged and her ministers increased.

JON: Not at all. It was more the other way. That was when the Devil got into the game.

OLD WOMAN: But the blessed priests, they bring us the gospel of salvation.

JON: They have a go at it. Much help for the soul I'd say it was, to see them yawning before the altar and slobbering in their pulpits.

OLD WOMAN: Mind what you're saying, Jon dear.

PETER: We've often had trouble with this little people, and the Prince of Darkness expects much of it. But the fight's not over yet.

OLD WOMAN: Ah, but ain't a lot of these here transgressions more pranks than real crimes? But it's nothing but the truth—we makes a very bad use of God's gifts.

PETER: Perhaps you have met some of your acquaintances who were on the way down?

(*The Old Woman sighs.*)

JON: I hope you're not going to compare me to that damned riffraff. Do you happen to know who I am and what my stock is, Peter old chap?

PETER (*taking up the ledger*): I'm pretty well informed of it, Jon Jonsson.

JON: Certainly my name's Jon, son of Jon Jonsson the rich, son of Svein the hymn-writer, son of Grim the lawman, son of Klaeng, son of Kari, son of Bishop Brand. I come in the direct male line from the kings of Norway.

PETER: You Icelanders don't exactly lack family pride.

JON: Do you know anything about family history?

PETER: I know this much, that some of your ancestors went straight to hell.

JON: Who told you that lie? But on the other hand, the Norse vikings didn't ever spend their time torturing sticklebacks and minnows to death, like your countrymen in Galilee. When you put to sea and had a tiny bit of a tossing, you fell to praying, shaking in your shoes and in a blue funk!

OLD WOMAN: You should be ashamed of that kind of talk to this holy man. (*To Peter.*) But seeing as he was born with this taint in his blood, and bad instincts in his body, you should make more allowances for him.

PETER: He was granted full intelligence.

JON: And plenty of it.

PETER: He was given sense to choose or reject.

JON: And I've done it too, proper.

PETER (*turning the pages of the ledger*): Now that I know your reason for coming, I will, in accordance with my official duty, and for the further revision of your record, as it is set down in the protocol of heaven, put a few questions of conscience to you, Jon Jonsson, which I ask you to answer directly and definitely.

OLD WOMAN: Remember you're standing before your judge.

PETER: Do you acknowledge that you have received in your youth the ten commandments of God, and have also had a Christian education?

JON: Yes. And for every commandment I learnt, I got ten whacks from my masters.

OLD WOMAN: That was all the Christianity he had.

PETER: Do you admit the validity of the ten commandments?

JON: What do you think? Need you ask?

PETER: Do you claim to have acted in accordance with these commandments and lived your life as befits a child of God?

JON: Yes, you can put that down.

PETER: Do you remember any sins which you have committed and need to confess?

JON: Oh no. I don't think I remember anything of the sort. Though I might perhaps admit that I've sometimes happened to make a little slip, like everyone else. But I'm sure you're not smallminded enough to take account of that sort of thing.

PETER: Do you call it a little slip to take God's name in vain?

JON: Have I done that? Besides, I've always thought the Creator was above eavesdropping.

PETER: Do you call it a little slip to covet the goods of another?

JON: Everyone in the world does that—every man jack of them. I've never had anything of my own—not a brass farthing.

OLD WOMAN: There you're telling the truth, Jon dear. We lived on starvation level.

PETER: What are the words of the eighth commandment?

JON: The eighth? Is there anything special about it?

PETER: Do you remember having broken that holy commandment?

JON: Oh no.

OLD WOMAN: What about that leg of mutton, Jon?

JON: Who cares about one leg of mutton? Do you think the Heavenly Father is some kind of miser?

PETER: But what about the sheep?

JON: What damned sheep? Do you mean when I mistook the earmarks of those two or three scraggy sheep? That's all done with now!

PETER: Are you ready of your own will to confess your principal sins to me?

JON: I'll get along without admitting sins I never committed.

OLD WOMAN: But perhaps you might remember a few trifles, Jon dear.

JON: Shut up, woman.

PETER: Do you remember no sins which you committed with a woman?

JON: With a woman? Now you're joking, Peter old boy. Do you mean with my old gal?

PETER: With the wife of another man.

JON: That's the way! You sniff out everything. Do you suppose I've got no natural instincts? I can tell you, Peter Johannesson old boy, that every single man on earth is intimate with more than one woman. Fellows that had no leanings that way would be damned feeble creatures—more like. It's not the will they lack. You can write that down.

OLD WOMAN: That's true what you say, Jon dear. There's not many that don't have plenty of trouble with their bodies.

JON: And I asks myself—ought you to count against us as sins those instincts we've had put in our blood on purpose to keep life going in heaven and earth? Why, no child comes of itself. Is it wrong for a man to give in to a law of nature?

(*The Enemy appears on the watch, dressed as before.*)

PETER: Do you consider that is serving God, Jon Jonsson?

JON: And you can talk like that, you who denied your Saviour three times while the bloody cock crowed twice!

OLD WOMAN (*falling on her knees*): O Lord, have mercy on him. Draw, in thy mercy, a bloodred stroke through the record of his sins, and bathe him in the gracious fountain of salvation!

PETER (*at the gate*): In the name of the Holy Trinity, I close the Golden Gate. (*Goes in; the gate is heard to lock.*)

OLD WOMAN (*gets up, in tears*): Oh, Jon dear!

JON: I thought he wanted taking down a peg.

OLD WOMAN: You talked just like a raving lunatic. You might
have known it don't pay to quarrel with the judge.

JON: There was nothing else for me to do, if I wasn't to let him
get the best of me. I couldn't see any different but that he
was a man, same as myself.

OLD WOMAN: Have you given up all hope, then?

JON: I dunno as I've ever had any hope.

ENEMY: Here you can see which is the better
And stronger man—myself or Peter.
Often enough he has fled the fray. (*Laughs.*)
Checkmate! The board may be put away.
The gate is locked in the heavenly city,
Mine's open.

JON: It's Master!

OLD WOMAN: Oh God, have pity! (*Seizes hold of Jon.*)

ENEMY: Away with these heavenly trappings vain!
(*Tearing off the angel disguise.*)
For all that is heaven's I here disdain.
I left it young, and I hate and scorn
Its blind insistence on creeds outworn.
'Tis not my nature to cringe and crawl:
I was made to conquer—the Lord of all!
(*The Old Woman crosses herself and Jon.*)

ENEMY: I need no Michael to be my guide,
Though the crags be steep, on the other side.
I stick to my slave with the scourge-scored back;
I have followed Jon, I have dogged his track;
For often the dross from the soul is cleared
At the final moment—

JON (*shaking his fist at the Enemy*):   I ain't afeard!
(*Tries to tear himself from his Old Woman.*)

ENEMY: Your wife's endeavors are vain to save you;
You are weighed and damned—come Jon, I'll have you.
Though the cross be marked upon belly and breast,
Nor life nor record are changed the least.

For ever and ever you bear my brand,
My cringing bondman, in heart and hand.
'Tis I that have fooled you altogether,
And beaten the Lord—
JON: Oh, hold your blather!
(*Old Woman draws Jon toward the gate.*)
ENEMY: For both of you, 'twould have been much better
To have followed my counsels to the letter:
Yet, true to a good time-honored custom,
Folks will start climbing, till down we thrust 'em.
And if anyone's hurt, and his wounds afflict him,
I've plenty of brimstone to treat the victim.
(*The Old Woman knocks three times on the gate.*)
I'll soon singe the cross-mark from your pate,
So come now, Jon, they have shut the gate.
OLD WOMAN: I trust you to talk like a Christian, if anyone
should come out. (*Knocks again.*)
JON: It's no use knocking.
OLD WOMAN: Why, it looks just as if you was desperate to get
down into the brimstone. There's someone coming.
(*The gate opens. Paul the Apostle comes out and shuts the
gate. He is in a long red robe, and has a grey beard and a
heroic appearance.*)
PAUL: Paul the apostle greets you in the Lord.
(*The Enemy hides.*)
OLD WOMAN: God be with you, great preacher to the heathens,
rock of help to all that's in trouble. I knew you wouldn't
disappoint me.
PAUL: On the earth I dwelt among heathens. I journeyed from
land to land, to save them who dwell in the habitation of
unrighteousness which is their heart, and preached faith to
infidels. Many I drew up from wallowing in the mire and
abomination of their sins and made them the finest of God's
creatures. But what was my reward? On behalf of these
sinful worms of earth, I had to endure scorn and torments,

and finally I was beheaded by the Roman axe. Though many gave ear to my words, yet more have refused my message, and have hidden their infirmity in the darkness instead of being clothed in the armor of light.

JON: If the clergy spoke up like you do, the faith wouldn't be all smothered by the coughing in church. I'll stand by that. You're a fine speaker.

PAUL: My speech and my preaching were not with enticing words of man's wisdom, but in demonstration of the Spirit and of power, that your faith should not stand in the wisdom of men, but in the power of God.

OLD WOMAN: Where should we be without Him? We have Him to thank—and His apostles—that the world ain't like a whited sepulchre.

PAUL: Do men believe those who preach the truth better than false prophets? Far from it. Where is the wise? Where is the scribe? Where is the disputer of this world? Hath not God made foolish the wisdom of this world?

JON: Yes, that's for certain. Everyone on earth is a damned ass.

OLD WOMAN: We're ignorant folks. But didn't you say once: He that is weak in the faith should be cared for and not shaken in his conscience?

PAUL: That is so.

OLD WOMAN: And in your Epistle to the Romans it says: Be not wise in your own conceits. Recompense to no man evil for evil. And—as much as lieth in you, live peaceably with all men.

PAUL: That is true likewise. Hath God cast away his people? God forbid.

JON: Well, but it takes two to make friends.

PAUL: I have heard your discourse with the apostle Peter, my fellow-worker and brother, and know your business in coming hither. Wherefore I ask you, Jon Jonsson: Do you not yet know that the all-seeing God is a searcher of the hearts and reins, while we are his servants? Have you not yet been

convinced that you are unworthy to enter and consort with
the elect?

JON: Not in the least. Certainly not.

OLD WOMAN: I implores you, sir. Show mercy to my husband,
and open the Golden Gate to him.

PAUL: Wherefore should I transgress the laws of heaven?
Wherefore should I despise the decision and act of my
fellow-worker? Know you not that the unrighteous shall not
inherit the kingdom of God? Be not deceived: neither forni-
cators, nor idolaters, nor adulterers, nor the effeminate, nor
abusers of themselves with mankind, nor thieves, nor the
covetous, nor drunkards, nor revilers nor extortioners shall
inherit the kingdom of God.

(*The Enemy, on the watch, chuckles with delight.*)

JON: You're a proof of that, or rather the opposite. It can't
hardly be so. To the best of my knowledge you was yourself
an idolater and a reviler. Wasn't you pleased, when the
martyr Stephen was stoned to death? Didn't you persecute
Christian folks and want to wipe out the gospel of Christ
from the earth? Perhaps that's not reckoned as sin?

OLD WOMAN (*who has stared at Jon in consternation*): You're
behaving like a brute and not a man. (*Produces the bag and
shows it to Paul.*) You knows my thoughts, sir. This is my
last wish.

(*Old Woman crouches down in front of Jon with the open
bag. Paul raises his hand. Jon, covered by his wife, sinks
down into the bag with a cry.*)

OLD WOMAN (*stands up, gathers the mouth of the bag together
and ties it up*): This is the best place to keep you, you
bundle of rubbish!

JON: Open, open at once!

PAUL: You hear my words, Jon Jonsson. By no means would I
contend with you, but if you had altogether turned from
your way of life instead of becoming hardened, had pre-
ferred truth to lies and purged your heart, then these merci-

ful doors of salvation would stand open to you. Let no one deceive himself. Those who defile the temple of God, them shall God destroy. (*Goes to the gate.*) To this my conscience in the Holy Spirit bears me witness. (*Goes in and shuts the gate. The Enemy laughs.*)

JON (*roars*): Open the bag, you devil of a woman!

OLD WOMAN: Be quiet, you brute.

THE ENEMY: Mine art thou, Jon, and I better merit
To claim thee kin than the Holy Spirit.
Though great St. Paul may have cause to feel
Thy manly courage and voice of steel,
Though priests their pages with ink may stain,
Beside my wisdom it all is vain.
Nor peace nor mercy thy soul shall know,
O'er screes and lava thy road must go,
Back to the north and down below. (*Laughs.*)
And down below!

OLD WOMAN: God must have forsaken you, Jon dear.

JON: Open the bag! It's all the same to me, damn it!

OLD WOMAN (*taking a hasty look at the Enemy*): Now he's stretching out his claws. This is what I came here for, to save you from everlasting damnation.

JON: Nice sort of saving I call it! Now then, open the bag, I tell you.

OLD WOMAN: I don't believe as how Mary the mother of God won't take pity on you, if I can manage to get a word with her. (*Knocks three times on the gate.*)

JON: Surely you're not going to knock for the third time?

OLD WOMAN: Don't you say a single word, and hold your breath.

(*Soft music and ringing of bells*)

THE ENEMY (*starts, stretches out his claws, hisses*): Jon, Jon. (*Withdraws into cover.*)

OLD WOMAN: Now, be humble, like a child. (*Goes a few steps from the gate.*)

CHOIR OF ANGELS:

O Mary, mild and great,
The mother of Our Lord,
To thee we consecrate
Our song of thanks outpoured.
Thou breathest faith and heat
Upon earth's frozen sward,
O Mary, mild and great,
The mother of Our Lord.

(*The gate opens of its own accord. The Virgin Mary comes out before the end of the song. She is in a snow-white silk robe, with her hair hanging down and a wreath of flowers on her head. Accompanying her are angels and saints, who arrange themselves behind her in the gateway.*)

OLD WOMAN (*falling on her knees*): Holy Queen of Heaven! Merciful mother!

MARY: I heard thy sighing.

OLD WOMAN (*in tears*): You wept by the cross. Have pity on me!

MARY: All shall be well with those who love most fervently.

OLD WOMAN: I would sacrifice my salvation for him—will you speak to your blessed Son, and ask his help?

MARY: I will speak to my Son. God bless thy love and care, and give thee peace. (*Exit with her escort, who finish their song. The music dies away gradually.*)

OLD WOMAN (*crossing herself and standing up*): I've never seen a more godlike face.

JON (*shyly*): It was like a sweet breath of spring playing round me.

THE ENEMY (*on the watch*):

Come now, Jon, it's a woman's way
To kneel and grovel and whine and pray.
Your soul's my prize—though it wants inflating,
And the end of the story needs no stating.
So come this minute, I'm tired of waiting.

JON: Who asks you to wait?

PETER (*comes out and shuts the gate*): So you're still here, my good woman.

OLD WOMAN (*hopefully*): Mary the mother of God was going to plead my cause with her beloved Son.

PETER: You can trust my verdict. It will not be changed.

(*The Enemy gesticulates exultantly to the Old Woman.*)

OLD WOMAN: Ah well, them as lives by the land has plenty of troubles, in heaven as well as on earth. But its not your fault that things went wrong. I mustn't think how grand it would have been for my Jon, to come to live in bliss among the angels. Isn't the glory inside the gate quite unspeakable? I guess I needn't ask. And is every soul, what gets in, allowed to live there for ever?

PETER: World without end.

OLD WOMAN: And it'll never be thrown into the fire, no matter what it does, and whatever happens?

PETER: No, never.

OLD WOMAN: I suppose it'd be sinfully forward of me, if I was to ask you just to let me peep in—through ever so little a chink?

PETER (*considering*): Why should I refuse you that?

OLD WOMAN: I'd like so dreadfully to have a look in.

(*Peter opens the door slightly. Music in the distance.*)

OLD WOMAN: Oh! Oh! Are the flowers of gold? I'm thinking what a joy it would have been to my Jon to be here. And then of course, as I see, it must be many times more lovely the nearer you get to the Lamb's throne and the shining choir of glory. (*Peter nods his head in assent.*) Do you think my eyes would be dazzled too much, if you was to open it just a tiny bit more?

PETER (*complying with her wish*): The light of heaven heals all the ills of Christian people.

(*In the beams of light are seen many-colored flowers and shrubs. Angels and other beings in white move to and fro.*)

OLD WOMAN: My Lord and my God! There I see my blessed little lads! (*Moves a few steps backwards as she speaks.*) And there's my father and mother, and the priest, and the farmer, and my friend Helga, and the Wild Swan, and—(*as she makes a spring and throws the bag as far as she can into heaven*) and in you shall go too, my Jon—and may God have mercy upon you!

(*Cries of welcome. Peter is thunderstruck.*)

THE ENEMY (*in a furious rage*):

Heaven's pages are torn, and can ne'er be mended,
Commandments are lies, all justice ended,
And the laws of heaven and hell suspended!

(*Disappears.*)

PETER: Do you know what you have done, woman?

OLD WOMAN (*as she runs away*): Good-bye, Peter dear, and give my love to my Jon!

(*Exit. Music begins at this point, and lasts to the end of the play.*)

PAUL (*entering*): Great things have been happening here.

PETER (*bowed*):—which will probably cost me my post and my job?

PAUL: God forbid. Love suffereth long, believeth all things, hopeth all things, endureth all things. To Him be the power and the glory.

CHOIR OF ANGELS: Amen, Hallelujah!

(*The apostles stand one on each side of the gate.*)

JON (*appears in the gateway. He is dressed in white, and holds a palm branch to his breast. Behind him are angels and saints. He makes as if he did not see the apostles, and looks round on both sides.*): What, has my old gal gone, dear old bird? (*Looks mockingly at the apostles.*) So here you are, you men of God?

(*The apostles say nothing. Jon flourishes his palm branch, and goes quickly into heaven. The Angels and Saints dance round Jon, singing "Eia! eia!"*)

JON (*gazing in all directions, as if the glory was only now apparent to him, notices his attire, half-bewildered*): Why have I now become as white as driven snow?

THE REST (*sing*): Thou art a child at heart, and all of us are so. Eia, eia!

JON: Why have I now been given this palm-branch, fair and green?

THE REST: This is to testify thy conscience now is clean.

JON: Why do the flowers I see appear like burnished gold?

THE REST: Because the soil is rich with mercies manifold.

JON: Who in those homes reside, whose gables this way face?

THE REST: This is the city of heaven, the Godhead's dwelling-place.

JON: Come they from stars or sun—these ever-dazzling beams?

THE REST: From the Lamb's glorious throne this holy radiance streams.

JON (*rejoicing*): What, like a snowcapped isle, is yonder lofty tower?

THE REST: That is our Mary's home, the blessed Virgin's bower. (*The music grows louder. Ringing of bells. Jon is resplendent.*)

THE REST: With joy the vault of heaven is trembling, as you see.

FIDDLER: " 'Tis blithe beneath the birches that grow by Greenwood Lea!"

ALL: Eia! Eia!

(*As the singing ends, the apostles close the gate slowly and quietly.*)

CURTAIN

ATOMS
AND
MADAMS

A Comedy in Four Acts

Kjarnorka og kvenhylli,
by Agnar Thórðarson

Translated from Icelandic by Einar Haugen

First published in Icelandic 1957

Introduction

The third play in our collection, *Atoms and Madams* (*Kjarnorka og kvenhylli,* 1955), by Agnar Þórðarson, leaps right into the modern age. This is Iceland after World War II, catapulted against her own will into an atomic world. From being a country at the edge of civilization she suddenly became a crossroads.

On May 10, 1940, the inhabitants of Reykjavík awoke to find their country occupied by a British expeditionary force. This was not wholly surprising, except to the Icelanders, since Norway had been occupied by the Germans just one month earlier, and the British realized that they ought not to be caught napping again. By agreement with the Icelandic government the United States took over the defense of Iceland from the British on July 1, 1941, to the mutual satisfaction of all parties concerned. It is impossible to exaggerate the effect of the war on Icelandic life. From having been the remote "saga island" of romance and mystery, poor in worldly goods and unspoiled by tourism, it turned into a stepping-stone of East-West traffic. Full independence from Denmark was attained even before the end of the war, in 1944, and membership in NATO in 1949. Iceland's position on the great circle midway between Washington and Moscow gave it in the age of the airplane a strategic importance it had never before held, unless we hark back to the Viking Age a thousand years earlier. An occupying force which at times was larger than the male population could not help but alter the pattern of life and bring this former dependency of Denmark into a new Anglo-Saxon world atmosphere.[1]

The main quality of this atmosphere can be characterized as *prosperity*. Ready money was rare in prewar Iceland, where the rural population made its living primarily by sheep ranching and horse raising and the urban population by catching and processing fish for export. The towns were all small, even the largest, Reykjavík, with about 31 per cent of the inhabitants of the whole country, having only 38,000 inhabitants in 1940.[2] Twenty-five years later the population had doubled, and the city had changed its aspect in every way. Served by two airfields built during the war (Reykjavík by the British, Keflavík by the Americans), the city now has a well-built harbor, abundant electric power from the waterfalls, luxury hotels and restaurants, high-rise apartment houses and elegant homes, traffic problems with its many automobiles and buses, and, in short, a standard of living which for many equals that of Britain and America. The prosperity is in some ways a precarious one, being built on the price of fish on the world market, the demand for Icelandic services by American forces at Keflavík, and the success of Icelandic Airlines as an economy conveyor of passengers from America to Europe.

The war and its aftermath were hectic years of transition, with sharp economic and political conflict, crises of confidence which led to inflation in money as well as governments. Iceland here offered a sharp contrast to the postwar stability of the other Scandinavian countries, where Social Democratic governments kept inflation in check and allowed prosperity to return slowly and surely. In Iceland alone was society torn by the growth of a large and ably-led Communist party, which vigorously resisted all measures designed to bring Iceland into closer contact with the Anglo-Saxon powers. Its intellectual

[1] For a detailed account of these events see Nuechterlein, *Iceland, Reluctant Ally.*

[2] *Árbók Reykjavíkurbæjar 1945* (Reykjavík, 1945), p. 2.

leadership succeeded in winning considerable control of the labor movement, to the disadvantage of the more moderate Social Democrats. The rural population was represented largely by the Progressive Party and the middle-class urban population by the Independence Party, both moderately conservative in their views. During most of this period no party had sufficient strength to rule alone, so that the governments were usually coalitions of two or more of the four major parties. Each party had its own Reykjavík newspaper, circulated throughout the country, in which violent political invective was the staple diet.

Agnar Thórðarson is a man of this new world, one of its most successful chroniclers. Another is Nobel Prize Winner Halldor Laxness, who gave an acid picture of postwar profiteering and high life in Reykjavík in his novel *Atomstöðin* (*The Atom Station*, 1948, Eng. tr., 1961). In the play here presented by Agnar Thórðarson we see the same distaste for the new capitalism, with its conspicuous consumption, its moral decay, and its cultural emptiness. Against its glittering but corrupt facade the author sets up the old moral values represented by unspoiled rural Iceland. Senator Thorleifur Olafsson and his empty-headed wife Karitas represent the bourgeoisie and its failure to meet the challenge of the new age. As a result their daughter Sigrun turns away from them and finds in the comic but honest peasant Sigmundur Jonsson an antidote to their well-meaning but essentially poisonous view of life. The satire is well-turned and proved to be enormously popular, having an extraordinarily long run in the theater of the Dramatic Society of Reykjavík on its appearance in 1955–56 and being constantly performed again by dramatic groups around the country.

Agnar was born in Reykjavík in 1917, the son of an Icelandic physician and a Danish mother, and studied at the University of Iceland on and off from 1937 until the last year of the war, 1945, when he took his degree in Icelandic language and literature. In the meanwhile he had been back and forth to London and Oxford, where he alternately studied and worked for the

BBC and the Ministry of Information. He won a prize for a
short story written while he was still a student. In 1947 he
received a British Council scholarship to study drama and
English literature at Worcester College, Oxford, for a year; he
spent the following year in France and elsewhere on the con-
tinent. At this time he visited the theater diligently, became
acquainted (*inter alia*) with the work of Eugene O'Neill, and
decided to devote himself primarily to the writing of plays for
the new Icelandic theater and radio. In 1953 he became a
librarian at the National Library, where he has successfully
combined librarianship and a writing career. He visited Algiers
in 1952, the Soviet Union in 1956, and in 1960–61 he studied
drama with Professor John Gassner at the Yale University
School of Drama.

Before he turned to plays, Agnar published two novels. The
first of these, *Haninn galar tvisvar* (*The Cock Crows Twice*,
1949), is the story of a young man of good family who is
attracted to the teachings of Communism, but in the end marries
a wealthy girl whom he does not really love. The world in
which he moves is a hard-drinking, car-driving, girl-chasing
one, but the vacillating hero is portrayed as a weakling who
in the end betrays the basic moral values. A more mature
and tragic treatment of a similar theme is to be found in his
second novel, *Ef sverð thitt er stutt* (*If Your Sword Is Short*,
1953). In the words of his translator, Paul Schach: "Since the
Icelander cannot escape from his past, he must . . . choose
between accepting or rejecting its stern ethical dictates."[3] The
same theme dominates his first major play, *Spretthlauparinn*
(*The Sprinter*, 1954), in which a minister is unmasked as a
man without principle. Three of his plays draw their materials
from Icelandic history, *Their koma í haust* (*They Are Coming
This Fall*, 1955) about the dying out of the Icelandic population
in Greenland, *Goðorðamálið* (*The Chieftaincy*, 1959), which
was broadcast for the fifteenth anniversary of Icelandic independence, and *Hæstráðandi til sjós og lands* (*Commander-in-*

[3] *The Prairie Schooner*, vol. 33 (1959), p. 137.

Chief at Sea and on Land, 1965), about Iceland's short-lived dicator, Jørgen Jørgensen. Most of his plays, including two serials, have been written for the radio, and these have in general not been published. Agnar is widely recognized in Iceland as the one writer of this generation who has successfully exploited the possibilities of the modern radio and theater. He has used these devices of urban culture to remind his countrymen of the vices of their new prosperity and has held up the satirical mirror which he hopes will bring them back to their moral senses.

While the satire may seem obvious enough, its effect is enriched by the special Icelandic quality that permits a comic confrontation of an old and self-conscious culture with the problems of the atomic age. The politicians glibly mouth the well-worn phrases of Icelandic patriotism, showering compliments on the viking yeomen who for a millennium have inhabited the Hermit of the Atlantic, also called the Mountain Maid, at the same time as they are fleecing them for their own profit. In the figure of Sigmundur the city folk see only a comic bumpkin, who is too limited in horizon to understand the new age and therefore the ready victim of their schemes. In the snuff-taking, earthbound Sigmundur the author has underlined many of the amusing features of his rural countrymen, to whom the viking past and their own immediate ancestors are virtually indistinguishable. Sigmundur refers in passing to the *Book of Settlement,* a roll of the founding families of ninth-century Iceland; to Egill Skallagrímsson, the fierce viking chieftain of one of the greatest family sagas; to Thorgeirr Ljósvetningagoði, the lawgiver who in the year 1000 slept for a day and a night on the question of whether the Icelanders should remain pagans or become Christians; to Snorri Sturluson, author of the *Prose Edda,* in which the difficult forms of skaldic poetry are expounded, including metaphors called "kennings" of the type that make obscure reference to a woman as "the lily of the serpent's hide." Sigmundur, like many of his countrymen of the older generation even today, is not only a rich source of folklore (he has his "dream lady" and his grandfather who slew the "Iranes monster"), but a poet and a saga teller in his own right. While his urbanized friends either laugh at or are bored by these activities, they are in the end forced to recognize that through this body of traditional lore he has preserved a core of solid moral values without which the country could well be lost.

E. H.

Agnar Thórðarson: Bibliography

IN ICELANDIC

Haninn galar tvisvar (*The Cock Crows Twice*). Novel. Reykjavík: Helgafell, 1949.
Ef sverð thitt er stutt (*If Your Sword is Short*). Novel. Reykjavík: Mál og Menning, 1953.
Förin til Brazilíu (*Voyage to Brazil*). Comedy for radio. Performed, Icelandic Broadcasting, 1953.
Spretthlauparinn (*The Sprinter*). Play in three acts. Performed, Icelandic Broadcasting, 1954; The Summer Theater, Reykjavík, 1958. Reykjavík: Bókaútgáfa Menningarsjóðs, 1959.
Their koma í haust (*They Are Coming This Fall*). Play. Performed, National Theater, 1955. Act I printed in *Tímarit Máls og Menningar*, 1952.
Kjarnorka og kvenhylli (*Atoms and Madams*). Play in four acts. Performed, Dramatic Society of Reykjavík, 1955–56. Reykjavík: Bókaútgáfa Menningarsjóðs, 1957.
Andri. One-act play for radio. Performed, Icelandic Broadcasting, 1955.
Tónsnillingurinn (*The Musical Genius*). One-act play for radio. Performed, Icelandic Broadcasting, 1955.
Víxlar með afföllum (*Notes at Discount*). Radio serial in nine

parts. Performed, Icelandic Broadcasting, 1958; Dramatic Society, Selfoss, 1963.

Gauksklukkan (*The Cuckoo Clock*). Play in two acts. Performed, National Theater, 1958. Reykjavík: Helgafell, 1962.

Goðorðamálið (*The Chieftaincy*). Play for radio. Performed, Icelandic Broadcasting, June 17, 1959.

Ekið fyrir stapann (*Over the Cliff*). Radio serial in thirteen parts. Performed, Icelandic Broadcasting, 1960.

Sannleikur í gifsi (*Truth in Plaster*). Play in three acts. Performed, National Theater, 1965.

Hæstráðandi til sjós og lands (*Commander-in-Chief at Sea and on Land*). Historical play. Performed, Icelandic Broadcasting, 1965–66.

IN ENGLISH

"The Thief." Short story, tr. by Paul Schach. *The Prairie Schooner*, vol. 32 (1958), 210–16. Reprinted in *Best Articles and Stories* (Spencer, Indiana, 1957–   ).

"Episode from *If Your Sword is Short*." Tr. by Paul Schach, with an introductory note. *The Prairie Schooner*, vol. 33 (1959), pp. 136–47.

Characters

Senator Thorleifur Olafsson*
Karitas, his wife
Sigrun, their daughter
Sigmundur Jonsson, a farmer
Dr. Alfreds
Kristin, a maid
Valdimar, a political leader
Elias, a sailor
Addi, housewife
Kamilla, housewife
Gunna, housewife
Boas, Senate caretaker
Professor Epihara, atomic expert
Paper Boy

Originally written in 1955 and performed by the Dramatic
Society of Reykjavík during the season 1955–56; printed
at Reykjavík in 1957, under the title *Kjarnorka og
kvenhylli* (literally, "Atomic Power and Female Charms").

* Translator's note: Thorleifur is in fact an *althingismaður*, or member of the Icelandic *althingi* ("parliament"). Throughout, "Senator"
and "Senate" have been substituted, as simple terms, hallowed by
Roman and American tradition as something imposing but occa-
sionally hollow.

Act I

The time of the play is the present. The scene is in the countryside, somewhere in southern Iceland.

As the curtain rises, the first strains of "Iceland, Happy Land" in the arrangement of Jon Leifs are heard. The backdrop is a view of distant, snowcapped mountains, with lava fields in the foreground. A bright summer's day.

Senator Thorleifur Olafsson is standing with a palette in one hand, a paintbrush in the other. In front of him is a half-finished oil painting on an easel; in its upper corner is fastened a postcard.

Thorleifur is a man of middle age, with graying visage, quite handsome, though a bit flabby. His features reflect a weak character, but when he looks at the mountains, his expression is one of sadness and nostalgia. He wears a hat with a wide, upturned brim.

His daughter, Sigrun, barely eighteen, lolls in the grass nearby, chewing on a straw. It is evident that there is a good rapport between father and daughter.

As Thorleifur surveys his work, an explosion is heard. He starts a little, looks toward the mountains, and is about to continue painting.

His daughter has also looked up.

SIGRUN: Do you hear that? He's still blasting.

THORLEIFUR (*without paying much attention*): Yes, I suppose so.

SIGRUN: Just imagine! What if he should find some ore!

THORLEIFUR (*mumbling absentmindedly*): M-hm.

SIGRUN (*gets up*): Well? Do you really think so, daddy? Do you think he may find ore?

THORLEIFUR: Naw, not much danger of that.

SIGRUN: But you were all talking about it in the car on the way out here.

THORLEIFUR (*still absentminded and intent on the painting*): We were? Oh sure, just theoretically. Vordufell is a remarkable mountain in more ways than one. But of course there isn't any ore in it. Well, well. (*Triumphantly steps back from the painting.*) Now look: how do you like it?

SIGRUN: Gee, daddy, you're a real artist. The glacier is so bright in your picture. Why, it looks just like it was made of nylon!

THORLEIFUR (*proudly viewing his picture*): Yes, doesn't it! (*Mixes his colors.*) It is exactly as if rays flashed from the mountain, for you know—there *are* mystic beings living in it.

SIGRUN: Oh, it's always such a thrill to be out here in the country again! I could shout or cry, or I don't know what—

THORLEIFUR: True. Here no one treads with workaday shoes. Here there is holiday in the very air.

SIGRUN: And it's always Sunday on the almanac! Oh, I wish we never had to leave the red-letter days and go back to the black ones! (*She looks up and calls out.*) Hi there, Sigmundur!

THORLEIFUR (*looks up*): Well, Sigmundur my friend, so there you are.

(*Farmer Sigmundur comes on stage from the left. He is stocky, ruddy, weatherbeaten, with heavy mustaches, a man in his fifties, who makes free with his snuffbox while he is talking.*)

SIGMUNDUR: What a hell of a racket that fellow is making!

He's going to scare the devil out of my ewes if this keeps up.

THORLEIFUR: The fellow? You mean Doctor Alfreds?

SIGMUNDUR: Oh yeah, you have some fancy titles out there in Reykjavik.

THORLEIFUR: Dr. Alfreds is a great scientist, and he was sent here by the International Scientific Commission.

SIGMUNDUR: Scientist, you say? Very well, but after all, isn't it more important to be a human being?

THORLEIFUR: We Icelanders have become a modern nation, Sigmundur my friend, and have to take part in international cooperation.

SIGMUNDUR: You don't say. Well, I guess I don't know much about these things. But it sure didn't do us any good with this international cooperation when they brought in mink and let them raise hell with our sheep. Well, (*takes snuff*) I know it's all right, or you wouldn't be backing him.

THORLEIFUR (*laughs*): Well, I should hope not, Sigmundur; I should most certainly hope not. (*A new explosion is heard.*)

SIGMUNDUR: They're not exactly noiseless now, are they?

SIGRUN: That's the third blast.

SIGMUNDUR: Well, I'll have to get back and look after old grey-stripes. She might have got scared, and here I'm busy weaning her. (*He leaves.*)

THORLEIFUR (*calls after him*): O.K., Sigmundur, don't let us take you away from your work.

SIGRUN (*rolls over in the grass*): Lord, what a funny fellow he is.

THORLEIFUR: Good old Sigmundur. He's a character, but he's one of my staunchest supporters.

SIGRUN: Oh daddy, you should never have gone into politics.

THORLEIFUR: Why do you say that?

SIGRUN: Oh—I just feel it somehow.

THORLEIFUR: A person cannot refuse to assume the duties and responsibilities of society when he is chosen to do so. Besides, I don't see that we have anything to complain about.

SIGRUN: No, it's not that.

THORLEIFUR: I have worked for various improvements here—

SIGRUN: I remember once—a long time ago—I bawled because the kids teased me. They said you had gotten into the Senate by buying silk bloomers for all the old women in the district. They had read it in some paper or other.

THORLEIFUR (*chuckles*): My opponents have charged me with worse crimes than that!

SIGRUN: But you've never struck back at them so that it did any good. You haven't been tough or hardboiled enough. You're so sweet and cute, daddy. I know you're the nicest man in the world, and yet—it's cheap, somehow, to be so nice. I wish you were just a little bad, then you would understand what I mean.

THORLEIFUR: Yes, Sigrun dear, I do understand. And this may be just the reason why I plan to retire from the political arena.

SIGRUN: Do you really intend to resign?

THORLEIFUR: I recall when I was about to enter upon my political career—then I thought that honor was an unwritten law in public life. Yes, that's how childish my ideas were; but I quickly learned better.

SIGRUN: You must have had disappointments, daddy.

THORLEIFUR: I had great faith in men in those days. I thought, for example, that Valdimar really had the welfare of the people at heart—

SIGRUN: Valdimar, he's repulsive. I've never been able to stand him.

THORLEIFUR: Valdimar is a two-edged sword, that's certain. He's a great hand at cowing his own party members, by good means or bad, all except me—But why should I start raking up all that business? A man just gets himself into a temper.

SIGRUN: And you stood up against him all by yourself.

THORLEIFUR (*bitterly*): Yes, they all ran except me, the milksops!

SIGRUN: Daddy, you really ought to go through with it and resign.

THORLEIFUR (*paints*): Maybe I will, and then devote myself to my art.

SIGRUN: It would be such fun, daddy, if you should get to be a regular artist and painter.

THORLEIFUR (*dignified*): It has always burned in my blood, even though I haven't had time to pursue this calling before now. Sometimes I have been on the verge of secluding myself so I could do nothing but paint—transform all existence into color—paint just like Toulouse-Lautrec.

SIGRUN: You mean the man we saw in the movies?

THORLEIFUR: That was an unforgettable picture. Imagine: he was a wealthy nobleman, but that is all forgotten, while his art and his name as an artist live on.

SIGRUN: Oh, daddy, how thrilling that would be!

THORLEIFUR (*in a lower tone*): Hush. Here comes your mother.

SIGRUN: Yes, daddy, you ought to resign from the Senate and then we could go away somewhere, far far away.

THORLEIFUR: Hush, we mustn't talk any more about this now.

SIGRUN: Just the two of us, somewhere far, far—

THORLEIFUR (*uneasy*): No, no, not now, maybe later—

SIGRUN (*pouting*): Oh, daddy, you always say "later."

(*Madame Karitas comes on stage, dressed in party clothes. She is blonde, superior, and sophisticated in manner.*)

KARITAS: Have you seen anything of Dr. Alfreds?

THORLEIFUR (*paints*): Seems to me I heard some cracks from him just now.

KARITAS (*scornfully*): Oh, indeed, so you heard that. My, how observant you have been getting lately.

(*Sigrun sits with downcast face, as if she were ashamed of her father's performance.*)

THORLEIFUR: Well, I suppose the chap will come back here after a while.

KARITAS (*looks angrily at him*): What a clod you are, Thorleifur. Just think if the doctor should find some valuable metals.

THORLEIFUR (*paints*): Oh, not much danger of that.

KARITAS: Well, just the same, I don't suppose that this institution sends out men at random! What's the name of it again?

THORLEIFUR: The International Metals Investigations Commission, IMIC for short.

KARITAS: Yes, of course, IMIC. (*She looks away with her hand shading her eyes.*) And then all this mystery about the doctor's coming here. A person actually has to read foreign newspapers to keep up on what is happening in this country.

THORLEIFUR (*with some pride*): Oh well, a man has his connections.

KARITAS: As if it weren't a sensation when IMIC sends a specialist here.

THORLEIFUR: Could be, could be. (*Steps back from his painting and points at it.*) But this is more of a sensation for me right now.

(*His wife looks astounded at him, and Sigrun gazes hopefully at him as if she expects a great decision.*)

KARITAS: What?

THORLEIFUR (*elated*): The painting. I feel as if I have succeeded in picturing the majestic calm of the glacier.

KARITAS (*bursts out laughing, scornfully*): My good, dear Thorleifur—now don't begin to imagine that you're an artist, just because you can copy a postcard.

THORLEIFUR (*hurt*): Well, why not? I have the postcard here, well, it's just a little help for me. I've never believed in caricaturing nature, and you can't deny that the beauties of nature are incomparable here.

KARITAS (*peevishly*): As if we hadn't seen it before.

THORLEIFUR (*without letting her rude remarks affect him*): I'll tell you, wife, I was just thinking that it is now sixteen years since I first looked out over this district as its representative in the Senate.

KARITAS (*looking through her spyglass*): Yes, you did succeed in getting elected, Thorleifur dear, but what have you succeeded in since?

THORLEIFUR: Well, I think I can say that I have worked out various improvements for the district; what do you say about the bridge and the road?

KARITAS (*contemptuously*): Senator for sixteen years, and that's all?

THORLEIFUR: I have been the only senator in the party who dared to oppose Valdimar.

KARITAS: And what did you get for your trouble? Nothing except that you are excluded from everything; the end will be that *I* will have to go to Valdimar and straighten things out.

THORLEIFUR (*downcast*): No Karitas, you will never do that.

KARITAS (*coldly*): Why not? (*She turns quickly to her daughter.*) Why are you lolling around like that, child?

(*Sigrun doesn't answer, but looks at her mother defiantly.*)

KARITAS: Why don't you answer?

THORLEIFUR (*pleading*): Please, Sigrun dear, answer your mother.

SIGRUN (*as if in a dream*): Daddy, I can hear the river murmuring under the lava.

THORLEIFUR (*solemnly*): Nature is speaking to herself—but few understand what she is saying.

(*Sigmundur on stage, with a tuft of wool in his hands.*)

SIGMUNDUR: Well, old gray-stripes was plenty fiery. She was a regular old bitch today.

THORLEIFUR: And I see you have been shearing too.

SIGMUNDUR: Yes, I was relieving old Somi of his wool. He was getting so damn lousy with wool, poor fellow, that he could hardly move. (*Looks at the painting.*) And here our good senator has just fixed the glacier on his canvas.

THORLEIFUR: Yes, the majesty of the great wilderness always enthralls me when I come out here.

SIGMUNDUR (*takes a pinch of snuff*): A person can certainly see that.

(*The wife is reconnoitering with the spyglass; acts as if she were on pins and needles.*)

SIGMUNDUR (*looks at the painting, contemplates it from every angle*): It's real artistic, you sure can't deny that. But haven't you ever tried to make a picture of the madam here, she's real dressy.

KARITAS (*quickly*): Thorleifur? Not on your life.

SIGMUNDUR: Well, you know she wouldn't look at all bad, and that reminds me—I sure would like a picture of my old ram Somi. He's a first-class ram, with a big belly and fat all over. Every lamb he sired ran to forty or fifty pound.

THORLEIFUR (*uncomprehending*): Well, that's really quite a bit, isn't it?

SIGMUNDUR: And I've been thinking of sending him to the ram show at Reykjavik this fall.

THORLEIFUR: Yes, you really ought to do that. But tell me now, wasn't it in that canyon over there that old Hroar the pioneer is supposed to have stopped the avalanche?

SIGMUNDUR: Yes, sir, that's the place. That's where he slit up the cat down in the canyon, and with that trick he made the avalanche run over the sands way to the east. (*Points.*)

SIGRUN: But where did he get the cat?

SIGMUNDUR: The *Book of Settlement* doesn't mention that; but I wouldn't mind if he had moved the river, too, while he was at it.

THORLEIFUR (*paints*): Yes, the river has been a great obstacle to traffic in this district.

SIGMUNDUR: And we farmers are going to remember for a long time that our senator squeezed the money for the road out of the Senate.

THORLEIFUR: It was an uphill fight, but it was crowned with success.

SIGMUNDUR: Our blessings on him for that and everything else that issues from him!

KARITAS (*impatiently peering in all directions*): How was that again, Sigmundur, didn't they say the Germans found some ore here before the war?

SIGMUNDUR: Well, I wouldn't be surprised. The soil is rich enough here even though you have to work for what you get. But the best German I know was old man Molkti, who sent us that wonderful rheumatism salve, and you know, the best thing about the salve was that it was the finest cure we had for worms in the lambs. You just stuck a tablespoon of it into their rear ends. But as for ore, well, damned if I know.

KARITAS (*tosses her head*): But of course they didn't have as good instruments as Dr. Alfreds.

SIGMUNDUR: I can't say about that, but the Germans are pretty smart; I've always thought Germany was like a giant eagle that wouldn't let itself be chained.

THORLEIFUR: But civilization was on the brink of destruction when the Nazis nearly defeated England.

SIGMUNDUR: Civilization? (*He takes some snuff.*) Well—I wonder if it wasn't more as if the Insane Asylum had attacked the Old Folks' Home? It makes me think of what Laugi was saying the other day—

KARITAS (*cries out rapturously*): He's coming—he's coming—up the canyon—

THORLEIFUR (*does not show much interest, but looks to where she points*): Well, part of him, anyway.

SIGMUNDUR: Then maybe we can hope that all this clatter of his will stop. I'd better hurry home and get the hired girl to put on a pot of coffee. Maybe there will be a drop for our good senator.

THORLEIFUR: It's always the same old hospitality from you, Sigmundur.

SIGMUNDUR: Oh, we farmers owe you this a thousand times.

KARITAS: My husband never spares himself any effort when it comes to doing things for you people up here.

SIGMUNDUR: Oh, I know that, I sure do.

THORLEIFUR: And yet a man can never do enough. I feel that most strongly whenever I come out here and stand face to face with the glory of the wilderness.

SIGMUNDUR: Well, well. (*He plods away.*)

KARITAS (*calls excitedly*): Hello, Dr. Alfreds!

DR. ALFREDS (*from a distance*): Hello, hello!

KARITAS: How did it come out?

THORLEIFUR: Aren't those instruments of yours pretty heavy? (*Dr. Alfreds on stage with a knapsack on his back and technical equipment of all kinds; he is a young man with glasses, his face grimy, dressed in a leather jacket and high laced boots, with a jockey's cap of large-checked material.*)

DR. ALFREDS: Elephants—herds of elephants.

THORLEIFUR: Surely you didn't see any elephants, Dr. Alfreds?

DR. ALFREDS (*takes off his earphones*): Elephants—yes, I think that's exactly it.

KARITAS (*laughs*): Oh, you're just *so* funny, Dr. Alfreds.

DR. ALFREDS: You must excuse me if I use code words, but that is necessary.

KARITAS: What? Did you find something?

DR. ALFREDS: Sorry—I can say nothing in public before I have reported to Professor Popoff.

KARITAS (*ingratiatingly*): Not even to me? In all confidence?

DR. ALFREDS: The Geiger counter bubbled and shook all the time I was in the canyon.

THORLEIFUR: You don't mean to say that you have found any traces of—uranium?

DR. ALFREDS: Well—I'm afraid I've already said too much. But it is not unreasonable that you who are the senator of this district should be the first man to learn about my discoveries.

KARITAS (*excitedly*): Uranium? Is it really true?

DR. ALFREDS (*quietly*): The Geiger never lies.

THORLEIFUR: If I understand you rightly, Dr. Alfreds, this is a big piece of news?

DR. ALFREDS: But whatever you do, only in confidence, as I said. I think one could say that this is just as remarkable as the find that was made in Madagascar this winter.

THORLEIFUR: Uranium, here in this mountain? I can hardly believe it.

KARITAS (*offended*): But of course, when the doctor says so.

THORLEIFUR (*embarrassed*): Well, I just mean, a man wouldn't have—

DR. ALFREDS: This has come as a surprise even to me. But the samples will of course have to be more thoroughly examined.

THORLEIFUR: Remarkable. Most remarkable indeed.

DR. ALFREDS: But this must remain a secret, for at least a week or ten days, until I have new instructions from Professor Popoff. (*He takes a stone from his back pocket.*) I'm sure the old man would jump with joy if he saw this.

BOTH OF THEM: Is this uranium?

DR. ALFREDS: I took a few crystals with me as samples. (*Hands them over.*)

KARITAS (*steps back*): Oh, no. Aren't they radioactive?

DR. ALFREDS: No danger as they occur in nature's kingdom. I would judge they contain about ten per cent uranium.

KARITAS (*looks at the stone*): Isn't that wonderful? Uranium, fancy that.

THORLEIFUR: So this is how it looks.

KARITAS: Isn't uranium awfully expensive?

DR. ALFREDS: Yes, rather. (*In a didactic tone.*) One may say that the whole future of mankind builds on this, now that the coal beds and the oil wells of the earth are about to dry out. Just one pound of uranium can give us power that corresponds to the burning of twenty million pounds of coal.

THORLEIFUR: Really?

DR. ALFREDS: But ordinary uranium does not undergo fission, and it is a highly complex and difficult process to separate the isotopes, for fission occurs only with uranium 235, and this is found only in the proportion of one out of 140. Or in other words, in order to secure one pound of pure uranium 235, it takes 140 pounds of ordinary uranium–

KARITAS (*open-mouthed*): Heavens above! This is beyond my understanding. (*Sigrun snickers.*)

KARITAS (*quickly turns on the daughter*): Why are you snickering, child?

THORLEIFUR (*who has been looking at the stone*): Oh, I don't think it will do any harm to let her laugh.

KARITAS: How can the girl ever learn good manners when you always encourage her rudeness? (*Turns to Dr. Alfreds.*) I shall have to apologize to you for our daughter, Dr. Alfreds, but she is at that age—

DR. ALFREDS (*makes a courteous gesture*): Oh, my dear madam, it is on the contrary I who ought to ask your forgiveness. I know only too well that we scientists often make fools of ourselves in the eyes of laymen when we try to expound the laws of the physical universe.

KARITAS (*to her daughter*): Go and get my mink cape in the car, and the blue veil. I'm just a little cold.

(*Sigrun gets up and walks off defiantly.*)

THORLEIFUR (*calls to her*): But remember, Sigrun dear, not a word about what Dr. Alfreds has told us in confidence.

SIGRUN (*from afar*): O.K., daddy.

DR. ALFREDS (*listening to the counter again*): Does the farmer here own the land?

THORLEIFUR: Yes, at least in name.

KARITAS: But you have always been signing notes for him; wasn't it for the barn last time?

THORLEIFUR: Hush, I've never complained about that.

DR. ALFREDS (*listens again*): So he owns the land. Yes, indeed. So IMIC should turn directly to him?

THORLEIFUR: Well, that's as you might take it.

(*Karitas whispers eagerly to Thorleifur while Dr. Alfreds is bent over his equipment. Thorleifur nods.*)

THORLEIFUR (*clears his throat and starts to fold up his easel*): I want to tell you, Dr. Alfreds, that once upon a time I introduced a bill to secure support from the government for industrial enterprises. Without any real capital for the support of Icelandic industry we will forever stay in the same rut, here where all investment goes into building houses and churches.

DR. ALFREDS: This is exactly what has struck me most forcibly here, and you are the first influential person I have heard speak with so much vision and understanding of the age we live in.

KARITAS: That's true. The Icelanders are so unimaginative that they think you can't make money on anything except real estate and huckstering.

DR. ALFREDS: These people simply can't afford to leave all the power in their country unbridled; there are millions of kilowatts.

THORLEIFUR: Now the Great Powers will of course race each other to bid for these uranium beds when your results are made public.

DR. ALFREDS (*smiles slyly*): If they aren't too late.

KARITAS: But you're here on behalf of IMIC. (*Makes a sign to her husband, who looks troubled.*)

THORLEIFUR: The wealth of Iceland's nature is first and foremost the property of the people which has pitted its strength against this harsh land for more than a thousand years.

DR. ALFREDS: Naturally, if there were enterprise and capital enough, for this will be a costly undertaking. But as a senator you would of course have access to funds.

THORLEIFUR: (*eagerly*): I have always fought to secure the economic independence of our people in the present and in the future.

(*Dr. Alfreds looks thoughtfully at him for a moment.*)

KARITAS (*brightly*): I tell you, my husband has always been a great idealist.

DR. ALFREDS: That I understand very well. All good scientists are also idealists in their way, true idealists.

THORLEIFUR (*solemnly*): I have always had an unwavering faith in the country, and I shall never evade my responsibility for seeing that my people may enjoy a great and glorious future.

DR. ALFREDS (*looks to the side*): Well, there comes the farmer himself. (*Starts off stage towards him, but Thorleifur taps him on the shoulder and keeps him back.*)

THORLEIFUR: Dr. Alfreds, we need to talk this matter over at leisure and alone. The fellow is unquestionably rather stubborn and peculiar, so that I think it might be most rewarding if you let me handle the negotiations. Above all, we mustn't rush into anything.

DR. ALFREDS: No, of course not.

THORLEIFUR: But as soon as we get to Reykjavik—I'll get you a car right away, and support from the government, and of course we'll pay all your bills. We might work out some real cooperation here.

DR. ALFREDS (*shakes his hand firmly*): I see that you are really a man of our time.

SIGMUNDUR (*comes from the farm*): And what does science say?

THORLEIFUR: Science? (*Laughing.*) Bless you, no one can get to the bottom of that any more than the virgin birth and the Holy Trinity.

DR. ALFREDS: My investigations are only in their infancy yet—

SIGMUNDUR: Well, well.

KARITAS: So, Sigmundur, we were just going to drink a toast to the marvellous beauties of nature here at Hofstadir.

DR. ALFREDS: The place is incomparable.

SIGMUNDUR (*with his snuffbox*): Beauties of nature, eh? Well, the pastures aren't too bad here when the weather is right. I didn't start feeding the sheep hay until late in Advent and I stopped long before the first Summer Day.

DR. ALFREDS (*confused*): What? Did you stop?

SIGMUNDUR: Yes, you bet.

THORLEIFUR (*takes out glasses and a bottle*): Now we're going to skoal all together. (*Fills the glasses.*)

KARITAS (*cheerily*): Sigmundur, our friend, we're overcome with admiration.

THORLEIFUR: We shall drink a toast for the industriousness, the contentment, and the honesty which characterizes the labors of our farmers and their families. As the poet says, "The farmer is the pillar of agriculture, and agriculture is the pillar of the nation." Skoal, a toast to both!

KARITAS AND DR. ALFREDS (*seconding*): Skoal!

SIGMUNDUR: Well, I don't know what you call industriousness down there in Reykjavik, but for my part I think idleness is man's greatest curse, and I often think about how badly it all turned out for Alli at Gil, a promising lad—I really do—so careful he was with the cattle and such a handy fellow with the scythe, but now they say he's tooting a trumpet in some dance hall. Pfui!

THORLEIFUR: Very true, very true indeed. (*To Dr. Alfreds.*) Farmer Sigmundur is one of my staunchest supporters, descended from a fine old family. I will never forget the blessed Sigthrud who traced our family connections.

KARITAS: She was such a delightful woman.

SIGMUNDUR (*strokes his beard*): Well, I won't say whose family I think is the most remarkable, but this I do know, that

my grandfather Simon the Strong laid low the Iranes monster which had long been a terror to the people.
(*Karitas laughs.*)

DR. ALFREDS: The Iranes monster, just so, that's extraordinary.

THORLEIFUR: A regular viking that Simon.

SIGMUNDUR: Yes, a viking. And he got a medal for it which now is kept in one of the safes in the Capitol.

THORLEIFUR: Yes, that's right. But what I was going to say—hm, Sigmundur my friend—Dr. Alfreds took a few samples down there in the canyon. All his wisdom is in rock, you know. (*Laughs.*)

SIGMUNDUR: Well, I won't miss the rocks. I've carried plenty of them out of the meadow here. But I don't like all these scientific blasts around here. I could lose the value of my ewes in all the bedlam.

DR. ALFREDS: I'm very sorry, but it was quite unavoidable.

SIGMUNDUR: Of course I don't understand all this science business, but I wouldn't be unhappy if they put water in all the gunpowder, for it's real nasty the way they seem to be using it abroad, according to what I hear. (*They laugh.*) But won't you please come over to the farm now, though there isn't much to offer better folks.

KARITAS: Thank you so much, Sigmundur. (*She takes her bag and leaves the stage.*)

THORLEIFUR: Thank you. (*He picks up his easel.*)

SIGMUNDUR: Shouldn't I carry something for the good senator? (*Thorleifur hands him the easel.*)

THORLEIFUR: Thank you. Maybe you'll take the easel and the paint box. (*Leaves.*)

DR. ALFREDS (*collects his equipment*): There is plenty of grass here for the sheep and such?

SIGMUNDUR: Oh yes, but the stock gets pretty slim in winter, and at Runolf's place they got a sickness of the sheep (*They leave the stage.*) but they tell a story about the lambs—

(*For a moment the stage is empty, then the daughter comes*

from the left with the cape on her arm and the blue veil in her hand. She looks down and picks up an instrument which Dr. Alfreds has forgotten. Dr. Alfreds comes running.)

SIGRUN (*hands him the instrument*): Did you forget this?

DR. ALFREDS: Yes, thank you so much. (*Is about to leave.*)

SIGRUN (*stops*): Dr. Alfreds.

DR. ALFREDS: Yes? (*He stops and turns to her.*)

SIGRUN: You don't think I'm a child just because I got to laughing a while ago?

DR. ALFREDS: Heavens no. Quite the contrary, you are a lovely young lady.

SIGRUN: Mama always thinks I'm still a child. But I am really quite experienced.

DR. ALFREDS (*somewhat puzzled*): I see?

SIGRUN: I've smoked marijuana! Do *you* have any dope?

DR. ALFREDS (*astounded*): Dope?

SIGRUN: I want some kind of exciting drug, something really exciting.

DR. ALFREDS: You mustn't talk like that.

SIGRUN: You won't believe me. But I intend to do something awful, something perfectly terrible, something that nobody has ever done before. I just don't know yet what it should be.

KARITAS (*comes noisily back on the stage*): What is this, child? Why are you so poky in bringing my minks? (*She puts on the cape.*)

DR. ALFREDS: I forgot this instrument here. (*Leaves.*)

KARITAS (*sharply*): The coffee is waiting, Dr. Alfreds. Come, little one. You'll get fresh milk right from the cow at Sigmundur's place!

CURTAIN

Act II
Scene 1

A few days later in Reykjavik. In the senator's home. Up stage a roomy hallway with hunting gear and rifles on the walls, pictures of ducks, grouse, and fish, and a set of reindeer antlers over one door. Tables and benches in rustic style; a telephone on a small table. Wide staircase leading up to the next floor.

On this side of the hallway a large living room, comfortably furnished and decorated. Landscape paintings on the walls, with Thorleifur's painting from the first act in an especially prominent place. Doors leading offstage left and right. When the doorbell rings, no one walks through the living room.

Sigmundur sits in an easy chair with the snuff box in his hands, waiting. He has left his knapsack and a little bag in the hall; both of them look very much out of place.

Thorleifur comes into the room. He is noticeably livelier and more energetic in manner than he was in Act I. Confidence and self-satisfaction emanate from him. He is dressed in a sports outfit.

THORLEIFUR: I hope you will forgive me, Sigmundur, for making you wait. How are you, anyway, old man? It's wonderful to see you. (*Claps him on the back.*)
SIGMUNDUR: Greetings! Wonderful to see *you*, senator! Everything's just fine.

THORLEIFUR: Kristin, will you bring the coffee, please?

KRISTIN (*in the hall, through the open door*): Yes, it's all ready.

THORLEIFUR: And you have just come to town? (*Sits down.*)

SIGMUNDUR: I got here this morning with Laugi.

THORLEIFUR: And what's new?

SIGMUNDUR: What's new? Well, I heard on the radio that there's been a big flood in Japan. I reckon it mighta washed away the whole business here in Reykjavik, even including the Capitol. Ain't nothin' can stand up against a big wave like that. (*Kristin comes in with the coffee.*) But the Jap's tough, that's what I've always said.

THORLEIFUR (*who has scarcely listened to Sigmundur*): Thank you, Kristin, that's just fine. Help yourself, Sigmundur. Have a roll.

SIGMUNDUR: Thank you.

THORLEIFUR: Flood, you say. Yes, there have been lots of floods.

SIGMUNDUR: And at that, the Japs have to pay through the nose to support the Emperor in his palace, on top of all they pay out for the common welfare.

THORLEIFUR: Yes, indeed. Yes, you're right. (*He turns to Sigmundur.*) But if I might change the subject—I sent you a message about the note. The people in the bank weren't very happy about extending it.

SIGMUNDUR: Now what in the devil . . . ? I had understood—

THORLEIFUR: Well, Sigmundur, these are difficult times. The herring seems to be failing us, and it looks as if the government is going to have to devaluate the krona.

SIGMUNDUR: Devaluate? Is our economy in such a mess?

THORLEIFUR: Somehow they will have to protect the income of our people.

SIGMUNDUR: And there can't be any mistake in their bookkeeping?

THORLEIFUR: No, you can be assured that everyone is doing his very utmost.

SIGMUNDUR: And so they have to devaluate? But if I may ask: what could I do when my farm burned down? And all without insurance? Could I devaluate my debts?

THORLEIFUR: Now, now, Sigmundur, let's take it calmly. If they do devaluate, you farmers are the ones who lose the least. And I reckon a fellow might give you a hand if the banks should fail us.

SIGMUNDUR: It's hardly advisable to add to what I already owe you.

THORLEIFUR: Oh, don't worry about it, my friend.

SIGMUNDUR: Well, I know this, that if it hadn't been for your good heart, I would have gone to hell a long time ago with all my household.

THORLEIFUR: I have never considered it anything more than my simple duty to help you as much as I could, Sigmundur.

SIGMUNDUR: Your big heart has always been the same, and I don't think there's anyone in our country who can equal you. In my humble opinion, I want to say that I think you'd adorn the highest throne this country could give you.

THORLEIFUR (*laughs*): You don't say. Here I've made out a note so that we can let the fellows in the bank go hang. (*Hands him a document.*)

SIGMUNDUR (*puts on his iron-rimmed glasses and reads, then lays the paper down*): Uh-huh. That's right. Now I don't understand this at all. You haven't asked for any security?

THORLEIFUR (*gets up and rests his hand on Sigmundur's shoulder*): Your name is sufficient security for me, Sigmundur my friend. (*Picks up the note.*) And here is the note all paid.

SIGMUNDUR (*leans back in amazement*): Oh, but this is just too much!

THORLEIFUR: I just wanted to show you what complete and unconditional confidence I have in you.

SIGMUNDUR: Well, I've often said to Laugi that trust is the cornerstone everything else has to be built on, but that anyone should trust me that far is more than I would ever have believed.

THORLEIFUR: You certainly deserve it.

SIGMUNDUR: And I sign here?

THORLEIFUR: Right here. (*Sigmundur writes.*)

SIGMUNDUR: A fellow can't deny that his head is never free so long as he owes another, and there's nothing like these little debts to take the starch out of a man.

THORLEIFUR: But in that case, why not solve the whole problem in a simple way?

SIGMUNDUR: What do you mean?

THORLEIFUR: You know, I have often said to myself when I have been out there with you that there is no place on earth I would rather have a summer home than on Vordufell. From there one can gaze far out over the mountain landscape, and those mountains—when the evening sun tints them with gold—they are unforgettable.

SIGMUNDUR (*glances at the new painting*): Yes, your picture tells its story.

THORLEIFUR: And therefore it just occurred to me that you might sell me the mountain.

SIGMUNDUR: What? Vordufell?

THORLEIFUR: I would like to make forests grow there, clothe the mountain as it was in the pioneer days of our first settlers. The bitter truth is that it is we who have failed our country, not the country that has failed us.

SIGMUNDUR: Yes, but Vordufell has gone with the Hofstadir farm from the beginning of our history. We couldn't get along without those pastures.

THORLEIFUR: Unless maybe you would sell me the whole farm?

SIGMUNDUR (*startled*): Now I'm sure you're just teasing me.

THORLEIFUR: No. I'm serious, Sigmundur, very serious. Isolated farms are constantly falling in price, and it's quite certain

that you won't get out from under your debts very soon
unless something is done. But I'm ready to make you so good
an offer that you can get along and even improve your
position. I think you yourself hinted you might like to stop
farming and move to Reykjavik for good.

SIGMUNDUR: Well, I have talked sometimes about having to
leave, since this trek to the city never seems to stop. But I
still think it's healthier to wrestle with your lot in life, as a
man should, than to run away from the fight. And I wonder
if poor Joseph is any happier since he left to work in that
kitchen than he was when he lived at Upper Holt. Even
though he can wave bills in your face now, the poor devil.

THORLEIFUR: You aren't running away from the battle, Sigmundur, just because you choose a worthier role in life, one
that corresponds better to your skill and experience than to
be forever slaving away in the hopeless and solitary struggle
with the soil. I haven't brought up this subject without a
purpose, for right now you might have a chance to take over
a position which it seems to me would suit you brilliantly.
(*Pats his shoulder.*) Yes, it would suit you brilliantly.

SIGMUNDUR (*uncomprehending*): A position? A position for
me? Well, I'll be blasted—

THORLEIFUR: You know old man Boas, the senate caretaker—

SIGMUNDUR: Oh, sure. I've known him—he's from Loustadir
farm. He comes of the Viking River family. Torfhildur at
Skarfafell was a half-sister of my grandmother—

THORLEIFUR: Right. So he is. And it's been decided that Boas is
going to give up his position this coming winter.

SIGMUNDUR: Fine old gentleman, and well has he served his
country.

THORLEIFUR: Yes. (*Sits down.*) But what would you say to
taking over after him?

SIGMUNDUR (*jumps up, makes a full turn*): Me? No, you just
can't be serious.

THORLEIFUR: Dead serious. You're just the man for this job. Trustworthy, hardworking, reliable.

SIGMUNDUR: Well, I don't think it's any great virtue for a man to be faithful to what's been entrusted him. But to step into the shoes of old Boas. (*Shakes his head.*) No, that just won't do.

THORLEIFUR: You'll make it all right, no danger of that.

SIGMUNDUR (*can't conceal his pleasure*): I can just see myself in the senate with all those statesmen—a man isn't used to such elegant folks.

KARITAS (*comes into the room*): Well, if it isn't my friend Sigmundur! (*Greets him with unusual warmth.*)

SIGMUNDUR (*rises*): Good evening, ma'am.

THORLEIFUR: Well, Sigmundur, we'll just let this idea simmer a while, and then we'll talk it over this fall and settle it before the Senate meets. (*Sigmundur is about to say something, but Thorleifur does not give him a chance and pats him on his shoulder in a fatherly way.*) It would certainly be a great honor for your countrymen out there if you get this position, and you are more than welcome to it. Don't worry about it, and have confidence in me. (*Turns to his wife.*) You see, this is our new Senate caretaker.

KARITAS: You don't say so! Senate caretaker? May I congratulate you? How delightful!

SIGMUNDUR (*completely confused*): Well now, I really don't know, to tell you the truth.

THORLEIFUR: I am really looking forward to introducing you to the cabinet members and the presidents of the Senate, and I am positive that they will think I have made a good choice. It is not unfitting that the Senate caretaker should first and foremost be a true representative of the yeomanry of our country, whose solid culture has been the torchlight of the Icelandic people for more than a thousand winters. (*Sigmundur tries to interrupt, but Thorleifur does not let him speak.*

He hands him the note.) And there you have the note fully
paid so that you have no more worries about the bank.

SIGMUNDUR (*stammers*): Thanks, but I'm—I'm completely
bowled over.

THORLEIFUR: Oh, it's nothing at all. It's a pleasure to know that
you will get a well-deserved reward for all your faith and
confidence in years past. (*Rests his hand on his shoulder.*)
But as I have said, we'll make the final settlement in the fall.
You will excuse me now, for I'm going salmon fishing with a
friend of mine. You'll stay here tonight of course. Don't you
have some business to take care of while you're in town?

SIGMUNDUR: Thank you. I guess I did have some errands. I
mustn't forget that crowbar Gisli asked me to get.

KARITAS: You know, Sigmundur, that our house will always be
open to all you men from Nupa.

THORLEIFUR (*chuckling, as he gathers his equipment for the
trip*): And not least when they are about to become officials
of the august Senate. (*Leaves.*)

SIGMUNDUR (*half to himself*): I really was surprised about old
Boas—

KARITAS: But how about it, didn't you just get engaged? I
thought we heard something about that?

SIGMUNDUR: Oh no, no. That was Laugi and Ranka who have
been working for me. They got engaged the other day.

KARITAS (*laughs*): And then you'll be next.

SIGMUNDUR: No, no. I haven't been chasing skirts so far. There
isn't much of that kind out where we live anyway.

KARITAS: Oh, I wonder if you don't keep a pretty sharp look-
out. (*Laughs.*) Yes, indeed. (*Kristin comes to the door.*)
Kristin, will you please show Sigmundur to the guest room
upstairs. Didn't you have some baggage?

(*Sigmundur absentmindedly hums to himself*).

KARITAS: Sigmundur?

SIGMUNDUR (*jumps up*): Yes, my saddle bag and the little

suitcase are out front here. (*Goes out and Kristin after him.*)

(*Thorleifur comes back in, is making ready for the trip.*)

KARITAS: And what did the fellow say?

THORLEIFUR: It will all go according to plan, have no fear.

KARITAS: How well you can handle these men, queer birds they are.

THORLEIFUR (*satisfied with himself*): This is because I have intuition. I have always had intuition.

KARITAS: But have you seen the newspapers?

THORLEIFUR: Well, what about it?

KARITAS: It's all about Dr. Alfreds.

THORLEIFUR: What's that, wife?

KARITAS (*picks up a paper*): Look here. (*Reads.*) "Specialist commissioned by IMIC finds rich uranium deposits in Iceland. Dr. Alfreds refuses to answer questions, but prophesies a brilliant future for the nation. An atomic age is about to dawn on the Hermit of the Atlantic."

THORLEIFUR (*grabs the paper from her*): Let me see (*Reads avidly.*)

KARITAS (*takes another paper*): And here. (*Reads.*) "Dr. Alfreds awakens the Mountain Maid from her thousand years of sleep"—(*Thorleifur seizes the paper.*)

THORLEIFUR: Well, I'll be—

KARITAS: And here. (*Reads.*) "The Icelandic people hail the victory of science." And here's a big picture of him. (*Seizes another paper and reads.*) "You rode into our courtyard on your white charger."

THORLEIFUR (*glancing at one paper after the other*): It's all right. He just says "somewhere in Iceland", nothing more. "Somewhere in Iceland", that's just the way they talked during the war.

KARITAS: He's so clever. "Somewhere in Iceland". That's really smart of him.

THORLEIFUR: But in any case don't let *our* man get a peek at the
newspapers. That is unnecessary. (*Tosses them aside.*) We
just have to keep the place a secret until this fall.

KARITAS: But my darling, do you really think Valdimar doesn't
have his connections? All he needs to do, for that matter, is
to call the research lab at the University.

THORLEIFUR: But they don't know *where* the ore is. (*Laughs.*)
This time I really hold the trump card. (*At that moment the
door bell rings.*)

KRISTIN (*comes down the stairs in the hall, opens the outside
door*): Come right in.

KARITAS (*hesitating at the door, remembers she is not made
up*): Wonder if that could be Dr. Alfreds?

THORLEIFUR: No, it's Valdimar. Best he doesn't see you. I'll say
you're taking a bath.

(*Valdimar is heard booming his greeting, comes into the
hall. Thorleifur takes his wife by the arm, pushes her away
from the door, but does not open it. Valdimar is white-
haired, vigorous, and roguish in manner.*)

VALDIMAR (*in the hall to Kristin*): You haven't been swimming
in the 200-meter race, have you, miss?

KRISTIN (*outside*): No, not yet.

VALDIMAR: But you really should, you know, for your nation
and for my sake. (*Pinches her thigh, she squeals a little and
slaps him.*) And remember to let *me* know first so I can get a
chance to see you in a swimming suit. (*Pinches her again and
laughs.*)

THORLEIFUR (*opens the door out to the hall*): Well, Valdimar!
Hello, and how are you, anyway?

VALDIMAR: Greetings, old man. (*They embrace and come into
the room.*)

THORLEIFUR: It's always a pleasure to see you.

VALDIMAR: As it says in the *Edda,* "A brotherless back is bare
indeed." (*Laughs.*)

THORLEIFUR: Find yourself a place to sit. A cigar?

VALDIMAR: Thanks. (*Sits down.*) Well, old boy, it's really been a year and a day since we talked together.

THORLEIFUR: Right you are. And now I've just about decided to retire from politics.

(*Valdimar lights his cigar and gives Thorleifur a light.*)

VALDIMAR: So? Is it your stomach?

THORLEIFUR (*surprised*): My stomach?

VALDIMAR: Yes, old Vardi was talking about some stomach ailment. He said you didn't show up after the last joint session.

THORLEIFUR (*gloomily*): No, I didn't show up.

VALDIMAR: Nothing at all with your stomach then?

THORLEIFUR: Just a little short on hydrochloric acid is all.

VALDIMAR (*chortles*): I understand. But then every man has to fly according to his feathers. Or rather, some come plunking down to earth without feathers and don't exactly make an eagle's flight. (*Laughs.*) Well, well, I'm glad you aren't ill.

THORLEIFUR: How about yourself?

VALDIMAR: O, what is man but a reed. (*Looks around in the room.*) But what's this: isn't that a new picture, or am I mistaken?

THORLEIFUR (*wishes to minimize it*): Oh yes, I slapped it together this spring, just for fun.

VALDIMAR: And where is it from?

THORLEIFUR: Oh, it's sort of imaginary.

VALDIMAR (*pretends to be surprised*): You have artistic skill, man.

THORLEIFUR: Heavens no, I don't take this kind of thing seriously.

VALDIMAR: But you really should. I mean it. Old political hacks like me aren't good for anything but to keep struggling as long as we can. But art lives. "Ars longa, vita brevis," as they say. Yes, even if they cut off their ears like this crazy guy, what was his name?

THORLEIFUR: Oh no, that's not for me. That's not my calling in life.

VALDIMAR: Calling, you say? Praise your good fortune. It's just the inferior artists who think they have a calling. The true artist is always modest. There is so much depth, such unusual depth and self-immersion in this picture. You really owe it to the nation to make use of your gifts.

THORLEIFUR: No, no, it doesn't amount to anything; and I'll have to put it aside now.

VALDIMAR: I've just had an idea. Now listen to me. Iceland has been given the privilege of appointing the chairman of an international commission for the extermination of beasts of prey, with headquarters in the Hague. We have plenty of experience with the minks now, don't you think? The vice chairmen will be from Pakistan and Nicaragua.

THORLEIFUR: And how does this concern me?

VALDIMAR: But don't you see, man! This is the ideal position for you. With headquarters in the Hague you would have a marvellous chance to study the old Dutch masters. (*Thorleifur is sunk in thought.*) A great honor for the country—it would correspond fully to an ambassador's rank—income non-taxable—I see Karitas in my mind's eye as an ambassador's wife in Central Europe—a magnificent and unique opportunity. I'm convinced that with this beginning you will wind up as Secretary-General of the United Nations.

THORLEIFUR (*looks up*): No, Valdimar, I reject the offer.

VALDIMAR: Think it over for a while. You don't get an offer like this every day. If only I had been younger—

THORLEIFUR (*gets up and brings his fist down on the table*): No, I reject the offer.

VALDIMAR: Don't be childish now, Thorleifur. You're always inclined to be a little hasty.

THORLEIFUR: No, Valdimar. I value your offer very much indeed and thank you for the confidence you have shown me. But, as I said, I reject the offer.

VALDIMAR: And what do you think Karitas will say about this?

THORLEIFUR: She entrusts such decisions to me.

VALDIMAR: Call her in anyway.

THORLEIFUR: She's in her bath.

VALDIMAR: The rosy-fingered goddess of dawn rises from her depths, ah yes. As old Odysseus put it. I thought you would have set greater store by all she has done for you.

THORLEIFUR: And so I do. I value her very highly.

VALDIMAR: I never had a better secretary, never had anyone as quick and clever. There's nobody like her.

THORLEIFUR: No, I know that.

VALDIMAR: I remember how she wrinkled up her nose when I pointed out to her what a promising young man you were.

THORLEIFUR (*astounded*): You did?

VALDIMAR: You were a pretty miserable speaker in those days.

THORLEIFUR: I had too much to say.

VALDIMAR: Colic, I suspect. Well, you got over it pretty successfully, but without Karitas—that's something else again. Doesn't she still go over your speeches?

THORLEIFUR (*angrily*): Valdimar, I thought you had learned that you can't talk this way to me.

VALDIMAR (*laughs*): I think I can usually recognize her style. (*Sigmundur meanwhile comes down the stairs and knocks on the door.*)

THORLEIFUR (*jumps up and calls out*): Come in.

SIGMUNDUR: I just got to thinking about this mountain—

THORLEIFUR (*interrupts him quickly*): Yes indeed, Sigmundur, we had better talk about that later, not now. (*Pushes him out the door.*) Right now there is a visitor here, and I am just about to leave.

SIGMUNDUR: I was just going to—

THORLEIFUR: Yes, later, not now. (*Closes the door. Sigmundur stands a few moments in the hall, mumbles something to himself, takes some snuff, puts on his visored cap, and goes upstairs again.*)

VALDIMAR: You certainly slammed that door right on his nose.

THORLEIFUR: Well, you know, the usual squawk, just when a fellow has other fish to fry.

VALDIMAR: Are you referring to uranium fish?

THORLEIFUR (*surprised*): Who says so?

VALDIMAR: Now now, you might as well pull your uranium man out of the icebox, so we can stop playing hide-and-go-seek.

THORLEIFUR: I doubt that I know any more about Dr. Alfreds than you, Valdimar.

VALDIMAR (*chuckles*): "Somewhere in Iceland"—that was pretty smart. Reminds me of the good old war days.

THORLEIFUR: I want to tell you one thing, Valdimar: when a man gets too far into the woods, it ends with his going out again on the other side.

VALDIMAR (*laughs*): Yes, Little Red Ridinghood ought not to venture in by herself. But if you, old man, think you are going to play the wolf, I refuse categorically to play the grandmother, you understand?

THORLEIFUR: I don't trim my sails to every wind.

VALDIMAR: If you have any sails left.

THORLEIFUR: What I do on my own time is surely my own business.

VALDIMAR: Unless it turns out to be other people's business too.

THORLEIFUR: If you imagine you can give me orders, you are badly mistaken.

VALDIMAR: Gingerbread boy.

THORLEIFUR: You can mock me all you wish. Go right ahead. For you nothing is sacred. You wouldn't stop at anything to get your way, not even a crime.

VALDIMAR (*starts to rise*): This is too much—

THORLEIFUR (*pounds the table*): Yes, not even a crime. You are undermining the foundations of democracy by making the legislature superior to the executive power. You don't care about the division of power, but want to concentrate it all in the hands of a few. You're heading straight in the direction of a dictatorship.

VALDIMAR (*gets up*): Well, if I don't seem to see wings growing on you, my boy.

THORLEIFUR (*backs away from him*): I had decided to withdraw from politics. It seemed to me that the struggle for the rights of the people and for the ideals of democracy was so hopeless. But now I find after all that it is my duty to fight on, and never give in. . . .

VALDIMAR: Well, well, so little Karitas has been mean to him lately. We men are always so vulnerable to female whims. That's our Achilles' heel. (*Laughs.*) But you are repaying me badly, my friend, if you take it out on this innocent old bystander. It doesn't suit your style to make faces and wave your sword at me. (*He pats Thorleifur on the shoulder.*)

THORLEIFUR (*jerks away*): Stop this comedy. You think I can't see through you.

VALDIMAR: Now I'm beginning to think that your shortage of hydrochloric acid is really serious. (*Goes to the door.*) But I repeat: come to me when you're tired of this strutting. (*Turns at the door.*) Please give my regards to our darling Karitas. Good-bye.

THORLEIFUR (*cries out*): You are like a corrosive acid. You have never understood ideals, never proposed any exalted tasks for land and people. No, you are hollow and rotten, while I have never failed the ideals of my youth—no, never.

VALDIMAR (*at the door*): Good-bye!

KARITAS (*comes running in*): Thorleifur, what's going on here anyway?

THORLEIFUR (*pounds the table*): Never, never!

KARITAS: What, has Valdimar left? (*She is dressed up and attractive.*)

THORLEIFUR (*doesn't answer at once, is occupied with his thoughts, and bursts out laughing*): He's scared, Valdimar is. He's scared, shaking in his pants.

KARITAS: Does he know about the company? I mean Icelandic Resources, Inc.? And about Dr. Alfreds?

THORLEIFUR: Not for sure. But he suspects something. And then that god damn Sigmundur had to come storming down here. That was a big help.

KARITAS: What did Valdimar say?

THORLEIFUR: He offered me a post abroad.

KARITAS: And you said?

THORLEIFUR: Do you think I don't see through him? Now at last when I have a stranglehold on him. No, I should say not.

KARITAS: A good post?

THORLEIFUR: What difference does that make? The old fox will soon find out who is the stronger. But he thought he was going to have it like Caesar and send his rivals far away from Rome as consuls. (*Throws out his hands in a wide gesture.*) But *I* will soon have conquered Rome.

KARITAS: Didn't he ask about me? I should really have said hello to him.

(*Just then the doorbell rings. Karitas hurries to the door. Thorleifur stands before a large ornate mirror and expands his chest.*)

KARITAS (*in a loud voice*): Well, Dr. Alfreds!

DR. ALFREDS: Hello, madame Karitas. What a pleasure to see you!

KARITAS: Same to you, doctor. Won't you come in?

(*Dr. Alfreds is dressed in a light-colored summer suit, is bareheaded, and wears a red carnation in his lapel. He kisses the lady's hand in a gallant manner.*)

THORLEIFUR (*greets him with enthusiasm*): John, come in, man. (*Picks up the document and points to the daily papers which have been laid aside.*) The city is in an uproar.

DR. ALFREDS (*modestly*): Yes, they were just a trifle curious at the research laboratory.

THORLEIFUR: And you certainly gave the newspapermen a clever answer.

DR. ALFREDS: Oh, in my position you learn not to let those chaps stick their noses into everything. I told them I would turn journalist only when I entered my second childhood. But they left that out in their interviews. (*They all laugh.*)

KARITAS: It was very clever of you to say "somewhere in Iceland."

DR. ALFREDS (*mysteriously*): Never say too much: that's my golden rule.

THORLEIFUR: And now we'll have a directors' meeting after the weekend.

DR. ALFREDS: A telegram arrived this A.M. from Professor Pop-off.

THORLEIFUR: And what did he say?

DR. ALFREDS: IMIC will of course pay for all preparatory research—if we have the capital. (*He pulls out the telegram.*)

THORLEIFUR: Splendid. But we can't publish any of this before everything is properly prepared. I'll settle the contract with Sigmundur this fall—that's clear. Investors will be very grateful for a chance to buy into the enterprise. But right now I don't intend to have Valdimar and his gang in on it.

DR. ALFREDS: The drills will be coming as soon as the bank has transferred funds to my men. (*Pulls a telegram out of his pocket.*) Here's the telegram.

THORLEIFUR (*looks hastily at it*): No trouble with that.

KARITAS: But don't you send the telegrams in code?

DR. ALFREDS: Of course, madame.

THORLEIFUR (*laughs*): Elephants, herds of elephants. (*Returns the telegram to Dr. Alfreds.*)

KARITAS: I still don't believe that you can fool old Valdimar.

THORLEIFUR: At last he missed the bus. (*Laughs.*) I'll send him a jar of jam for consolation. Now there will be a greater revolution in the industrial life of this country than ever before.

DR. ALFREDS: We scientists pin great hopes on the future of atomic power.

KARITAS: It's just wonderful!

THORLEIFUR (*puts his arm around Dr. Alfreds' shoulder, speaks seriously and with feeling*): All this I owe first and foremost to you.

DR. ALFREDS (*courteously*): No, not to me, but to science.

THORLEIFUR: You shall have no reason to regret our cooperation. Well, I think I had better start. Hilmar and I are going out fishing. (*Shakes his head knowingly.*) Even that could have its significance.

DR. ALFREDS (*alone with the wife*): My dear madame, I wonder if I could make a long distance call to the United States from here?

KARITAS: To the United States? For heaven's sakes, it's as if the world has shrunk since you came here, Dr. Alfreds.

DR. ALFREDS (*gallantly*): On the contrary, it seems to me rather as if it has expanded since I came to know you, madame. But this is just a little call to my dear Barbara Hutton. I mustn't deprive her of her Thursday call.

KARITAS (*deeply impressed*): Barbara Hutton—the richest woman in the world!

DR. ALFREDS: Oh, bless you—even so, she doesn't hesitate to let me pick up her check, most recently in the Stork Club—

KARITAS: The Stork Club—that's where I've always wanted to go.

DR. ALFREDS: It's not a bad place. But it's a shame the way that scoundrel Porfirio behaved last time.

KARITAS: Porfirio—isn't that her husband?

DR. ALFREDS: Porfirio Rubirosa—she can't move without his watching her. And somehow—I've never trusted him. He doesn't inspire confidence, or what was it old people used to say? Perfidious. (*Laughs.*) That's the word—just too perfidious!

KARITAS: How wonderfully well you speak our language.

DR. ALFREDS: I can never forget what I have once learned. (*Looks around.*) But as I was saying—the telephone—if you will excuse me—

KARITAS: Yes, of course. Right here, in the hall. (*Directs him to it, closes the door.*)

THORLEIFUR (*has been searching the rooms with some irritation*): Wife, where is my tackle box? I've mislaid it somewhere.

KARITAS (*looks around, turns towards him*): Listen, did you know that he is a friend of Barbara Hutton and Porfirio Rubirosa?

THORLEIFUR (*hunting*): And who the devil are they?

KARITAS: Please, Thorleifur, why do you always have to talk like a clod?

THORLEIFUR (*finds the box*): Here it is. Well, so I'm off.

KARITAS: But Thorleifur—

THORLEIFUR (*ready to leave*): Now what?

KARITAS: Well, it's about Dr. Alfreds. I really can't receive him when you aren't home. Won't you tell him so?

THORLEIFUR: How silly. Why can't he drop in? I'll be back tomorrow night.

KARITAS: I don't know. But I feel that he always looks at me in such a strange way.

THORLEIFUR: He's a man of the world. But beyond that—no, darling, don't act like that.

KARITAS (*kittenish*): Have you stopped being worried about me?

THORLEIFUR: I trust you. You know I have always trusted you.

KARITAS: Yes, I know that. And there's no one else but you.

THORLEIFUR (*chuckling*): You do believe in me now?

KARITAS (*looking at his hands*): But there's one thing I'd like to ask of you.

THORLEIFUR (*uneasy, is about to pick up his bag*): And what's that?

KARITAS: It is that you must remember to clip your finger nails.

THORLEIFUR (*laughs and kisses her*): You're priceless.

SIGRUN (*enters, starts when she sees them so loving, speaks almost sharply*): Daddy.

THORLEIFUR (*half starts, while his wife leans against him and looks inimically at her daughter*): Yes, I'll have to hurry now.

SIGRUN: Daddy—take me with you.

THORLEIFUR: But, my dear, I'm just rambling up the Salmon River with Hilmar, and I'll be back tomorrow night.

SIGRUN (*with deep emphasis*): Take me with you, or else—

KARITAS: What kind of a whim is this?

THORLEIFUR (*disturbed*): Or else what, Sigrun dear? Is something up?

SIGRUN (*turns gloomily away from him*): No, you never understand anything.

THORLEIFUR (*gives up, helplessly*): Well, well then.

KARITAS: She's half spoiled already by your coddling.

THORLEIFUR (*catches sight of the painting*): Oh, while I think of it (*Goes over to the painting and takes it down from the wall.*)

KARITAS: What are you doing with the painting?

THORLEIFUR: Sigrun dear, won't you take it up to your room? You can have it.

SIGRUN (*turns slowly and looks him full in the face*): No dad. I don't want it, not now.

THORLEIFUR: You don't want the painting? (*With an angry gesture.*) O.K., do what you wish with it. Give it to Sigmundur. But I don't want to see it again. (*Throws out his chest.*) Now I won't deviate one hair's breadth from my course— (*Leaves the painting on the floor. Dr. Alfreds comes in.*)

THORLEIFUR (*kisses his wife*): Good-bye, my love. (*Strokes his daughter lightly on the shoulder and makes ready to kiss her cheek, but she turns away.*) Good-bye, Sigrun dear. (*Turns to Dr. Alfreds.*) And good-bye to you, John.

DR. ALFREDS: Have a good trip, and good fishing.

THORLEIFUR: Thank you, and get my wife to find you a cigar. So long. (*Leaves.*)

DR. ALFREDS (*gives the daughter some conspicuous glances while he is waving goodbye*): Good-bye.

KARITAS (*who has noticed the glances, speaks sharply*): Have you taken your cod-liver oil, my dear?

SIGRUN: No, I don't feel like it now, I have such a hangover.

KARITAS: How you do talk, child. Dr. Alfreds, I hope you don't take her seriously.

DR. ALFREDS: Don't all women say the opposite of what they mean?

KARITAS (*angrily to her daughter*): Now please stop hanging around here. Why don't you find something to do?

SIGRUN: I'm going.

KARITAS (*in an admonishing tone*): And be sure to take that cod-liver oil.

(*The daughter doesn't dare disobey and leaves.*)

DR. ALFREDS: What a pleasure it would have been to know you, madame, when you were her age.

KARITAS: What do you mean? That I have grown so old?

DR. ALFREDS: No no, quite the opposite. I mean, in your teens.

KARITAS: Sigrun is such a child yet, really much more inexperienced than you would think from her appearance.

DR. ALFREDS: And when I stand before you, I too feel inexperienced.

KARITAS (*takes a cigarette and offers one to Dr. Alfreds*): Do take one.

DR. ALFREDS: Thank you. (*Lights a match.*) May I?

KARITAS (*takes his hand*): Do you enjoy playing with fire?

DR. ALFREDS: Yes, unless it's the kind that you burn yourself on. (*Tosses away the match.*)

KARITAS (*leaves him*): And now my husband has left on his fishing trip.

DR. ALFREDS: Sorry, but I'm going to have to leave, too.

KRISTIN (*comes in*): Excuse me.

KARITAS: Kristin, my dear, won't you vacuum the room please. It's full of snuff from that impossible fellow.

KRISTIN: Yes, here it is. (*She brings in the vacuum cleaner.*)

DR. ALFREDS (*bows and kisses her hand*): Au revoir, madame.

KARITAS: Some ladies are coming here this evening. I know they are just dying to meet you.

DR. ALFREDS: Thank you, madame. An irresistible force draws me back here again.

(*The vacuum cleaner starts up.*)

CURTAIN

Act II
Scene 2

Evening of the same day. Scene unchanged. Sigmundur is shouting into the telephone in the hall, and in the living room four ladies are playing bridge. They are obviously well-heeled and rather overdressed.

A small cart on wheels stands near the bridge table. On this Karitas has placed various sweets in a silver bowl and sherry in a crystal decanter. Wine glasses at each place before the ladies. Now and then they lift the glasses and sip gingerly.

SIGMUNDUR (*shouts at the same time as the ladies are playing in the living room and converse together*): I asked Laugi there about the bag—(*Louder*) about the bag. What? Can't you hear me, Gisli? Hell of a racket on this line. (*Lower.*) Manga dear, can't you give Gisli this message? I sent the bag on the milk truck. Laugi was going to leave it at the gate. (*Louder.*) Hello. Hello. At the gate. Manga. Hello. Gisli. I was just telling Manga. About the bag. Yes, and about the crowbar. No, no. Not the gocart. The crowbar. Hello, hello. And the bag by the gate. Laugi. Leave it behind. On the truck. Well. (*Lower, to himself.*) What a big hurry they were in. But you can't spend another long distance call on them. (*Takes some snuff, and then walks slowly up the stairs.*)

(*The racket from Sigmundur has bothered the ladies, who have been glancing at the door as if they hoped for some peace. The players are Karitas, Gunna, Kamilla, and Addi. Kamilla is the dummy.*)

ALL: At last.

GUNNA: What were we talking about? Oh, yes, Porfirio Rubirosa.

ADDI (*plump and new-rich*): What was that you said? Porfirio Rubirosa? What's that?

KARITAS: That's her husband, of course.

GUNNA (*dressed like a chorus girl, with tasteless exaggeration*): Dear, Barbara Hutton, but isn't she the richest woman in the world?

KARITAS: Oh, I don't suppose she's anything more than a human being like the rest of us.

GUNNA: She's the one who changes husbands to match the seasons.

KAMILLA: What do you mean?

GUNNA: A shaggy one in winter, of course, and a short-haired one in summer. (*Snickers.*)

KARITAS (*half-scandalized*): Please, Gunna.

ADDI: Well, it's your play, Gunna.

GUNNA: No, it can't be.

ADDI: Yes, darling, just try for once to keep track of the game.

GUNNA: That guy out there has just about cracked my eardrums.

KARITAS: I won't have you saying anything nasty about one of my husband's constituents. They're sacred in this house.

KAMILLA: Yes, of course.

GUNNA: But aren't you frightened to be alone in the house with him?

ADDI (*laughs*): Oh, I don't see that he would be so dangerous, not for *me*.

KARITAS (*laughs*): Sigmundur? Oh no, and then my husband is coming home late tonight. Well, and whose play was it? (*Plays.*)

KAMILLA: What time is it? The airplane ought to be landing about now.

ADDI: I just can't wait to see Tobba. She wrote me she had just bought a new mink.

GUNNA: No, don't tell me. She's always dressed fit to kill.

ADDI: She was just like a shorn sheep in her last creation—the yellow one, you remember? (*They snicker.*)

KAMILLA: But Karitas, do you think Dr. Alfreds will come after this?

KARITAS: I just don't understand it. He could scarcely afford to come much later. I told him to come right after nine.

ADDI: Tell us, how is he dressed?

GUNNA (*snickering*): You mean undressed, don't you, Addi dear?

ADDI (*offended*): Gunna!

KAMILLA: There's been so much talk about these discoveries of his. I'd like to have a personal interview with him.

KARITAS: Yes, you really ought to.

KAMILLA: I've heard that IMIC has been granted a monopoly from the government on all the uranium that will be found here. (*Turns to Karitas.*) Do you know anything about it?

KARITAS: No, darling. I don't know any more about these matters than you do. Though of course my husband couldn't avoid getting acquainted with Dr. Alfreds on account of his position. Well, we took this game. (*Gathers in the cards.*)

ADDI (*to Gunna*): Why didn't you play the jack of clubs, my dear? You knew that I was out of them.

GUNNA: Darling, have you ever been anything but out?

ADDI: But I had four hearts, and if—

KARITAS: No no, please don't start quarreling again. Let's have a taste of this instead. (*They sip from the sherry glasses.*)

KAMILLA (*starts to deal*): I want to say one thing: I think all this mystery about the uranium discovery is a regular scandal. In a healthy society such a thing wouldn't be tolerated.

KARITAS (*shuffles the cards*): I don't think Dr. Alfreds is anywhere near finished with all his researches and investigations.

GUNNA (*looking at the cards in her hand*): Isn't he just awfully learned?

KARITAS: My dear, in the world of science we know only a very few names. But of course he is very well educated.

ADDI: Otherwise IMIC would hardly have sent him here.

KAMILLA: A person is always filled with involuntary pride when men of Icelandic stock gain fame in the great world.

ADDI: They say that Lord Nuffield once travelled around in the Icelandic settlements of Canada, and there he came to a school where he listened to little John Alfreds reciting. After that he adopted him and paid all the expenses of his education.

(*They express their astonishment and admiration. Just then Sigmundur comes in.*)

SIGMUNDUR: It just struck me that I wanted to take a peek into the parlor, before I hit the hay.

KARITAS: Yes, Sigmundur, please come in. You've already met the ladies. Did you talk with your people at home?

SIGMUNDUR: I was talking with Gisli. Laugi was supposed to take a little package for me, but don't you suppose I had

trouble getting that crowbar? It wasn't before I got down to
the Co-op store—

KARITAS: Yes indeed, why don't you find yourself a seat, Sigmundur?

SIGMUNDUR: Thanks a lot. (*Stubs his toe on a chair, stands
there obviously overcome by all the splendor of the living
room.*) Oh, excuse me.

KARITAS (*looking at her cards*): What was it?

SIGMUNDUR: I happened to run my toe up against the chair. I
hope I didn't scratch it.

KARITAS: Oh, no, that won't do any harm.

(*Gunna snickers.*)

ADDI: One heart.

KARITAS: One spade.

SIGMUNDUR (*with his snuffbox*): Seems to me they're puffing
up this fool doctor to beat the band. I don't think for a
minute that he found any uranium, damn if I do. And where
in the world do you suppose he really came from, and who is
he?

KARITAS (*eager to stop this conversation*): Yes, indeed, Sigmundur, it was a fine thing that you got hold of that—that
crowbar.

SIGMUNDUR (*plays with his snuffbox*): Yes, I finally made it.
(*Gets up.*)

KAMILLA: But Sigmundur, don't you think we can trust the
scientists from the famous international institutions more
than ourselves?

SIGMUNDUR: Well, who did Egill Skallagrimsson trust more
than himself, and aren't we all descended from him?

ADDI: But Dr. Alfreds is a highly educated man, isn't he, Karitas?

KARITAS: Why yes, of course, what else? (*They pay no attention to Sigmundur.*)

SIGMUNDUR: Uhhuh. He's gone to school. But wisdom isn't
learned in school. Conceit is what most people learn there.

KARITAS (*tries to change the conversation*): Sigmundur, you should give Kamilla a chance to hear some of your stories. You know Kamilla from the national radio, she is so fond of all kinds of folklore.

KAMILLA (*in a magisterial tone*): Nothing human is foreign to me. Life is so magnificent when one understands it aright.

SIGMUNDUR: That's exactly it, when one understands it aright. (*Takes out from his inner breast pocket a packet wrapped in many layers of protective paper.*) Well, I suppose it ought to be this story which I composed this spring.

KARITAS: Yes, let's hear it. (*To the others.*) Sigmundur has such a marvellous memory.

SIGMUNDUR (*thumbs through the pages and moistens his fingertips with his tongue*): Will you excuse me if I blow my nose first?

KARITAS: By all means.

(*Sigmundur blows his nose loudly, then draws in some snuff and grunts. They speak in a low voice about the game and begin playing.*)

SIGMUNDUR: May I begin?

KARITAS: Please do. (*They play.*)

SIGMUNDUR (*reads*): In the year 1897 there lived in eastern Stafholt Sigurdur Paulsson, a knight of the Dannebrog order, and his wife Groa daughter of Sigurhans, who was beyond the age of childbearing when this saga took place. Their ancestors are not known to me. Sigurdur spent his boyhood years in Hornafjord, and there lived Magnus who had descendants in Faskrudsfjord, hardworking folks. One of Groa's brothers was John, the father of sheriff Bjorgvin at Cross River in Eyrarsveit and the rest of his brothers and sisters. Sigurdur and Groa had had one child, Fridny, who now lives in Brotherborg Street in Reykjavik, an elderly widow. She was married to Judge Johannes who was in the entourage of King Frederik at Thingvellir in 1907 and was the son of the Reverend Larus at Eid who was the son of Sigurd the son of Bjarnhedin at Nes. It was the Reverend Larus who chased the Eida ghost from the parsonage, as is reported in the annals. The children of Fridny and Johan are now for the most part of middle age. (*Blows his nose.*) Olgeir is a carpenter in Reykjavik, Baldur is an outstanding wrestler, and Tryggvi is a cantor in the male chorus The Harp and won a prize on their trip to Stockholm as everyone knows, and I have not yet mentioned four sisters who died in childhood. And now the saga turns to John the sheriff of Eyrarsveit, son of John, son of Einar.

KARITAS (*desperate*): No, Sigmundur, I'm afraid this is going to be a little too lengthy. You should rather give us the privilege of hearing some of your poetry. (*To the others.*) Sigmundur is such a fine poet.

KAMILLA: Oh, so you're a poet.

SIGMUNDUR: Oh, bless you, ladies, I would never dream of being called a poet. But at that I do think my ear for good verse isn't too far below that of these moaning poets that are most in fashion at the present time.

GUNNA: Have you never made a poem about love?

SIGMUNDUR: Not exactly that, but I did hammer out a little ditty just for the dickens of it when Laugi and Ranka plighted their troth. One verse ran like this:

> One maid there was who all outshone,
> One lily of the serpent's hide,
> Whom all men wished that they might own,
> 'Twas more than flesh could e'er abide.

GUNNA: Serpent's hide—isn't that the same as snakeskin?

SIGMUNDUR: Lily of the serpent's hide is a poetic figure for a woman, naturally.

(*Gunna stares.*)

KARITAS: Of course it's a figure for woman, but Gunna doesn't quite understand how you mean it.

SIGMUNDUR: Now how could a fellow mean that in more than one way? (*He looks at them, and they look at each other.*) Snorri asks: to what shall one compare a woman?

GUNNA: Compare? Can woman be compared to anything at all?

SIGMUNDUR (*forges on undaunted*): In poetry, woman may be compared to gold, and "the serpent's hide" is naturally gold, and so "the lily of the serpent's hide" is a woman!

KAMILLA: Yes, of course, a woman may be compared to gold.

KARITAS: Naturally. Do you understand it now?

SIGMUNDUR: It's as plain as a wart on the nose.

(*Just then the doorbell rings.*)

KARITAS (*exclaims*): Well, guests are coming (*She turns to Sigmundur.*) Excuse me, all of you. I have to go to the door, the maid's off. Now, Sigmundur, we thank you for all the entertainment.

SIGMUNDUR: I guess I better go hit the hay. I really had thought I would let you hear some ballad verses I made a while back about Alexander the Great and the heroes of Thebes.

KARITAS: No, not now, Sigmundur. (*The bell rings again.*) Later.

SIGMUNDUR: O.K. then. Goodbye everybody.

THE LADIES: Thank you for the entertainment.

KARITAS: We thank you ever so much.

SIGMUNDUR: Oh, it was nothing at all.

KARITAS: Would you mind very much going up the back way?

SIGMUNDUR: Oh sure, that's quite all right with me. (*He leaves.*)

KARITAS (*whispers as she walks to the door*): If he had seen the doctor, no-one else would have gotten a word in edgewise. (*Goes out, opens the front door, exclaims.*) Dr. Alfreds!

DR. ALFREDS: My apologies, madame.

KARITAS: That's perfectly all right. Come in.

(*Dr. Alfreds comes in, bareheaded and without overcoat, as earlier in Act II*).

KARITAS: We were beginning to think you had forgotten—

DR. ALFREDS: I was beleaguered by journalists there in the hotel. At last I had to escape by the window.

KARITAS: Poor Dr. Alfreds. You never get any peace.

DR. ALFREDS: That is how it is to be a scientist nowadays. We, too, have become accustomed to traveling incognito.

KARITAS: But won't you come in? (*They go into the living room, where the others stare expectantly at Dr. Alfreds and smile.*) May I present Gudrun, the wife of bank president Bjartmar.

DR. ALFREDS (*bows*): I am afraid I would be an indifferent bank president if I had so beautiful a wife.

GUNNA: Oh no, not at all, my husband loves me just like a bankbook. (*Giggling, while the others look half scandalized at each other.*)

KARITAS (*continues the introductions*): This is Adalheidur, the wife of architect Sofonias—he's the one who designed the church with the four steeples.

DR. ALFREDS: It's a pleasure. I too have always been an enemy of the trivial. "Excelsior sursum corda," as it is written. (*They bow.*)

KARITAS: And this is Kamilla, who read the famous story of "The Secrets of Pollyanna" on the radio.

(*Dr. Alfreds bows.*)

KAMILLA (*excited*): Tell me, Dr. Alfreds, why do you keep it a secret where the uranium was found in this country?

DR. ALFREDS: I'm sorry, but I have no control over that.

KARITAS: That's IMIC, of course. But please find yourself a place to sit, Dr. Alfreds. What may I offer you, whisky or sherry?

DR. ALFREDS: Just sherry, thank you. I am expecting a call from Professor Brown-Turning any moment now. (*Looks at his watch.*)

GUNNA: Oh, Dr. Alfreds, you must promise me to come to a party at our house one of these evenings. My husband always invites his colleagues, the bank directors, and then Valdimar comes and some of the cabinet and director Thorleifur and—

KARITAS: My dear, Dr. Alfreds is much too busy—

DR. ALFREDS: Unfortunately, I have just been ordered to prepare for a trip to Siam after the first of next month.

ADDI: To Siam?

DR. ALFREDS: We scientists are rarely able to determine our own travel plans. But it has been a rare pleasure to come home here to the old sod. Nowhere in the world are women as charming and as hospitable as here in the land of ice and fire—unless it be in Panama.

GUNNA: We are so southern in our temperament.

KAMILLA: How delightful that you should say this, Dr. Alfreds—you who have taken such high degrees!

DR. ALFREDS: I am not one of those who boast of their degrees. To tell you the truth, there was a student over there in Princeton who was almost a match for me, a Russian. He was a sharp rascal and he slipped behind the iron curtain with all his learning. I met him at the international congress in Moscow again last year. He had become a specialist in gamma rays and was director of the research laboratory in Sverdlovsk.

ADDI: Think of that! They made you a professor right away, didn't they?

DR. ALFREDS: Oh, that was pretty much a matter of course. But life is just an endless schooling for me, and I wonder if a man doesn't end up saying with Socrates, "I know that I know nothing."

KAMILLA: You are so wonderfully modest, Dr. Alfreds. But may I ask you just one little personal question?

DR. ALFREDS: Yes, of course.

KAMILLA: We have heard that it was Lord Nuffield who discovered your genius and paid for your education. Isn't that true?

DR. ALFREDS (*clears his throat*): My benefactor once said to me: never speak of what I have done for you. That is my private affair. But let mankind enjoy the benefits.

KAMILLA: Now isn't that just like Lord Nuffield? He was so noble.

ADDI: Yes, that is so beautifully spoken.

DR. ALFREDS (*in deep thought*): He was a man without compare.

ADDI: Oh, Dr. Alfreds, I do wish you could meet my husband. You see, he has invented a new stucco mixture.

DR. ALFREDS: A stucco mixture—yes, indeed—

ADDI: It's just like ice cream.

GUNNA: I do so want to ask you, Dr. Alfreds—tell me, have you ever been in love?

DR. ALFREDS: My love is the goddess of science.

GUNNA: I mean, have you ever been in love with a real physical woman and all that?

KARITAS (*scandalized*): But my dear Gunna, you really mustn't ask questions like that.

GUNNA: Oh, why not?

DR. ALFREDS (*in a lofty tone*): Those who become scientists must renounce their personal happiness.

ADDI: How touching.

KARITAS: Dr. Alfreds, you must have been worn out long ago by all these questions—

DR. ALFREDS: Oh, that's quite all right.

KARITAS: But tell us then, how was it out there in the state of New Mexico?

DR. ALFREDS: At Los Alamos?

KAMILLA: What an entrancing name—Los Alamos—it is like hearing the rustling of palm leaves in the dark of evening, outside the veranda door—

KARITAS (*impatiently*): Yes yes, Kamilla, let the doctor talk now.

DR. ALFREDS: Oh, it's really nothing to talk about, nothing but cactus and desert sands.

KAMILLA (*dreaming*): Cactus and desert sands, I can just see it in my mind's eye.

(*Karitas gives her an angry look.*)

DR. ALFREDS: Cactus and desert sands, wherever you look.

KARITAS: More, Dr. Alfreds.

DR. ALFREDS: And insects as big as your fist.

GUNNA (*screams*): Good God, cockroaches!

KARITAS: Tell us all about it.

KAMILLA: It's so very thrilling. I see it so plainly before me. (*Karitas signals to her to be silent.*)

DR. ALFREDS (*clears his throat*): I will tell you: for reasons of security we got very little opportunity to look around us. Our eyes were blindfolded each time we traveled between Santa Fe and Los Alamos.

KARITAS: Your eyes were blindfolded?

DR. ALFREDS: Yes, blindfolded, for reasons of security. Nowadays you always have to think of security first and foremost, so nothing leaks out.

KAMILLA: But then in Los Alamos itself?

DR. ALFREDS (*laughs*): You ask, madame.

KAMILLA: And you don't dare to answer. Perhaps you think I'm another Mata Hari?

KARITAS (*with a touch of sarcasm*): No, darling, I'm sure that wouldn't occur to anyone about you, Kamilla. (*The others laugh.*)

DR. ALFREDS: You mustn't laugh at me. I assure you that careless talk can have terrible consequences these days. Remember what happened to my friend Bob Oppenheimer.

KARITAS: Do you know Robert Oppenheimer?

DR. ALFREDS: Yes, I should rather say I did. I was a sponsor when his younger daughter Alice was baptized. It was rather strange, you know; we had been working together for months before either of us knew about the other. We all went under secret names, and were all dressed alike, in white. Even Dr. Kristiakovski—but now I'm saying too much.

KAMILLA: This must be just awfully exciting.

DR. ALFREDS: Undeniably. The life of the scientist can in truth be "awfully exciting," as you put it.

KAMILLA: I mean fabulously exciting.

DR. ALFREDS: Certainly. We scientists are only human after all. We feel our responsibility to mankind. But progress naturally can't be stopped, as my friend Einstein once said to me.

(*Just then the telephone rings.*)

KARITAS (*goes out*): Excuse me.

GUNNA: But Dr. Alfreds, you haven't answered my question yet.

DR. ALFREDS: I'm afraid that further details would take far too much time.

KAMILLA: It has been *so* lovely to talk with you, Dr. Alfreds. You are so unusually straightforward.

DR. ALFREDS: If I may say so, madame, face to face with the riddle of life I have always felt my own insignificance, and yet the human spirit—

KARITAS (*comes in*): That was from the airfield. The plane is about to land.

KAMILLA: Well, then we'll have to hurry off. (*To Dr. Alfreds.*) A friend of ours is coming in from Paris. But I hope I shall have an opportunity to meet you again, Dr. Alfreds.

DR. ALFREDS: I certainly hope the same. (*To Karitas.*) I wonder, my dear madame Karitas, if I could use the phone a moment. It is quite urgent.

KARITAS: Yes, of course, help yourself. (*She shows him the phone.*)

GUNNA: Excuse me, could we give you a ride somewhere?

DR. ALFREDS: Thank you, madame, but I think I would prefer to enjoy the autumn eve of old Iceland and walk home.

GUNNA: But as I said, we will get in touch with you—

DR. ALFREDS: Thank you so much. It is always a pleasure to get acquainted with one's countrymen.

ADDI: And you mustn't forget *me*. We really didn't get a chance to talk together this evening.

DR. ALFREDS: "Happy the man who has his best meal uneaten," as the poet says.

ADDI (*confused*): Yes, perhaps we can make it for dinner.

KAMILLA (*shoves Addi aside, to Karitas*): You aren't joining us?

KARITAS: No, I can't make it. Tell Tobba I'll call her in the morning.

(*Dr. Alfreds is seated by the phone.*)

GUNNA: Bye-bye. (*Nods her head lovingly at Dr. Alfreds as Karitas stands in the doorway and bids them good-bye.*)

DR. ALFREDS (*in the telephone*): This is Dr. Alfreds. A telegram. O.K., etc.

KARITAS (*looking at the weather*): There will be a marvellous sunset tonight.

ELIAS (*is heard shouting right outside*): Hiya, gals. You want nylon stockings, whisky?

KAMILLA: What is this, man?

ELIAS: Gunna darling (*She is heard screaming.*)—I'll put 'em on you myself. (*She squeals, and the others shush him.*) What is this, man, what kind of talk is this, etc.

ELIAS (*from outside*): Oh, I wonder if Gunna doesn't know me. You did once upon a time, Gunna, didn't you?

ADDI: Come on all, he's crazy.

KARITAS (*as if frozen in her tracks, stands in the doorway, clearly recognizing the voice, calls out*): Elias. (*Retreats from the door, and then goes back to it.*)

ELIAS (*appears. He is wearing a gaudy tie, is sailor-like in manner, limps and staggers*): Hi, sister Carrie.

KARITAS: Merciful God, is that you, Elias?

(*Dr. Alfreds turns aside, busily speaking in the telephone.*)

ELIAS: Just as you see. I've come home. Home, do you understand?

KARITAS: I thought you were out at sea.

ELIAS: And now you're so glad to see me. (*Approaches her, but she backs away.*) You'll give me a great big welcome, won't you, Carrie dear? (*Tries to embrace her, but she pushes him away.*)

KARITAS: No, Elias. I can't receive you now. I swear it.

ELIAS: O.K. And how did you receive me last time? It's just three years ago. It makes a difference, doesn't it? In the war years I smuggled all your junk through the danger zone for you. Then I was welcome. Then I was good enough for you.

KARITAS: Elias, we've always tried to help you as much as we could. You remember it was us you could thank for—

ELIAS: Thank you? (*Walks toward her.*) Yes, I can thank you that I lost my eye. Is that what you refer to? Not quite so pretty in the face any more. Or that my arm was wrecked like this, huh? (*Rolls up his sleeve and shakes the arm in her face.*) Answer me, sister Carrie. (*Laughs bitterly.*) Yes, I think that's what I can thank you for.

KARITAS: Oh Elias, tomorrow, just not tonight. Tomorrow—

ELIAS (*makes a broad gesture with his arm in the direction of the spectators*): No, I didn't save the world so it would look like this.

KARITAS: Elias, I have guests.

ELIAS: Do you mean that shrimp over there? (*Points to Dr. Alfreds.*)

KARITAS (*horrified*): Don't talk like that, Elias. This is Dr. Alfreds, a specialist who is here on behalf of IMIC. (*Dr. Alfreds says good-bye in the telephone and puts down the receiver*).

ELIAS: And poor old Thorleifur, are there any signs of life left in him? (*Stares sharply at Dr. Alfreds.*) Well, what the devil—can I believe my own eyes? Is that you, Nick? (*Laughs raucously.*)

DR. ALFREDS (*in a superior tone, but still visibly shaken*): What do you want, my good man?

ELIAS: Hell's bells, man, how you have straightened yourself out. Where did you get that fancy outfit? (*Tries to put his hands on him.*) You surely didn't steal it?

KARITAS (*rushes at him, tears his hair, and slaps him*): You ought to be ashamed of yourself, shame on you.

ELIAS: Now now, take it easy, kid.

KARITAS: Get out of here. Oh, Dr. Alfreds—

DR. ALFREDS (*picks up his courage*): Now, my good man, why don't you leave peacefully, or else—

ELIAS (*knocks him away*): Or else what? You haven't even got the strength of a woman, Nick my boy. Remember in Panama when you were kicked off the *Clara* from Haugesund—

KARITAS: Elias—

DR. ALFREDS: If you're looking for money, my man, here are fifty kronur.

KARITAS: No no, Dr. Alfreds, don't give him money. He doesn't need it.

ELIAS: I have all the filthy money I want. But have you paid for the shoes you stole from that bitch with the buck teeth? Huh, now tell me that, Nick?

DR. ALFREDS: You're suffering from delirium tremens, my good man.

ELIAS (*laughs*): Ha ha ha. Delirium tremens. You don't say.

KARITAS (*shouts*): You are such a beast that I'm going to call the police.

ELIAS: Have you told Nick about the time we used to help dear old daddy pick over the junk piles?

KARITAS (*cries out tremulously*): Elias.

ELIAS: And mummy lost her mind because she couldn't sleep at night when he was jingling his money? Yes, Nick, old boy, there are other big shots besides you. What about a drink? (*Starts to take out his pocket flask.*)

KARITAS: Now get out of here, right away. (*Pushes him.*)

DR. ALFREDS: Out with you.

ELIAS (*paying no attention, sings*):

> I came home to my mountain valley,
> I came home in tattered shoes,
> I came home to see my mother—

Mother? So this is the reception I get? (*Leaves, calls from outside.*) But anything's good enough for a bum like me.

KARITAS (*slams the door, groans*): Oh, Elias, he had such a bad

accident during the war. He's always so awful when he's on
land. I didn't know but he was on a Norwegian
freighter—

DR. ALFREDS (*shakes his head*): All this drunkenness here in
Iceland!

KARITAS: You will have to excuse him, Dr. Alfreds.

DR. ALFREDS: Nobody pays attention to the ravings of a drunkard.

KARITAS: Once upon a time he was first mate on a big ship, but
now he always talks nonsense.

DR. ALFREDS: Pitiful, very pitiful indeed.

KARITAS: I do think it might be better if you went out the back
way.

DR. ALFREDS: Yes—(*They come into the living room, he hesitates a moment.*) Yes, I suppose so—

KARITAS: If you are in a hurry?

DR. ALFREDS (*looks at his watch*): I spoke with the hotel, so for
that matter—

KARITAS: Well, in that case you don't have to rush off. Please
come in. (*Shows him in.*)

DR. ALFREDS: Thank you.

KARITAS: Here is a good place to sit. Won't you have a glass of
sherry before you go?

DR. ALFREDS: Maybe so. Thank you.

KARITAS (*sits down next to him in the sofa and pours out two
glasses*): Skoal! Here's to you.

DR. ALFREDS: And to you! (*A moment's silence. Karitas puts
her hand to her head and moans.*) What is it?

KARITAS: Oh, nothing at all, really.

DR. ALFREDS: That nonsense from the drunk just now, I mean—

KARITAS: No no, we won't talk any more about him. That
doesn't matter.

DR. ALFREDS: Then what is the matter? (*He puts his hand
sympathetically on her arm.*)

KARITAS: I'm just tired.

DR. ALFREDS: Tired?

KARITAS (*collects herself, conspicuously removes his hand*): Here, have a cigarette.

DR. ALFREDS: Thank you.

KARITAS (*pouting*): You certainly made a hit with the women tonight.

DR. ALFREDS: I? A hit? Now I don't understand you—

KARITAS: Yes, indeed. Kamilla was right on the point of swallowing you whole. Did you really find her that exciting?

DR. ALFREDS: Oh, the one with the nose?

KARITAS: How can you pretend so? You ought to be ashamed of yourself.

DR. ALFREDS (*at a loss*): Well, to tell the truth—

KARITAS (*working herself up*): And I really ought to have chased you away when the women left.

DR. ALFREDS: But my dear lady, what have I done?

KARITAS: Oh, don't put on any pretences. If they had known that my husband was out salmon fishing and wouldn't come back before tomorrow! Then it would have looked pretty suspicious.

DR. ALFREDS: Oh, so that is what you mean. I am as innocent as—

KARITAS: You have been seeking opportunities to see me alone, Dr. Alfreds. You think you can seduce me. But I can tell you once and for all that I am not one of those women who let themselves be seduced.

DR. ALFREDS (*gets up*): You misunderstand me, madame. You misunderstand me dreadfully.

KARITAS: Oh come, come. (*Laughs in a low and ingratiating voice.*) Sit down. I wonder if I don't understand you only too well. (*Puts out a glass for him.*) Help yourself.

DR. ALFREDS (*sits down hesitantly*): Thank you.

KARITAS (*lifts her glass*): And whom shall we toast now?

DR. ALFREDS: For the moment you have made me completely speechless.

KARITAS: I was a little angry before, and you deserved it. But now it's over. And shouldn't we now toast your friend Barbara Hutton?

DR. ALFREDS (*recovers himself*): No, we should rather toast you.

KARITAS: All right. *Our* toast. Skoal!

DR. ALFREDS: Skoal.

KARITAS: Shouldn't we two be frank with each other? I rather feel that we see through each other.

DR. ALFREDS (*uneasily*): Yes, perhaps we do.

KARITAS: May I read your palm?

DR. ALFREDS (*holds out his hand a little hesitantly, she looks searchingly at it*): What do you see?

KARITAS (*laughs softly to herself*): Didn't I know it?

DR. ALFREDS: Know what?

KARITAS: It would really be fun to hypnotize you and see what came out.

DR. ALFREDS: I was hypnotized once. Never again.

KARITAS: You must have had some kind of vision. Tell me about it.

DR. ALFREDS (*slowly and dramatically*): I saw before me an event of long ago. The skyscrapers of New York tower against the dimming evening sky. It is winter. A young man is standing by the East River, staring out over the water into the falling snow. "Should I," he says to himself and sips from the brandy bottle in his hand. "Should I?" Then he sees before him the girl he loves, sees her standing before the high altar in white bridal dress, white as the snow around him. This is the evening she is to be married to the rich packing-house man from Chicago, because she thinks a poor scientist has nothing to offer her. "Should I?" says the young man again and again, and looks out over the water. Then suddenly it is as if he makes a decision. He flings the bottle away, turns from the river and hurries with rapid steps back into the city—to life. The snow crunches under his feet. Never, never again. From now on nothing but work—

KARITAS (*laughs*): But my dear friend, you surely don't think I'm sentimental. Do I look like that?

DR. ALFREDS: You wound me deeply by saying this, for this experience of mine was indeed grievously bitter.

KARITAS: Tell me rather that you get your fun necking with girls at the movies. That would be something from our own age. This is nothing but old warmed-over broth.

DR. ALFREDS: Don't you believe in love at all?

KARITAS: No, not when you ask like that.

DR. ALFREDS: How, then?

KARITAS (*laughs seductively and lovingly*): Do you know, Dr. Alfreds, I dreamt of you last night.

DR. ALFREDS: What did you dream?

KARITAS: We were sitting together just like this, and then all of a sudden you put your arms around me (*She gets up on his lap*) and I allowed you to put your arms around me. I just couldn't do otherwise. It was so wonderful.

DR. ALFREDS (*puts his arm cautiously around her*): Like this?

KARITAS: No, much firmer. Yes, that way, just that way, and then you kissed me. (*She takes his head and they kiss.*) Just as we are doing now.

DR. ALFREDS (*can scarcely catch his breath*): That was a funny dream.

KARITAS: There is an old saying about making your dreams come true. (*Kisses him eagerly.*)

DR. ALFREDS: Karitas—

KARITAS (*overwhelms him with her kisses*): No, no, not here—wait, wait, come—

DR. ALFREDS: You are so enchanting, so unusual—I have never —(*She kisses him again so that he cannot finish his sentence.*)

KARITAS (*groans*): Not here—you must be mad—(*But she is still the one who makes the advances.*) Heavens, are you

going to devour me? (*Squeezes him tight, then jumps up.*)
No, no, not here. Wait, wait, then come.

(*She hurries off into the room on stage right and gives him a
signal to follow her. Dr. Alfreds gets up half confused,
strokes his hair back with a surprised air, loosens his necktie,
hesitates, pats himself on the chest as if to assure himself of
his manliness. He hears a noise, starts, listens, peeks out into
the hall. He sees the daughter sneaking up the stairs with her
shoes in her hand. Dr. Alfreds goes out, closes the door
quietly behind him. They look into each other's eyes, Sigrun
gives him a sign not to say anything, and he goes up the
stairs after her.*)

KARITAS (*is heard off stage, calls lovingly*): John, John—
(*The daughter and Dr. Alfreds kiss on the stairs and disappear.*)

KARITAS (*comes out in her nightgown*): John, John, what
happened to you? (*Looks out into the hall.*)

(*Sigmundur at this moment comes in from the kitchen, bare-
foot, in his undershirt and long underwear, and crawls
around on the floor, hunting for something. Karitas hears
him and thinks it is the doctor.*)

KARITAS (*bends down and whispers*): Why are you hiding,
darling? Come.

SIGMUNDUR (*gets up on his feet*): Huh?

KARITAS (*screams*): Good God!

SIGMUNDUR: I forgot my snuffbox down here, lost it on the
floor. (*Holds up the snuffbox, while Karitas flees crying
from the stage.*)

CURTAIN

Act III

The Square in Reykjavik (Austurvöllur). Benches, walks, flower beds. Hotel Borg and the Senate House (Althingishúsið) in the background. Neon lights when it starts to grow dark. Late afternoon.

Sigmundur and Senate Caretaker Boas come walking from the Senate House. Boas is enfeebled and rheumatic, dressed like an official of the nineteenth century, with a gold-embroidered visored cap on his head. The Cathedral clock is striking.

BOAS: We won't go any further. It's safest to be on hand if anything should come up in the Senate.

SIGMUNDUR: Twenty-seven years. That's certainly a long time you've been taking part in legislating and other high affairs of state.

BOAS: Yes sir. There's been plenty of cabinets come and gone since I was made a guard of the august Senate.

SIGMUNDUR: I know—and always having to make peace between opponents. You know what I think: old man Snorri would have cut a fine figure in the cabinet.

BOAS (*sits down, puffing*): Snorri, you say. No, I would rather have chosen Chief Thorgeir from Lightwater. And sometimes I actually thought he must have been there when old Valdimar was sleeping most soundly during the speeches of his opponents.

SIGMUNDUR: What, do they sleep in the Senate?

BOAS: Oh, it happens now and then that Valdimar takes himself a snooze. And I suspect that he sometimes thinks up smarter ideas when he's asleep than when he's awake, just like the ancient chiefs.

SIGMUNDUR: Right you are. There's a lot to be learned from dreams. (*He takes some snuff, hands the box to Boas, cocks his head in various directions, stares at Boas's cap.*) You know, Boas, I'm most afraid I'd get dizzy wearing such a fancy headgear. It's hardly for me to jump straight from the cow yard and way up the social ladder.

BOAS (*proudly*): Oh—you get used to it. (*Puts his hand up to the visor.*) You get used to it.

SIGMUNDUR: Did you put it on when they had those riots last year?

BOAS: I always wear it when I appear on behalf of my office. But now when I take it off, I speak as a private citizen. (*Takes it off.*)

SIGMUNDUR: It would be fun to take a look at it.

BOAS (*hands it to him*): Be sure you handle it with care. It's national property.

SIGMUNDUR: When I look at this, I get to thinking: the national treasury certainly has to pay for a lot of different things.

BOAS: Bless you, my friend, you don't know the half of it. And yet for my part I've always tried to be economical. (*Shakes his head.*) But the waste of electric lights in this building is just awful, for those senators always forget to turn off the lights. And the way they waste paper! You can't imagine it, and now they say the price of paper has gone up in Finland.

SIGMUNDUR: What will be the end of it all?

BOAS: Oh, I guess they will be as they have always been—half way between poverty and comfort. That reminds me: I brought with me the Senate debates. It would be well if you peeked a little at these. (*Hands him the debates.*) You read the newspapers, I suppose?

SIGMUNDUR: No, I could hardly say so. Oh, a fellow takes a look at these sheets that Laugi brings now and then. But you don't gain much wisdom from that stuff.

BOAS (*horrified*): No, Sigmundur, it won't do to talk like that if you intend to win promotion here. You will have to read the papers and learn all about the struggles between the Great Powers.

SIGMUNDUR: Well, I had really thought we could let them do as they please.

BOAS: No sirree, I tell you I can feel the draught from those struggles all the way to my office sometimes.

SIGMUNDUR: To your office, you say. Well, well. To your office.

BOAS (*in a confidential tone*): Just between you and me, I won't deny that many a time I've been the intermediary who prevented trouble when the parties just couldn't agree.

SIGMUNDUR: And then the problems have been solved?

BOAS: I remember when we had the cabinet crisis three years ago, and the President of the Senate was just about to—but no, that's classified material. Certain it is that those who make the most noise are not always the ones who have the most influence. It's rather the ones who stand behind the scenes and don't say much. Here in the Senate we call that being a diplomat!

SIGMUNDUR: Diplomat, you say. You sure have a lot of strange words down here. I'm not up on foreign languages, you know, and I never did understand foreigners, except maybe some of those shipwrecked sailors.

BOAS: Well, Sigmundur, you don't get to be a bishop without a beating. (*Blows his nose.*) But when do you think you'll be coming down here for good?

SIGMUNDUR: You see, I wanted to agitate this with you a little before anything was settled. (*Scratches himself.*) Some way or other, I feel bad about giving up my land.

BOAS: Where could you do better than to become my successor? Lots of people would jump at the chance.

SIGMUNDUR: That's not what I meant, Boas. The offer is good, no doubt about it. But somehow I feel it in my bones. A fellow has his roots in the sod. And just lately my dream lady has visited me constantly, looking reproachfully at me and talking angrily to me.

BOAS: Just why should she be upset because you become the senate caretaker?

SIGMUNDUR: No, not exactly that. But then there is another thing: Laugi was repeating some chatter about Thorleifur being in cahoots with that doctor what's his name.

BOAS (*a light dawns on him*): Aha, you said it. Surely it wouldn't be on *your* farm that they found this uranium, and that this is why Thorleifur wants to buy the land from you? I'd be surprised if that wasn't it.

SIGMUNDUR (*thoughtfully*): No, it's out of the question that Thorleifur should have planned to hoodwink me. Oh no. Not such a spotless and upright man as he. But I wouldn't put it past the doctor. No, not my friend Thorleifur. I just won't believe that—

BOAS: Well—it might just be that he's a diplomat—

SIGMUNDUR (*troubled and thoughtful*): I don't give a damn about any diplomat. (*Just then the clock strikes eight.*)

BOAS (*gets up*): It's getting late. I can't sit around any longer. There's lots of work awaiting. Well, you'll come up to my office.

(*Sigmundur is going through an inner struggle and does not pay attention.*)

BOAS: Farewell, friend, and remember to look at those papers. (*Points to the Senate debates on the bench. Touches his hand to his cap.*)

SIGMUNDUR: Pfui, I don't think I have any business there.

BOAS: Well, I can't stay any longer. (*Stalks off.*) Duty calls.

SIGMUNDUR (*looks after Boas, says to himself*): Damned nonsense this talk of his. Thorleifur? No, not my Thorleifur. (*Takes some snuff, looks around.*) Wonder if there's any place I can walk aside here. (*Puts down his stick on the bench next to the Senate debates and lays his cap there too.*)

PAPER BOY (*Comes on stage just as Sigmundur slowly leaves it, shouts.*) Dr. Alfreds' Discoveries Cause Stir in Japan and

Other Volcanic Countries. Multitude of Scientists Coming Here on Behalf of IMIC. (*Catches sight of Sigmundur.*) Fellow, have you read about Dr. Alfreds?

SIGMUNDUR (*as he leaves the stage*): No, I've had enough just seeing the man.

PAPER BOY (*as he leaves the stage*): Icelandic Enterprises Incorporated Secures Monopoly on Uranium Extraction!

(*Dr. Alfreds and Sigrun on stage from the other side. Sigrun walks quickly away from him, he follows and seizes her arm.*)

SIGRUN: No, I'm dead tired of all these parties.

DR. ALFREDS (*puts his hand to his head*): You're right. I'd rather land among headhunters and cannibals than in an Icelandic surprise party. But now let's go away. Let's just run away from it all. You understand? I have plenty of dough.

SIGRUN: Shall I tell you who you are?

DR. ALFREDS: You can't, my dear, for there is no one like me.

SIGRUN: You're just a big front and nothing else.

DR. ALFREDS (*tries to reason with her*): Come now, don't be jealous any more. I swear, it wasn't my fault that the woman got mad and locked the door. I have a distaste for her.

SIGRUN: As if I cared. (*Catches sight of Sigmundur, who is just then coming on stage, buttoning his trouser fly and wiping his hands on his trousers.*) Is that you, Sigmundur? (*Runs towards him.*) I'm so glad to see you. You know I've been begging daddy to let me go with you when you go back to the farm?

SIGMUNDUR: You will most certainly be welcome, my child. But isn't that the doctor?

DR. ALFREDS (*shortly*): Yes, how do you do. (*To Sigrun.*) Well, Sigrun, aren't you coming?

SIGRUN: No, you can go away. Sigmundur, tell him to go away. He won't leave me alone.

DR. ALFREDS (*angrily*): Oh, I haven't needed to chase you too hard so far.

SIGRUN: I slept with you just because I was angry, because I didn't know what to do. But don't think you have any claim on me for that reason.

DR. ALFREDS (*seizes her arm*): Come on now, we'll buy an airplane ticket, and you'll see that Dr. Alfreds is a man who knows the world and can make servants dance attendance on him.

SIGRUN (*tries to get loose*): Let me go. I've never cared for you. I can't stand you.

DR. ALFREDS: Aw, come on. (*Tries to pull her along. But she resists.*) You'll get all you want, just name it.

SIGRUN (*screams*): Sigmundur.

SIGMUNDUR: Here, here, you can't lay hands on a young girl.

DR. ALFREDS: You just keep out of this and mind your own business. (*Is about to pull her some more.*)

SIGRUN: Help, you're hurting me.

SIGMUNDUR: Now, my boy, you run along home and go to bed.

DR. ALFREDS: What do you mean, you hick, ordering me around? Or don't you know who I am?

SIGMUNDUR: I don't have any illusions about that any more.

DR. ALFREDS (*sticks out his chest*): I'm the one who's going to make a millionaire out of you—I, I—

SIGMUNDUR: Oh? A millionaire?

DR. ALFREDS: I'm the one who made that dump of yours into the most sought-after piece of land in this country, I and nobody else. You could become a millionaire if you had any imagination, a millionaire, do you know what that is?

SIGMUNDUR: Just what are you drooling about, man?

DR. ALFREDS: You peasants are so stupid that a fellow can't even talk to you. But if there is any gray matter at all in that noodle of yours, you should hurry up and sell before it's too late.

SIGMUNDUR: Well, well. (*A light dawns on him.*) So Boas guessed right then. A dog isn't angry when you beat him with a bone, but you should remember that I, Sigmundur Jonsson, am no jester at the court of Mammon, and I will never sell my birthright to a wretch like you, even though a visored cap is offered in the bargain.

DR. ALFREDS: (*has retreated from him*): What kind of a noise is this, man? All right, you just sit there like a turd on your filthy farm. You're welcome to it. But remember anyway that Dr. Alfreds gave you a chance—on credit, which I never do otherwise.

SIGRUN: But all this is just a big joke on your part, isn't it?

DR. ALFREDS: Don't worry. The money has gone to my men on the other side of the ocean. I'm safe. And I've sold both the cars.

SIGMUNDUR (*exit deeply shaken*): So this was the reason for everything.

SIGRUN (*runs after him*): Let me go with you.

DR. ALFREDS (*calls to her*): Sigrun. (*No answer.*) All right, you'll be sorry. I have plenty of women in other countries. Women who can appreciate what a man does for them. (*No answer, swears.*) The little bitch. There's no way of pounding sense into her. (*Trembles with anger.*)

PAPER BOY (*comes on stage again, shouts*): Specialists from IMIC and Professor Epihara Arrive Tomorrow.

DR. ALFREDS (*starts*): What was that, boy? Has the god-damned professor recovered from his jaundice?

PAPER BOY: What? Who?

DR. ALFREDS (*hands him a ten-kronur bill*): There, give me a paper.

(*Paper Boy hands him a paper, starts to give change.*)

DR. ALFREDS: Just keep it, son, you can use it.

(*Paper Boy stares at the bill and at Dr. Alfreds, full of admiration.*)

DR. ALFREDS (*reads, to himself*): Well, so it's getting hot under foot. (*Notices the boy.*) What are you gaping at, boy?

PAPER BOY: I? I just—

DR. ALFREDS: Do you know who I am?

PAPER BOY: N-no.

DR. ALFREDS: Once I was an unknown little boy just like you—
but now? Well, let that pass. But I don't need a coat of mail
to conquer the world, nor a rifle. I just shoot an invisible
bacteria into a man's ear. Ha ha! That's the whole magic, and
then all the walls of the city fall without a sound.
(*Paper Boy stares, speechless.*)

DR. ALFREDS: Run along now, but bow to me before you go.
(*The boy is a little slow in bowing, and Dr. Alfreds forces
him to do it.*) Bow now, just bow. You'll never see a man
like me again.
(*Paper Boy bows, terrified, runs away*).

DR. ALFREDS (*cries out*): Excellent, excellent. You show great
abilities. (*Lights a cigar and looks up at the lighted windows
of the Senate*). I shouldn't wonder if good old Thorleifur is
sitting up there with his companions now, figuring out the
profits. (*Laughs.*) In the end it may be fun to learn how
much they value a man's silence. (*Walks off stage whistling
proudly.*)

CURTAIN

Act IV

*About a month later. In Senator Thorleifur's home. Same
scene as in Act II. Thorleifur stands before his easel, painting
a still life of flowers in a vase. His wife sits in a chair,
listening to a newscast while she fixes her nails. Thorleifur
paints, steps back from the canvas each time he makes a
stroke with his brush and surveys the result.*

ANNOUNCER (*reading*): Professor Epihara, who came to this country on behalf of IMIC, the International Metals Investigations Commission, has been travelling around extensively in the South and East with his assistants. Professor Epihara—

THORLEIFUR (*has been wholly occupied in surveying his painting, suddenly becomes aware of the announcer's news report, hurries over to the radio with his brush in hand and turns it off*): We've heard enough of that.

KARITAS (*jumps up*): Thorleifur, I was listening.

THORLEIFUR: I don't want to hear about this affair again in my house.

KARITAS: What if *I* want to listen? (*Turns it on again.*)

ANNOUNCER (*goes on reading*): . . . but his investigations have not been as fruitful as he had hoped . . .

THORLEIFUR (*turns it off again*): I don't give a damn about this Hairy Ape or whatever his name is.

KARITAS: As if it was his fault that you let that Alfreds bamboozle you.

THORLEIFUR (*tries to paint*): Yes, indirectly.

KARITAS: Why you didn't think of asking a man like Alfreds for documents and evidence, that's what I don't understand.

THORLEIFUR: Well, what could a person do? Alfreds claimed he was here on behalf of IMIC, and we had read in the *Daily Mirror* and other English newspapers that IMIC was going to send an ore specialist to this country.

KARITAS: And that is this Professor Epihara?

THORLEIFUR: The rascal fell sick of jaundice this spring, so that his trip was postponed. But of course we didn't hear about that, and so when this Dr. Alfreds, I mean Alfreds—

KARITAS: Frankly, I think you should have had the means of getting factual information.

THORLEIFUR: Yes, my dear, but you know that nowadays such matters are handled with as much secrecy as possible.

KARITAS: And then to let a young squirt like Alfreds pull the wool over your eyes!

THORLEIFUR: Well, didn't the newspapermen fall for it, too, every single one of them?

KARITAS: I just can't understand it—

THORLEIFUR: I tell you again, wife, a person actually has no defence against scoundrels like that who sail under false colors.

KARITAS: And just what colors do you think you're sailing under, may I ask? Some kind of Sunday school banner?

THORLEIFUR: No, we won't talk any more about this. It doesn't do any good. (*Tries to start painting again.*)

KARITAS (*putting on nail polish, after a moment's silence*): But he did have all those instruments.

THORLEIFUR: It's no trick to get yourself a Geiger counter. They don't cost more than fifty or sixty dollars.

KARITAS: But he must have known how to work it.

THORLEIFUR: I'm not so sure.

KARITAS: But you remember, it sounded as if he knew everything about uranium, when he was talking about it.

THORLEIFUR: He naturally picked that up when he was a barber's apprentice in Uranium City. People there are as crazy about looking for uranium as they used to be about gold in Alaska.

KARITAS: But was that just a made-up story about his being from Canada too?

THORLEIFUR: Bless you, he was born and brought up on Linden Street in this town. He made himself notorious here one winter by breaking into a candy store. They put him in jail for it. Then he stole a horse from a farmer and sold it to the slaughter house. After that he became cook's helper on a Norwegian hulk right at the beginning of the war. Brilliant career, isn't it?

KARITAS: Fancy that—he even stole a horse! But what about his family name, Alfreds, John Alfreds?

THORLEIFUR: In the police records he bears the full name of Jörgen Nicholas Holm Alfredsson.

KARITAS: Jörgen Nicholas Holm—what a name!

THORLEIFUR: As many names as a member of royalty. We have further learned that he was once deported from Canada.

KARITAS: And this fellow you all allowed to twist you around his little finger. (*Vehemently.*) But why didn't you arrest him?

THORLEIFUR: My dear, a man doesn't willingly make a fool of himself before the general public. No, it was politically most advantageous that Jörgen Nicholas Holm should quietly vanish from the country as Dr. Alfreds. More than that: we had to buy an airplane ticket to Mexico for him.

KARITAS: An airplane ticket to Mexico!

THORLEIFUR: Yes, my dear. We can praise our lucky stars we got off as cheaply as that.

(*Just then the phone rings.*)

KARITAS: The phone.

THORLEIFUR: I'll take it. (*Hurries out, the door is open.*) Yes, hello. Yes, oh no, the doctor has left the country. No, I'm sorry to say, I don't know for sure. Yes, no, oh that's perfectly all right. Goodbye.

KARITAS: Was somebody asking about Dr. Alfreds?

THORLEIFUR (*shouts*): For heaven's sake, he's no god-damn doctor (*Calms down quickly.*) I mean—among ourselves. Outside, people only know that Dr. Alfreds was overly optimistic about uranium, and that further investigations have led to different conclusions.

KARITAS (*still working at her nails*): But this is intolerable— absolutely intolerable—you who licked the dust at his feet—that you didn't see through him.

THORLEIFUR: But weren't you the one, my dear, who showed such passionate interest in him?

KARITAS (*with disgust*): I? Of course I believed it when you said he was here on behalf of IMIC, but it was you who introduced him into our home.

THORLEIFUR: As things stood, it was a matter of course.

KARITAS: You left him behind here in our home even though I had warned you against him, and no one knows what might have happened—if—

THORLEIFUR (*anxious*): If—what?

KARITAS (*in a lowered voice*): He was offensive towards me this summer, right after you had left.

THORLEIFUR (*shocked*): Karitas, what are you saying? What really happened?

KARITAS: I have spared you the truth about this affair. Heaven knows how awful it was.

THORLEIFUR: The skunk surely didn't try to—violate you?

KARITAS: No, Thorleifur dear, I can't bear to talk about it. I shudder to think of it.

THORLEIFUR (*sits down beside her and puts his arm gently around her shoulder*): Karitas, tell me about it.

KARITAS (*at once becomes excited*): I burned him with the cigarette. I scratched him. I hit him. I told him he would remember that a woman had struck him. And he staggered out after he had torn off my dress. (*Buries her face in her hands.*)

THORLEIFUR: Oh, my darling, now now. (*Strokes her with emotion.*) My little defenceless dove. But why haven't you told me this before?

KARITAS (*sobbing*): I couldn't. I just couldn't. That scoundrel. You should have known how he grabbed hold of me—

THORLEIFUR: Now now, we won't think about this any more. You were able to protect your honor. That's what matters—

KARITAS: God, how I wish I might have seen that beast in prison—branded at hard labor—beaten up with a club—and then you pay for his airplane ticket to Mexico—the man who swindled you for big sums—this notorious house-breaker and criminal who almost dishonored me—you actually give him a prize for all his villainy!

(*Kristin comes in just then*).

KARITAS: Well, what is it, Kristin?

KRISTIN: I didn't exactly know what I ought to do with these stones that the doctor left behind.

KARITAS: Throw them in the ashcan.

KRISTIN (*hesitantly*): But aren't they valuable? I thought—

THORLEIFUR: It's all right. The doctor was through using them for his investigations.

KARITAS: Yes, and don't stand there gaping as if you had never seen people before. Or don't you understand what we have told you?

KRISTIN: Yes, yes. (*Leaves.*)

KARITAS: The bag—I'm sure he slept with her.

THORLEIFUR: Now, now, dear.

KARITAS: Oh Thorleifur dear—can't we go away somewhere, somewhere far, far off, where we could forget all this? I still haven't been able to calm my nerves after this business last summer.

THORLEIFUR: No, I'm afraid that's out just now. This has all cost me plenty of money. (*Tries to paint*).

KARITAS (*as she puts nail polish on her nails, a moment's silence*): But don't you think it'll leak out who he really was?

THORLEIFUR: No, we have all made an agreement to keep it strictly under cover, and Valdimar will certainly see to it that no one blabs. He's used to that, the old man.

KARITAS (*sarcastically*): You seem to have become a great admirer of his lately.

THORLEIFUR: Well, it can't be gainsaid that he saved the day for us, and if—

KARITAS: So of course you're going to support his bill.

THORLEIFUR (*in a resigned tone*): Yes—I'll have to do that.

KARITAS (*quickly excited*): Weakling. That's what you are. You had a chance to get the equivalent of an ambassador's position. We could now have been in Rome or on the Riviera or anywhere, if you hadn't played the clown before Valdimar. And now you have to crawl on your knees to him.

THORLEIFUR: Yes, it was my fault that I trusted another man.

But what value is life if such trust is excluded. (*Paints.*) I wanted to seize the opportunity for the benefit of my people. I felt I didn't have the right not to—

KARITAS: Oh, keep quiet. Don't you think I've seen through your hypocrisy a long time ago, all your talk about ideals and noble deeds? You just wanted to make yourself a bigger man than Valdimar, but you didn't have the stuff in you.

THORLEIFUR: You can pass judgment on me, Karitas, and I don't ask for mercy. But have you ever tried to understand me as I am?

KARITAS: I've tried to make a man of you, my dear.

THORLEIFUR: You aren't fair, Karitas. You know I've always tried to please you. I've even tried to be the man you wanted me to be even though it was entirely contrary to my nature. The trouble is that a man can't in the long run be anything else than what he is. But this you have never wanted to understand.

KARITAS: But what do you think you would have become without me?

THORLEIFUR: The problem is not really what a man becomes, but rather what he is—what a man is in relation to himself and his limitations—and there I was too many things at once.

KARITAS: Yes, you should have remained the tear-jerking singer at funerals that you used to be.

THORLEIFUR (*with a touch of pathos*): Yes, I could sing. And I could also write poetry. My schoolmates were amazed at my many talents. I myself lived in daydreams about all that awaited me. You understand—I couldn't grow up because I had too many possibilities to choose from, and I didn't choose. To grow up is to set one's course in a definite direction. But I saw mirages on all sides. If only I had had the fortitude to devote myself entirely to my art, to the calling which has always had and now, I find, still has the deepest attraction for me. (*Steps back from his painting and points at it.*)

KARITAS: Your art. (*Laughs scornfully.*) No, Thorleifur mine, you have never been able to live for anything. You have just dabbled at everything—dabbled at being a big shot. You never got beyond being director of an inactive herring oil factory. You have dabbled at art—when you had to give in too much to Valdimar. You have even dabbled with me, your wife, so that as far as you are concerned, I might as well have remained a virgin. Oh Lord, that I ever got married to you. It would almost have been better to let this candy thief take one by force.

THORLEIFUR (*jumps up shocked*): Wife, why do you say this?

KARITAS: You have never had any convictions about anything, no passions, not even any vices, for you are just a fake, a fake. That's what you are and nothing else.

(*Knocks his easel over in her excitement.*)

THORLEIFUR: Karitas, Karitas—

KARITAS: Fake, fake—

KRISTIN: Excuse me. (*She is standing in the doorway, unable to make herself heard.*)

KARITAS (*cries out when she catches sight of her*): What's this, girl? Why do you sneak in this way? Haven't you any manners?

KRISTIN: Forgive me, but I didn't know—

KARITAS: Didn't know what—what—?

KRISTIN: The architect's wife is here.

(*Thorleifur picks up the canvas and his paints.*)

KARITAS: Addi? What does *she* want?

KRISTIN: She's asking if the lady is at home.

(*Thorleifur hurriedly collects everything and carries it out into the room across the stage. Takes off his smock.*)

KARITAS (*hurries out*): Addi, darling, are you here—

(*Thorleifur comes out again, in his usual suit. Karitas and Addi come in.*)

ADDI: Could I possibly have a talk with you?

(*Embraces her.*) I had to—I just literally had to come and

see you. (*Looks at Thorleifur.*) Good morning, Thorleifur.

THORLEIFUR (*greets her*): Good morning.

ADDI: I hope I'm not interfering?

KARITAS: Oh no, no, not at all, far from it.

THORLEIFUR: And Sophonias is busy building?

ADDI: Yes, busy building.

KARITAS: My husband is so terribly busy, too, now that the Senate is in session.

THORLEIFUR: Yes, I have to look over some papers.

KARITAS: Don't wear yourself out now, my dear. Remember this evening.

THORLEIFUR: Yes, I remember.

(*Thorleifur off.*)

ADDI: Was something troubling him?

KARITAS: Oh, no, not at all. My dear Thorleifur is always in such good humor. He's just a little tired. He and Valdimar have been working on a new bill. But please have a cigarette. (*Hands her one.*)

ADDI: Thank you. (*Lights it.*) You two are always so harmonious.

KARITAS: We have always been satisfied with each other, and I think—though I shouldn't say it—that my Thorleifur is just as infatuated with me now as when he kissed me the first time back of the Free Church.

ADDI: Oh, a person can see that all over him. Men just can't hide anything like that.

KARITAS: I think he still remembers all my party dresses.

ADDI: That blue one you wore on New Year's Eve was a dream.

KARITAS: It was a model from New York. But your dresses are in such good taste also.

ADDI: Oh, Sophonias has good connections. But to get back to the relationship between you and your husband—the fact that you agree so well will make it easier to bear up under trouble.

KARITAS (*annoyed*): What do you mean?

ADDI: We have always been able to talk together so well and have told each other—

KARITAS: Well, what is it?

ADDI: I felt it was my plain duty to come and tell you—

KARITAS: What *are* you talking about?

ADDI: So you haven't noticed anything? My Tota said to me— now you mustn't be upset—

(*She leans over to her and whispers.*)

KARITAS (*starts*): Pregnant! My Sigrun? Never. That's impossible—the child.

ADDI: She has been pregnant since this summer.

KARITAS (*jumps up*): Well, what business is it of yours? *You* didn't make her that way.

ADDI: Now now, try to calm yourself.

KARITAS: Calm myself! (*Snorts.*) So the girl is engaged, and isn't it the fashion nowadays for engaged girls to get pregnant?

ADDI: Is she enaged? I didn't know that. But surely not to this Alfreds?

KARITAS: You mean Doctor Alfreds.

ADDI: Was he really a doctor?

KARITAS: Doctor Alfreds is certainly an outstanding man in his field—very outstanding indeed. But of course *you* wouldn't understand that in science it often takes very little to make the conclusions erroneous, and as far as Sigrun's engagement is concerned, I can tell you she is engaged to a young and promising student.

ADDI: A young and promising student?

KARITAS: Yes, such incredible things do happen nowadays— young girls get engaged to young students, but of course I don't suppose you ever heard of anything like that before.

ADDI: I just didn't know that—

KARITAS: No, you don't need to tell me that there are lots of things you don't know. I have always trusted my Sigrun, and

that's more than you can say about your daughter, that
trollop who has always been hanging around the American
soldiers, and sticks chewing gum under all the furniture.

ADDI: That you would dare—

KARITAS: I dare to trust my daughter, and even if she is pregnant, I still trust her, for she is engaged, do you understand
that, and not a prostitute like your Tota. I wish to God that
Sigrun had never made friends with your people, for in our
district among cultured people you outsiders ought never to
have been allowed. You ought to have to stay in the slums,
like tramps and gypsies.

(*Addi retreats to the door, terrified.*)

ADDI: I just wanted to—

KARITAS: Get out. Get out.

ADDI (*screams*): You should talk about a cultured district! You
who made love to this fake doctor! And made a cuckold of
your Thorleifur!

KARITAS (*opens the door*): Get out. Your Sophonias is nothing
but a hayseed who never learned to draw anything but silos,
as anybody can see by his churches. (*Laughs contemptuously and slams the door.*) That snake. (*Rushes into the
living room and calls to Thorleifur.*) Thorleifur.

THORLEIFUR (*comes in with a newspaper in his hand*): What's
wrong? What kind of a racket is this?

KARITAS: She's pregnant, she's pregnant.

THORLEIFUR: Who? Addi?

KARITAS: Your daughter.

THORLEIFUR: Sigrun?

KARITAS: And of course with this housebreaker, Jörgen Nicholas Holm. Isn't it just delightful to become in-laws to such
high nobility?

THORLEIFUR: It surely doesn't have to be him?

KARITAS: Yes, I rather think I noticed something like that. She
was always giving him the eye.

THORLEIFUR: The wretched scoundrel—

KARITAS: I wonder if we hadn't better begin calling him *Doctor* Alfreds, even among ourselves.

THORLEIFUR: I don't believe it. I can't believe it.

KARITAS (*half to herself*): Why she couldn't have been more careful—(*To Thorleifur.*) But this is what I kept saying to myself this summer. We should really have locked her up.

THORLEIFUR: My poor dear little Sigrun—and where is she now?

KARITAS: Oh, she went to this ram show with Sigmundur. Ever since she visited his farm this fall she doesn't talk about anything but farming. It was all just to deceive me and make herself appear innocent.

THORLEIFUR (*looks at his wrist watch*): They must be coming soon. Perhaps I ought to telephone. (*Starts to go out, but stops.*) No, of course there isn't any telephone there.

KARITAS (*sits down*): Oh Lord, that this too should have to happen. (*Wipes her eyes.*)

THORLEIFUR (*sits down beside her*): Now, now, my dear, we'll manage to get out of it somehow. We can send the girl away and then she will marry someone she has long been engaged to. (*Picks up the newspaper he has been reading.*) By the way, have you seen that they're getting divorced, Barbara Hutton and Porfirio Rubirosa?

KARITAS (*tears the paper away from him as she hisses*): Yes, and I ought to get divorced from you.

THORLEIFUR (*unhappy*): No, my love, you mustn't do that. You are all that I have, the most precious and the most incomparable. With you I'm still wealthy.

(*Just then Sigrun's voice is heard in the hall, bright and cheerful. Sigmundur and she are both in new parkas, and he is in every way more dressed-up than before.*)

SIGRUN: Come on in, Sigmundur.

KARITAS (*inside*): There they are.

SIGRUN (*comes in and holds up a document*): First prize—first prize!

SIGMUNDUR: And a testimonial from the Minister of Agriculture himself!

KARITAS: A prize?

SIGMUNDUR: My old Somi just wouldn't be denied.

THORLEIFUR: That is gratifying, Sigmundur, truly gratifying. May I congratulate you? (*Extends his hand.*)

SIGMUNDUR (*a little brusquely*): Yes, I suppose you may.

KARITAS (*sarcastically to Sigrun*): And I suppose I should congratulate you too?

SIGRUN: Yes indeed. I was *so* excited when the Minister got up on the platform to speak.

KARITAS (*spits out the words*): You ought to be ashamed of yourself.

SIGRUN: So? And what, pray tell, have I done?

KARITAS: You ought to know that best yourself, you who have brought disgrace on us. Addi came here just now, and told me what Tota had said to her—

SIGRUN: That I am pregnant. Yes, it's going to begin showing pretty soon. I was just picking out material for a maternity dress today.

KARITAS: So you don't even know enough to be ashamed of yourself?

THORLEIFUR: But daughter, what misfortune has befallen you?

SIGRUN: It is no misfortune, daddy. Children are no misfortune.

KARITAS: You don't seem to be clearly aware of your circumstances.

SIGMUNDUR: Well, doesn't the Creator bless those who increase and multiply the earth?

KARITAS: Please, Sigmundur, excuse us. We need to talk a little with our daughter.

SIGRUN: No, he stays here. He knows everything about this.

SIGMUNDUR: Yes, I always told Laugi that there are fine qualities in the young people, even when they're a little careless with their fun. But no one should be too hard on them for that.

KARITAS: Very well, but may I venture to ask who the lucky man was—surely not Dr. Alfreds?

SIGRUN: Perhaps you're jealous? (*Laughs sarcastically.*)

KARITAS (*gives her a box on the ears*): Maybe this will teach you not to shame your mother.

SIGRUN (*walks menacingly toward her*): You shall never slap me again. I am myself about to become a mother, and my children shall never be beaten.

KARITAS: But my dear, whose child is it?

SIGRUN: It's mine.

SIGMUNDUR: You know, it has always seemed to me that somehow children belong to all of us.

KARITAS: If you intend to stay any longer under your parents' roof you will at least have to let us know who has seduced you.

SIGRUN: I am no longer dependent on you. I am eighteen years old and can do as I please. Sigmundur has promised me that I can stay on his farm as long as I wish. I just came here to say goodbye and collect my baggage. It's all packed upstairs.

KARITAS: Sigmundur—can all this be true that the girl is saying? I hope you haven't been influencing her—she's such a weak character.

THORLEIFUR: Yes, you understand, Sigmundur, we'll have to find some way out, as things now stand—

SIGMUNDUR (*strokes Sigrun's hair clumsily*): Yes, she's welcome, the little one, to stay with us as long as she wants to. She behaved so well those weeks she was with us. But this I would like to say to the Senator—that I think he had better find "some way out" in other matters than what concerns her. And you were badly mistaken when you thought I was so blinded by ambition that you could pull the wool over my eyes.

THORLEIFUR: No no, Sigmundur, that was all a mere misunderstanding—

SIGMUNDUR: Well, it's a little late to say "amen" when all the deacons have fallen silent. But this I want to tell you, that little Sigrun shall have all she needs in the way of milk and nourishing food. Laugi and Ranka have contracted with me for another year, at least, so that the grub isn't going to be too bad even though it's a lonely place.

SIGRUN: Oh no, I love to stay with you. Ranka will teach me to spin on your mother's spinning wheel.

THORLEIFUR: But wouldn't it be advisable to be closer to a doctor—

SIGMUNDUR: Ranka has been a midwife whenever it was needed, and she's done right well by the women, too. If there has to be a doctor, there's one in the village, down by the sea.

KARITAS: Do you still refuse to name the father?

SIGRUN: Isn't it enough for you to know that you are going to become a grandmother?

KARITAS: Sigrun—

SIGRUN (*turns away from her mother*): Come Sigmundur, you'll have to help me with the bags.

KARITAS (*cries out after her*): That you would *dare* to do it— (*The doorbell rings.*)

SIGRUN (*on the stairs as they walk up*): I intend to take my parrot with me so he can listen to the thrushes in the brush-wood—

(*Out.*)

THORLEIFUR (*opens the outer door*): Valdimar!

VALDIMAR: Hello, old man.

KARITAS (*glad to see him*): Valdimar!

VALDIMAR (*embraces her*): Always like Venus just risen from her bath. May I introduce Professor Epihara, Frau Olafsson. Herr Olafsson.

PROFESSOR: Küss die Hand gnädige Frau.

KARITAS: Speek eenglees?

PROFESSOR: Speek leetle eenglees.

KARITAS: Nehmen Sie Platz. Won't you please sit down?

VALDIMAR: The Professor is Japanese and prefers to talk German. As you know he has been traveling around the country far and wide this fall, but his researches have so far uncovered nothing of interest. (*They enter the room.*) Nichts gefunden?

PROFESSOR: Nein, gar nichts.

THORLEIFUR (*offers cigars*): No, it's hardly to be expected that there should be uranium here.

VALDIMAR: His assistants and he have divided the work between them, taken samples and investigated everything in a strictly scientific way. It was an expedition under his leadership that found the uranium deposits in Madagascar last year.

PROFESSOR (*nods*): Oh ja ja. Madagascar, Madagascar.

THORLEIFUR: Yes indeed.

VALDIMAR: But in these investigations there is one spot which the professor did not get an opportunity to study, and that was at Hofstadir, just the area where Dr. Alfreds of blessed memory thought he had found uranium.

KARITAS (*bitterly*): Jörgen Nicholas Holm.

VALDIMAR (*nods to her*): It is not because the professor thinks that anything of importance will come to light, but rather for the sake of scientific precision and completeness in his reports. But the farmer was most unfriendly. He threatened us and forbade us all entry.

THORLEIFUR: The fellow has gotten a little uppity lately.

VALDIMAR: To put it bluntly: he aimed a gun at the professor. (*Pretends to aim a gun.*) Boom-boom.

PROFESSOR: Ja ja, boom-boom.

KARITAS: He aimed a gun!

VALDIMAR: They had to take to their heels to save their lives.

THORLEIFUR: What's this? They've been in danger of their lives?

KARITAS: Imagine Sigmundur acting like that—

VALDIMAR: Be that as it may. But in order not to have left this
one spot unstudied and in order to satisfy the professor's
scientific conscience, I told him that most likely Alfreds had
left behind some samples of the rock here with you. I
remember you said—

THORLEIFUR: Yes, of course, the rocks—

VALDIMAR: Yes, the rocks. Steine.

PROFESSOR: Ja ja, Steine.

THORLEIFUR: Wife, where are those rocks we used to have?

KARITAS: The maid threw them in the ashcan. (*Runs out and
shouts.*) Kristin!

VALDIMAR: Die Steine sind in die Aschentonne geworden.
(*Speaks in a low voice with the professor who nods, and
they all three go out into the kitchen after Karitas. Just then
Sigrun and Sigmundur come down the stairs. Sigrun is carrying a cage with a parrot in it.*)

SIGRUN (*to Sigmundur*): Will you carry out the bags while I
call a cab? (*Sigmundur takes the bags and goes out. Sigrun
on the telephone*): This is at Senator Thorleifur Olafsson's.
Will you send a cab, right away?

(*Karitas comes in the kitchen door.*)

KARITAS (*listens silently a moment while the daughter speaks*):
Are you leaving?

SIGRUN: Yes.

KARITAS: Then you're really serious?

SIGRUN: More serious, mother, than I have ever been about
anything else.

KARITAS: I don't understand you. (*Sits down.*) You have become so strange. What is really the matter with you?

SIGRUN: No, you can't understand me, and it is hardly to be
expected. I don't even know if I understand myself. But
what difference does that make, when I know that what I am
doing is right and the only right thing, and that nothing else
matters beside this. It is so strange. It is exactly as if I had been
under some kind of spell and hadn't known what I wanted,
until now I am freed from the spell.

KARITAS: I wonder if it isn't now that you are under the spell. You can't be yourself now, girl.

SIGRUN: Yes, for now I am about to begin a new life. (*She strokes her waist.*) And here, within, it is growing day and night. But you can't understand anything because you are vain and selfish.

KARITAS (*puts her hands over her eyes*): You hate me.

SIGRUN: No, I don't hate you. Once I was afraid of you, but now I only pity you, for everything you want and get is such unimportant trash—oh mother, I wish you hadn't forgotten to be a human being—

(*Just then enter Valdimar, Thorleifur, and the professor with his Geiger counter and equipment on his ears and a report in his hand.*)

VALDIMAR: This is marvellous—nearly unbelievable.

THORLEIFUR (*excited*): Karitas, it's uranium, real uranium.

PROFESSOR: Ja ja, uranium.

KARITAS (*depressed, apathetically*): Yes yes.

THORLEIFUR: The professor says that in these samples which Jörgen Nicholas Holm, no I mean Alfreds, took, there is uranium, real uranium, just think—

PROFESSOR (*looks up for a moment*): Uranium—ja ja— wunderbar—(*Bends down again over his instruments.*)

(*Valdimar and he speak in muffled tones. Valdimar is no longer jesting in manner, but is all afire with zeal and hopes of profit.*)

THORLEIFUR (*to his wife*): We have been a little too quick. The man did find uranium, even though he was quite a different person from what he seemed.

VALDIMAR: I don't think we're going to miss him very much, Thorleifur. (*Laughs.*) But this time there isn't any fly in the ointment. (*Sigmundur enters.*)

SIGRUN: Do you know what they're saying?

VALDIMAR (*goes towards him*): May I have the pleasure of congratulating you?

SIGMUNDUR: Thank you very much. (*Takes out the*

document.) And the seal of the Minister of Agriculture right underneath.

THORLEIFUR: No no, Sigmundur, he isn't referring to the ram.

SIGMUNDUR: Then what?

SIGRUN: They're going to start speculating with your mountain again.

VALDIMAR (*laughs*): Pretty girls should be seen and not heard. That adds to their charm. But as I was about to say, Sigmundur, the nation lays certain obligations upon our shoulders.

SIGMUNDUR: So it's the same old song, is it? Just as I had expected. No, my friend, it's nobody's business what happens to be inside that mountain. And I forbid all trespassing on my property.

VALDIMAR: Bravo, excellent. That is the right national spirit. But unfortunately we are no longer living in the viking age. Unfortunately, I say, for never was our people more Icelandic than then. But nowadays it says in that boring document called our Constitution that men can be required to give up their property if the general welfare requires it. That's how it is, my good Sigmundur. We all have to bow to the people's welfare, both you and I, no matter what heroes we are.

SIGMUNDER: I didn't think you big shots counted yourselves among the people, the way you put up your coxcombs. But we farmers are the people, and we need the pastures we've got. No, I won't give up a stone or a stick from my land.

VALDIMAR: Now let's not get excited over a little thing like this.

SIGMUNDUR: Yes, I'll get excited when I feel like it. My grandfather Simon the Strong slew the Iranes monster, and I have not degenerated so far from my ancestors that I can't give this gang of mollycoddles from Reykjavik the beating it deserves.

SIGRUN (*calls*): The cab is here.

THORLEIFUR (*goes to Sigmundur and puts his hand on his shoulder*): I hope that we won't part as enemies, Sigmundur my friend, even though Valdimar has raised this question with you.

SIGMUNDUR: Enemies—if we are, it's mostly your own fault. And you won't get anything but trouble if you tie up to a fox's tail. It would be much better for you, Thorleifur, if you got out of this bad company while there is still time. Then you'll be welcome at Hofstadir, both you and your good wife, and I won't mind if you putter around and paint the landscape, just to keep out of mischief.

VALDIMAR: I'm sure that Sigmundur and I can come to terms.

SIGMUNDUR: You can chatter all you want about precious metals as far as I'm concerned. But I wonder if the most precious thing of all isn't an honest people, though of course you wouldn't understand that.

SIGRUN (*takes hold of his wrist*): Come now.

SIGMUNDUR: Yes, I'm coming. (*Looks at Valdimar and shakes his fist in his face.*) They say that a man who fights with the devil has his hands full, but I don't intend to give in just the same—and that's it. (*Exit.*)

VALDIMAR (*laughs*): There's fire in the fellow, real honest-to-god fire.

THORLEIFUR: He gets pretty nasty sometimes.

VALDIMAR: Well, we're leaving now. (*Goes up and bows to Karitas, who pays little attention.*) Wir gehen jetzt.

PROFESSOR (*kisses the lady's hand*): Auf wiedersehen.

KARITAS (*dully*): Goodbye.

THORLEIFUR (*goes to the door with them*): Auf wiedersehen, Professor Epihara.

PROFESSOR: Auf wiedersehen.

VALDIMAR: The old boy is anything but dead. (*Pats Thorleifur on the shoulder.*) Too bad he isn't a senator, Thorleifur. (*Thorleifur starts.*) Well, we can talk about this tomorrow, instead. (*Nods to Karitas.*) Good-bye, beauty queen, good-bye.

KARITAS (*depressed*): Goodbye.

THORLEIFUR (*comes back in*): So it was right on the property of that confounded rascal he found the uranium after all.

KARITAS (*suddenly bursts out in unrestrained laughter*): How ridiculous all this is. How utterly fantastic. It's just exactly what you have coming. (*Collapses and bursts into tears.*)

THORLEIFUR (*doesn't dare touch her, but stands beside her helplessly*): Carrie, Carrie dear, what is it, Carrie—

KRISTIN (*enters*): There's a telegram.

THORLEIFUR: A telegram? (*Opens it, reads to himself.*)

KARITAS (*without looking up*): Who from?

THORLEIFUR: (*reads*): PLEASE SEND STONE SAMPLES STOP VERY URGENT STOP FORGOT THEM STOP GREETINGS DOCTOR ALFREDS HOTEL REY ALFONSO MEXICO CITY. (*Lays down the telegram.*) Now I don't understand a thing. He wants his stones sent to him?

KARITAS (*jumps up*): No, of course you don't ever understand anything. But it is Jörgen Nicholas Holm who conquers the world and finds uranium wherever he goes—in Iceland, Mexico, Siam, with stolen samples from Canada in his bag. (*Tears the telegram into little scraps.*) Jörgen Nicholas Holm—Porfirio Rubirosa—and Barbara Hutton—(*Tosses the scraps into the air as the curtain falls.*)

CURTAIN

Published in the Nordic Translation Series

FROM DENMARK

H. C. Branner, *Two Minutes of Silence.* Selected short stories, translated by Vera Lindholm Vance, with an introduction by Richard B. Vowles. 1966.

Jacob Paludan, *Jørgen Stein.* Translated by Carl Malmberg, with an introduction by P. M. Mitchell. 1966.

FROM FINLAND

Hagar Olsson, *The Woodcarver and Death. Träsnidaren och döden,* translated by George C. Schoolfield. 1965.

Toivo Pekkanen, *My Childhood. Lapsuuteni,* translated by Alan Blair, with an introduction by Thomas Warburton. 1966.

F. E. Sillanpää, *People in the Summer Night. Ihmiset suviyössä,* translated by Alan Blair, with an introduction by Thomas Warburton. 1966.

FROM ICELAND

Fire and Ice: Three Icelandic Plays, with Introductions by Einar Haugen. Jóhann Sigurjónsson, *The Wish (Galdra-Loftur),* translated by Einar Haugen. Davið Stefánsson, *The Golden Gate (Gullna hliðið),* translated by G. M. Gathorne-Hardy. Agnar Thórðarson, *Atoms and Madams (Kjarnorka og kvenhylli),* translated by Einar Haugen. 1967.

Gunnar Gunnarsson, *The Black Cliffs. Svartfugl,* translated by Cecil Wood, with an introduction by Richard N. Ringler. 1967.

FROM NORWAY

Aksel Sandemose, *The Werewolf. Varulven,* translated by Gustaf Lannestock, with an introduction by Harald S. Næss. 1966.
Tarjei Vesaas, *The Great Cycle. Det store spelet,* translated by Elizabeth Rokkan, with an introduction by Harald S. Næss. 1967.

FROM SWEDEN

Karin Boye, *Kallocain.* Translated by Gustaf Lannestock, with an introduction by Richard B. Vowles. 1966.
Peder Sjögren, *Bread of Love. Kärlekens bröd,* translated by Richard B. Vowles. 1965.

OTHER TRANSLATIONS TO COME